To: the Rogg Family —
Jeff — Father ... 2003

W9-CNV-176

EXPLORING ORTHODOX CHRISTIANITY

ORTHODOX CHRISTIAN BELIEFS
"Real Answers to Real Questions
from Real People"

by
Stanley Samuel Harakas
Archbishop Iakovos Professor of Orthodox Theology *Emeritus*
Holy Cross Greek Orthodox School of Theology

*And God said,
"Let there be light !!"
and there was light*

*Papa & Mama
(P. — G.)*

**LIGHT & LIFE PUBLIJHING COMPANY
MINNEAPOLIJ, MINNEJOTA**

Light & Life Publishing Company
P.O. Box 26421
Minneapolis, MN 55426-0421

ISBN No. 1-880971-71-2

TABLE OF CONTENTS

ONE GOD: A TRINITY OF DIVINE PERSONS

JESUS CHRIST

THE HOLY SPIRIT

THE CREATION

ANGELS AND DEVILS

HUMAN BEINGS

SUFFERING AND EVIL

ICONS

HEAVEN AND HELL

To Our Lord and Savior Jesus Christ,
"To Him be the glory both now and
to the day of eternity" (2 Peter 3:18).

And to
Zoë Katherine Parigian
Our beloved grand-daughter

PREFACE

Throughout the last half of the twentieth century, *The Hellenic Chronicle* served as the link for Americans of Greek descent across this country. It was a time when immigrants were assimilating and starting their own families and when first and second generation American Hellenes were struggling with ways to stay connected, married within their heritage and steeped in their faith.

Founded in 1950 by my late father, Peter Agris, and continued by members of his family until its closure in the Fall of 2000, *The Hellenic Chronicle* was among the primary sources for information about Hellenism and Orthodoxy in America.

The Religious Question Box was, without question, the paper's most popular feature. From its inception in 1955 by the late beloved Rev. Dr. George Tsoumas and throughout its continuation for almost three decades by distinguished theologian Rev. Dr. Stanley S. Harakas, the column stood as a vital resource for Orthodox Hellenes seeking to keep their faith alive amidst the growing tide of inter-marriages, interpret and share its beliefs with their non-Orthodox spouses and integrate it into the lives of their children.

Its form, question-and-answer rather than lengthy sermonizing, made it the reader's own. The content and direction of the column sprung from the concerns of the readership, always keeping it timely. We recall Fr. Harakas' concern when asked if he would continue to write from retirement in Florida. He humbly queried whether we wouldn't rather have someone younger, with fresher ideas. We said then that it was the wisdom and sensitivity of Fr. Harakas' responses that drove our readers to The Question Box. We believe that today's challenging times make his interpretations of our faith and its relevance in our lives ever more necessary.

The Agris family feels privileged to have been able to support the Greek American community and our Greek Orthodox Church in America for a half century through the pages of *The Hellenic Chronicle*. Among our proudest achievements was providing the space for the vital columns of The Religious Question Box.

Fr. Harakas' love and devotion to our Church and to its communicants in this great nation have left an indelible mark. He and Presbytera Emily have given tirelessly of themselves to our Archdiocese, our beloved Hellenic College/Holy Cross School of Theology and to the many parishes which they have served.

We extend our love and thanks to them both and to each of you our hope that you will use and reuse each volume as a force within your home for Orthodox spiritual guidance.

–Nancy Agris Savage, Former Editor, *The Hellenic Chronicle*

TO THE READER

This book is the first in the series – "Exploring Orthodox Christianity." Each volume in the series will be based on one or more themes regarding the teaching and practice of the Orthodox Church.

Orthodox Christian Beliefs contains seventy five questions and answers about the doctrine and beliefs of the Orthodox Christian Church. The questions and answers were written over a period of years from 1984 to 2000. They were published in the "Religious Question Box" column of *The Hellenic Chronicle* newspaper of Boston, MA.

Every column was written to provide "real answers to real questions from real people." The first four and a half years of the column–from 1980 to mid-1984–were published in the book *The Orthodox Church: 455 Questions and Answers*. There, the answers were mostly very short and undeveloped. Even so, the book has found a wide audience.

Following the first volume, and in response to readers' requests for fuller and more detailed responses to questions, the answers were written so that only one question per column was addressed. In some cases, several columns were used to answer a single question or several closely related questions.

You will find fuller treatments in this volume on questions dealing with:

- Religious Knowing
- One God: A Trinity of
    Divine Persons
- Jesus Christ
- The Holy Spirit
- The Creation
- Human Beings
- The Church

- Saints
- Salvation
- Suffering and Evil
- Icons
- Heaven and Hell
- End Times: Christ's
    Second Coming
- Theology and Life

However, on the one hand, this book is not a textbook on these subjects. On the other hand, the answers are not narrowly limited, either. Rather, the questions are always put in their religious and historical context. So, each response begins with a description of the general background of the topic under discussion. Then, the specific question is answered. If you carefully read the whole response, you will usually achieve a more complete understanding of the topic in a general way. But at the same time you will see what issues concern real people like you who have submitted these questions.

How should you use this book?

First, of course, you can read it just like any other book, from front to back. You will find that the questions express genuine concerns, including many that raise doubts, conflicts, and disagreements with accepted teachings. Regardless of the subject and tone of the questions, the answers try to deal with them honestly, sincerely and with respect.

Secondly, you may be interested only in a particular issue for which you are seeking information. Because this book is organized topically, you can go directly to the Table of Contents. Under each of the headings listed above are the titles of each of the questions. By reviewing these, you can narrow down your search. Beneath that title are the sub-titles for that topic. By reviewing these entries, you will have a good idea if that topic is the one that interests you and about which you can learn. But do remember that the answers try to cover a lot of material in the short space of a newspaper column. You will probably learn more about your question than you first expected!

Thirdly, if you want to follow up the topic of your concern more thoroughly, go to the index at the back of the book. There you will find the page numbers where your search topic is found in many different contexts.

You should know that Light and Life Publishing Company and I plan to publish a series of these books on other themes that have been treated over the years in "The Religious Question Box." For example, the next book in the "Exploring Orthodox Christianity" series will deal with the Bible.

No book is ever written without help from a lot of people. Especially a book like this one. So the greatest thanks are due to the people who submitted these questions. They made the column and this book possible.

Very special thanks also go to Fr. John Tsaras, who as a student at Holy Cross Greek Orthodox School of Theology was my Teaching Assistant. It was he who made the original classifications of the columns and ordered them into categories. Since his most valuable work, I wrote more columns while in retirement. Most of these have been included in this book. But without Fr. Tsaras' original labors, the book would not have the shape it presently has. I am grateful to him for his devoted work. Fr. John now serves the St. George Greek Orthodox Church in Oklahoma City, Oklahoma, as the Parish Priest.

I am particularly grateful to Victoria Smith who carefully read an early draft of this book, supplying valuable editorial corrections and clarifying comments.

Thanks also, to Nancy Agris Savage the Editor of *The Hellenic Chronicle* who has been always supportive, encouraging and helpful. Words cannot express my thanks to Fr. Anthony Coniaris, founder and spirit behind Light and Life Publishing Co., who repeatedly pushed me to complete this volume and who has encouraged me over the years in so many other writing projects. He is a good friend and a blessed example for all Orthodox Christians.

Over the many years that I wrote "The Religious Question Box," I did so in the name of Holy Cross Greek Orthodox School of Theology in Brookline, MA where I taught for almost 30 years. I am grateful for the support and help of its Presidents, Deans, Faculty Staff and Students, including His Eminence Archbishop Iakovos.

Many thanks, as well, to my beloved Presbytera Emily who patiently assisted me in uncountable ways in the writing of this book. For the helpful things written here, I thank God above all. For the errors in fact and judgment, I myself must accept all the responsibility.

Finally, I want to thank you, the reader of this book, for your interest in "Exploring Orthodox Christianity" and your desire to learn about "Orthodox Christian Beliefs."

+Stanley S. Harakas, Th.D, D.D.

Archbishop Iakovos Professor of Orthodox Theology, *Emeritus*

Holy Cross Greek Orthodox School of Theology, Brookline, MA

Feast of Sts. Cosmas and Damian, the Unmercenaries, November 1, 2001

Religious Knowing

1. KNOWING GOD

Q. Is God really "known" and is the experiencing of God verifiable? How is He experienced? How does one distinguish between "wish-fulthinking" or imaginings of God, and true understanding?

– J. T. B., Bridgewater, MA.

A. There are many different ways of "knowing" anything. Some are more appropriate to "knowing God," than others. I will take your questions one at a time, and respond to them.

Is God Really "Known"?

The most direct and absolute answer to that questions is "no," if what we are speaking about is the very being and essence of God. What this means is that according to Orthodox Theology we human beings who are creatures, can never really fully comprehend and understand the fullness and the mysterious truth of God's essential reality. Only God is Creator; everything else is creature (that is, something that has been created). God in His very being is so different and so much beyond us, that we will never be able to comprehend His inner nature.

But that does not mean we cannot know things about God, or that we cannot be in a knowing communion with God. Nevertheless, we experience a reality: God reaches out to His creation to commune with it, to sustain it, and to redeem it. Orthodox theology refers to this "reaching out" of God with two phrases: "Divine Energies" and "Divine Grace." The phrase "Divine Energies" refers to the "going out of Himself" by God to relate to what He has created. "Divine Grace," which is the same thing, emphasizes the motive of love and the outpouring of freely given goodwill with which God relates to His creatures. In Orthodox Christian theology the Divine Energies and Grace are not "things" other than God, they are God Himself.

So you see, if we are recipients of Divine Grace and the Divine Energies, we are in communion with God. This very communion is "knowledge of God." For to be in communion with God is to "know" God by way of that experience. Though God can never be fully and completely known and understood by human beings, nevertheless, we human beings may come to know God in some measure of our capabilities through communion with God.

Further, we can put this experience of God into words, which reflect that knowledge. In this sense we can say things about God that could be characterized as "knowledge" and "truth" about God.

So to summarize, in the deepest and most profound sense we cannot know God in the hidden recesses of His being; yet, as God relates with us, His creatures, through His Energies and His Grace, we can know him in that experience. This experience can be put into words and described, so in this more "thought oriented" way, we can say we do have restricted, but real knowledge of God.

How Is God Experienced?

Verification is essential to knowledge. For knowledge to be knowledge it must be something that can be shared and experienced by others. In science, this means that other scientists can repeat an experiment. In mathematics, this means that calculations properly exercised produce the same results when done by another mathematician. Only a small part of what we call knowledge fits this rigorous criterion. The larger part of our knowledge is less precise. Medicine is an example. In a significant way, medicine is scientific knowledge. But in many other ways, medicine is an art, governed as much by intuition, insight and wisdom.

Orthodox Christianity has what might be analogous to the "science part" in medicine (we'll speak of this below), but a much larger part of knowledge in the Christian faith is on the experienced "insight and wisdom" side. I speak of the experience and knowledge of God in prayer, in religious experience, in obedience to the Divine Will, in the communion of love for God and for His servants and His creation, in participation in the spiritual struggle for the good and against sin and evil, in the experience of love and self-sacrifice.

How is this knowledge of God verified? People are called within the life of the Church to enter into a living experience of faith, obedience to God, communion with Him in prayer and sacrament, spiritual growth, love for God, for our fellow human beings and for all of creation. We enter this life of faith on the basis of the witness of others who have walked the same path of faith. We hear from the greatest of these, the saints, that this path is one of light, and spiritual happiness, and victorious living.

Faith means we live this as a kind of experiment of belief in our daily existence till the time that its truth is impressed upon us on the basis of our own experience. We then verify its truth in our own lives, and share it with others. "Come and see" (John 1:39) is at the heart of the mission of the Church. Gordon Allport, a psychologist of religion put it this way: "...all accomplishment results from taking risks in advance of certainties. Chronic skepticism, inhibitory and depressive thoughts, are incompatible with everything excepting vegetative existence... Only by having expectations of consequences beyond the limits of certainty do we make these consequences more likely to occur. Faith engenders the energy which when applied to the task in hand enhances the probability of its success...In so doing, it finds that the successive acts of commitment, with their beneficent consequences, slowly strengthen the faith and cause the moments of doubt to disappear" (*The Individual and His Religion*, pp. 73-74).

Thinking and True Understanding

"How does one distinguish between 'wishful thinking' or imaginings about God, and true understanding?" In the very same way that we test our knowledge in other areas of human experience. We check our own experiences and perceptions against the experience of others. In our case, we must constantly check our own religious experience against the experience of those persons who have met and experienced God and who have received knowledge of God in universally recognized ways. In particular, we must check that experience with the masters of faith who have put their experience of God into words. In practice this means always being in touch with the Church's experience of God as it has been recorded in its living tradition.

Where do we find this record of the experience of the Church of the knowledge of God? In the Bible (the record of God's self-disclosure to humanity), the formal decisions of the Church in Councils, in the writings and lives of the Saints of the Church, in the Church's worship and sacramental life -its ongoing continuation of the saving work of Jesus Christ.

This means that in practice, the Revelation of God as mediated to us through His Church is the litmus test that helps us discern between true understanding and wishful thinking or subjective imagining. That is why the Bible refers to the Church as the "pillar and ground of the truth" (1 Timothy 3:15). We are guided and directed in our spiritual journey to meet, communicate with, and know God in our hearts and our minds by the Church. We are helped by its formal teaching; by the lifestyle it directs us to follow; by the Church's liturgical and sacramental life; by its fellowship and community life. The safest and surest way to know God is in the Church.

2. GOD: HOW DO WE KNOW ANYTHING . . . OR GOD?

Q. I have three questions: 1) In our Greek Orthodox Religion, is God more important than Jesus Christ, or is the reverse true? 2) Who created God? (Interesting article: "How Man Created God," *Time* magazine, September 27, 1993, based on the book *A History of God*, by Karen Armstrong) 3) As regards the seven Ecumenical Councils accepted by the Eastern and Western Churches, why and how should 318 MAN Bishops (1st Ecumenical Council) profess the view that Jesus Christ was of the "same substance" with the FATHER, be considered Orthodox? — *T.N.A., Akron, OH.*

A. These three questions are interrelated. In thinking about how to respond, it would be possible to start with any one of them and then go to the others. But before them all is the fundamental question of knowledge itself: knowledge of this world and knowledge of divine things.

So, today's column will address the basic question "How do we know anything?" Then, we will begin addressing the question regarding knowledge of divine things. Next week we will discuss divine knowledge more in detail. In subsequent columns we can then turn to the questions above.

The Value of Knowledge

"Knowing" is important to human beings. To "know" is to have some idea about how things are, and consequently to be able to deal with reality appropriately and effectively. For example, to "know" that it is raining makes it possible for us to dress appropriately. But to "know" is also perceived by most people as good in itself, whether we can immediately use the knowledge or not. What we "know" forms us, gives us a view on the world, influences our character, contributes to civilizing us, and is worth having for its own sake.

How Do We Know . . . Anything?

But, how do we know anything? There are several ways that we can come to some knowledge about things. These are: intuition, deduction, inference, experiment, experience and revelation.

Intuition is the direct and unmediated perception of some condition or reality. All of us experience intuition some times. We feel strongly that some situation "speaks directly to us," and our "gut feeling" conveys knowledge and conviction to us. The truths expressed by poets and artists are often arrived at intuitively. The problem with intuitive knowledge is that it is difficult to share intuitive knowledge effectively and convincingly with others.

Deduction is the rational (logical) process we use to move from an accepted proposition to a new affirmation on the basis of logical principles of reason, called syllogisms. Drawing on our logical abilities we reason from one premise to another. "A is twice the size of B; C is twice the size of B; therefore A and C are of the same size." But this form of knowledge is also difficult to apply in practice because we cannot always take into account all possible factors.

Inference is a looser way of coming to knowledge about something by noting apparent common points, and making assumptions that are not strictly logical but carry with them a semblance of plausibility. It is three o'clock in the morning and you drive by an appliance store. You see the front door of the store open and you see men moving appliances from the store into an unmarked truck. You infer that a robbery is taking place. So you call the police. It is a good inference, but, of course, there could also be another explanation: the owner had to make an early morning delivery to a far-away customer, but his own business truck is needed for other deliveries first thing after opening. We all use inferences and often they are right, but sometimes they are not. Yet, on the basis of inferences, we function in a practical way from day to day.

Experiment is a method by which people test ideas about how things happen or how they are in themselves. We call these ideas "hypotheses," which are assumptions about how things work based often on the previously discussed ways to knowledge. An experiment is a way of testing a hypothesis. Repeatedly verified hypotheses -provided the conditions of the experiment are the same- provide us with "scientific knowledge." But new conditions, or new hypotheses, can overturn "old scientific knowledge" and replace it with something else. Yet, some experimentally based knowledge is (almost) universally recognized as true knowledge. However, all scientific knowledge is held tentatively, as subject to change.

Experience is also an important way of "knowing." We say, "You don't really know what it means to (fill in the blank), until it has happened to you." To "know" what it means to be a mother is to experience it. Until then you have some idea about it, but you don't really "know" it. Different people will "know" the experiences described by others, precisely because they too have "experienced them." But it is also likely that their "experiences" are not exactly the same, and thus their "knowledge" is not the same either.

Revelation is a way of knowing something when someone tells us what we could not otherwise know. When you go to the doctor he asks you how you feel. You "reveal" to him your aches and pains. Or, you may reveal your innermost anxieties to a psychiatrist or your sins to a priest. The listener depends on the accuracy of what is said on the trustworthiness of the person who reveals it. Someone could lie to you or deceive you. So you use some of the other means of knowing mentioned above to assess the trustworthiness of the person who reveals something to you.

The point is, of course, is that we can "know" many things, but our "knowledge" is never absolute, regardless of the means that we use. We may have a working knowledge of some things without knowing them fully. In all likelihood, most of our knowledge is precisely like that. Absolute knowledge is probably impossible. Yet, we have enough knowledge in most cases to understand our situation, make decisions, create new things, plan for the future, and function in a reasonably stable way. For example, to drive a car you don't have to know all the details of how an internal combustion engine works.

How Do We Know About . . . God?

We know about God pretty much in the same ways that we know about other things, but the mix and emphasis is different, precisely because some of the methods are more applicable and some are less applicable to the reality of God.

Take the experimental method, for example. It is an excellent method to knowledge about physical and material things. Physics is, we say, "an exact science." But the experimental method gets into trouble and is less accurate when it seeks to deal with less measurable, tangible and experimentally controllable realities. For example, it is impossible to verify that all factors in a psychological experiment have been repeated in another experiment. The repeatability of the experiment can never be verified. As a result, the probability of accurate knowledge in a psychological experiment is much reduced.

Similarly, it is impossible to put God into a test tube, or control "divine variables" for any kind of human experiment. The experimental method is not as useful, yet it is not useless either. A form of the experimental method, in a limited way is, indeed, one method we can use to come to a knowledge of God.

3. WAYS OF KNOWING GOD

Q. I have three questions: 1) In our Greek Orthodox Religion, is God more important than Jesus Christ, or is the reverse true? 2) Who created God? (Interesting article: "How Man Created God," Time magazine, September 27, 1993, based on the book A History of God, by Karen Armstrong) 3) As regards the seven Ecumenical Councils accepted by the Eastern and Western Churches, why and how should 318 MAN Bishops (1st Ecumenical Council) profess the view that Jesus Christ was of the "same substance" with the FATHER, be considered Orthodox?   – T.N.A., Akron, OH.

A. Last week we began answering this question by asking the fundamental question, "How do we know . . . anything?" The column pointed to four main points: first, the importance of knowledge; second, that the means to knowing anything are intuition, deduction, inference, experience, experiment and revelation; third, that no knowledge that human beings have can be absolute; and, fourth, that our knowledge of the things of God is dependent on the same means to knowledge, but that in regard to divine things, the ranking of importance is different from the means we use to know these worldly things. Let us now look at each of these ways of knowing in relationship to God and to divine things.

Knowing God Intuitively

Throughout the ages, people have "intuited" knowledge of divine things. Nearly every culture, nation and race of people has had some "sense of the divine." Scholars call this "the numinous sense," in which people recognize a power or powers that go beyond ordinary human and this-worldly experience. Sometimes it is called an apprehension of the "transcendent." Though this is a common thing, it is also not very reliable in telling us just exactly what the "numinous" is, since there is such great variety among people as they try to describe it.

Knowing God Deductively

Sometimes, people argue for the existence of God on the basis of deductive reasoning. For instance, the great Church Father, St. John of Damascus (675-749), in his encyclopedic work *Fountain of Knowledge* has a large section called "The Exposition of the Orthodox Faith." There he presents many logical arguments for the existence of God, trying to "prove" this belief rationally. Not so long ago, a French Nobel Prize Biologist, LeCompte du Nouy, wrote several books seeking to show mathematically that a Creating God had to exist, because there is not enough time–according to mathematical probabilities–for the world and all that is in it to have come into being by chance. Yet, most theologians hold that one cannot adequately "prove" (or for that matter, "disprove") the existence of God. The reason is that the rational presuppositions are necessarily drawn from the created world. For God to be God, however, the logic of the world would not necessarily apply to divine reality.

Knowing God by Inference

It is a different thing, however, when we stand before a beautiful sunset, examine the loveliness of a flower, sense the depth of love, or forgiveness, or sacrificial human behavior and infer that such things cannot come into existence unless there is a Transcendent One that brings them into being. Often, it is the sense of holiness that provokes us to such deeply felt inferences. For example, in the book of Daniel, the pagan Babylonian King Belteshazzar says to the prophet Daniel, "You are that Daniel, one of the exiles of Judah, whom the king my father brought from Judah. I have heard of you that the spirit of the holy god is in you, and that light and understanding and excellent wisdom are found in you" (Daniel 5:13-14) (RSV). Sometimes this is very convincing to the person who "sees" the connections, but it is not easy to "prove."

Knowing God by Experience

Many people have had a profound personal experience of the presence of God in their lives. For many, it is the kind of quiet confidence produced by the experiences described in the preceding section: a sunset, the experience of being forgiven, the miracle of the birth of a child, etc. Others, experience some abrupt or totally unexpected healing, or escape from some impending evil. Often experiences such as these combine reason with inference, intuition and bits and pieces of knowledge absorbed through an existing religious culture. It seems that some mystical experience of God is in this category of knowledge. Mystical experience is usually understood as a direct and unmediated knowledge of transcendent divine reality. I suppose that the so-called "after death" experiences reported by some people are of this same quality. While personally convincing, these experiences are so subjective that they can be shared with others only with difficulty.

Knowing God by Experiment

Many years ago, I published an article titled "Faith." The theme of the argument was, that faith was like a personal experiment in which we consciously live according to the hypothesis that God does, indeed, exist and that God has expectations of us, and that following those expectations will produce not only good results for our lives, but also the unshakable conviction and personal knowledge that in truth God exists and that God is real. The "hypothesis" is that God exists and relates with us. The "experiment" is to live as if He does exist and concurrently to conform one's life to godly ways. The "proof" is found in the results it produces. For many who live this "experiment" it powerfully confirms knowledge of God. But since so much of it is subject to personal attitudes, values and experiences, it cannot be considered as fully objective verification of God's existence.

Knowing God By Revelation

We "know" God, also, when God makes Himself known to us. The Bible is a record of God's self-revelation to His creatures. The Old Testament is a witness of events in which God revealed Himself to the Hebrew people. Some of the most dramatic events of revelation were the ten plagues in Egypt, the giving of the Ten Commandments on Mt. Sinai, and the vision of God seen by the Prophet Isaiah. But God also revealed Himself through more ordinary historical events throughout the Old Testament period. In the New Testament period, the most striking divine revelation was the person of Jesus Christ. His disciples stood in Jesus' presence and could not help but acknowledge His divine nature. Thus, "Nathaniel answered him, 'Rabbi, you are the Son of God! You are the King of Israel!'" (John 1:49); and, after experiencing a remarkable miracle Peter said to Jesus, "Truly you are the Son of God" (Matthew 14:33). Revelation about God and divine things is the surest way of knowing about them, but like all other ways of knowing about anything or about God, it is not absolute knowledge. It points to much truth about God, but does not exhaust it.

Why No Absolute Knowledge of God?

There is a powerful reason why there is no absolute knowledge of God. Rejecting the truth of God's existence would then be a case of stupidity! But God wants us to be free to accept Him and to freely respond to what He is and what He has done for us. Only then, as freely choosing to believe in Him and His ways, can we become what we really are: God's image and likeness!

4. DIVINE REVELATION

Q. I have three questions: 1) In our Greek Orthodox Religion, is God more important than Jesus Christ, or is the reverse true? 2) Who created God? (Interesting article: "How Man Created God," *Time* magazine, September 27, 1993, based on the book *A History of God*, by Karen Armstrong) 3) As regards the seven Ecumenical Councils accepted by the Eastern and Western Churches, why and how should 318 MAN Bishops (1st Ecumenical Council) profess the view that Jesus Christ was of the "same substance" with the FATHER, be considered Orthodox? – *T.N.A., Akron, OH.*

A. The past two weeks we began answering this question by asking the fundamental question, "How do we know . . . anything?" and "How do we know anything about God?" In these articles four main points were made: first, the importance of knowledge; second, that the means to knowing anything are intuition, deduction, inference, experience, experiment and revelation; third, that no knowledge that human beings have can be absolute; and, fourth, that our knowledge of the things of God is also dependent on the same means to knowledge, but that in regard to divine things, the ranking of importance is different from the means we use to know these worldly things.

Of course, for the Christian faith, though all the other means are used in obtaining knowledge about God and the things of God, the most important of them is Divine Revelation.

Revelation and the Questions

If we look at the four questions included in the inquiry we have been responding to in these columns, we will see something very important. None of them can be addressed without reference to revelation. There is nothing in any form of human knowledge obtained through intuition, deduction, inference, experience, or experiment that can directly address these questions. The reason is that each of them is about the Trinitarian nature of God, something that has never been known to have been arrived at, except in the most vague speculations by intuition, never by deduction or inference or experiment, and only by experience in the revelatory process. There is no way to address these particular issues except through the witnesses to Divine Revelation!

Revelation of God in Holy Tradition and Scripture

Divine Revelation is God's self-disclosure to human beings. God has made Himself known (that is, has revealed some things about Himself) to human beings. Thus, Divine Revelation is inseparable from the experience of human beings. The revelation of God about Himself did not take place at the beginning in a book. It was God's communication with people in their historical experience and, in particular with persons who were vessels of God's revelatory experience.

These experiences of Divine Revelation were not seen by those who experienced them as private and subjective intuitions or insights. They were understood as a "breaking into" their conscious experience by God: precisely, as experiences in which God made Himself known. Those who had experiences of Divine Revelation understood them as a unique reality, distinct from other ways of knowing things, and often attributed the experience to God or the Word of God, or to the Holy Spirit of God.

The remembrance of these revelatory experiences formed a tradition of the word of God. Those who experienced its power understood that in that Divine Revelation, God was still present. Often that presence was identified as "the Spirit of God," or "the Holy Spirit."

Eventually, this experience and knowledge was written down into Scriptures. In the case of the Hebrew people, through whom God chose to make His Divine Revelation, it was written down in the books that make up the Old Testament, an account of the development of the covenant relationship between God and the Hebrews through a process of progressive revelation.

At a point in time, these Old Testament Scriptures "were fulfilled" in Jesus Christ. The most important passage of the New Testament that expresses this understanding is the following regarding Jesus Christ: "'The Spirit of the Lord is upon me, because he has anointed me to preach good news to the poor. He has sent me to proclaim release to the captives and recovering of sight to the blind, to set at liberty those who are oppressed, to proclaim the acceptable year of the Lord.' And he closed the book, and gave it back to the attendant, and sat down; and the eyes of all in the synagogue were fixed on him. And he began to say to them, 'Today this scripture has been fulfilled in your hearing.'" (Luke 4:18-21). (see also a few of many other examples in John 12:38, John 13:18, John 17:12.)

Thus, Divine Revelation was made manifest in the person, life and work of Jesus Christ. The Apostles were witnesses to that Revelation and conveyed it to the Church and those that continued their work, the Bishops and clergy of the Church. This living experience of the person, life, teaching and promises of Jesus Christ for the salvation of the world was preached, taught, and lived in the Church for decades before ever being written down. Eventually it was written down in the form of Gospels, a history (the book of the Acts of the Apostles) and in letters (Paul, Peter, John, James, etc.) and an apocalyptic writing (The Book of Revelation) to form the New Testament.

But, of course, anyone could read these writings, or Holy Scriptures, as they were called. Consequently, anyone could also try to understand them out of their own experience and with their own ideas, and not that of the Holy Tradition of the revelation that produced them. Further, people could mistakenly think that they too had revelations and write them down into false scriptures. Who could discern the false from the true? Only those who were already living in the original Holy Tradition. In fact, that is just what happened. The Church, by consulting its own experience of Holy Tradition under the guidance of the Holy Spirit, formed the canon or list of authentic writings of the New Testament. Without the Church, its Holy Tradition, its Church Fathers and Bishops, its unbroken historical experience of the Holy Spirit, there would be no Bible nor Holy Tradition and therefore no witnesses to God's self-disclosure. As a result, neither would there be any way to answer your questions in your inquiry above!

5. REVELATION IN THE CHURCH

Q. I have three questions: 1) In our Greek Orthodox Religion, is God more important than Jesus Christ, or is the reverse true? 2) Who created God? (Interesting article: "How Man Created God," Time magazine, September 27, 1993, based on the book A History of God, by Karen Armstrong) 3) As regards the seven Ecumenical Councils accepted by the Eastern and Western Churches, why and how should 318 MAN Bishops (1st Ecumenical Council) profess the view that

Jesus Christ was of the "same substance" with the FATHER, be considered Orthodox? – *T.N.A., Akron, OH.*

A. Over the past three weeks we have provided the questioner and
the readers of "The Religious Question Box" a background for
answering these questions. We've discussed different ways of obtaining knowledge and we have pointed out that the chief source of
knowledge about divine things comes primarily from Divine
Revelation. This is particularly true of the questions listed above. The
previous three columns have also helped us understand that human
beings have been, without question, involved in the revelatory
process, so that it is unavoidable that human beings, and in this case,
Bishops of the Church gathered in an Ecumenical Council, would be
the only competent persons capable of discerning the content of the
faith, based on Holy Tradition and the Holy Scriptures under the
guidance of the Holy Spirit.

What We've Done So Far

What we have done so far is to respond to the implication that
any answer given on the basis of Divine Revelation is "man made"
rather than revelatory. It is impossible to convey truths of Divine
Revelation without reference to human beings. But in the context of
Holy Tradition and the Holy Scriptures, it also means that the Holy
Spirit is also present in these revelatory truths and the human beings
that express them for us.

Trinitarian Questions

Thus, the only way to answer these three questions is out of the
Scriptural Tradition and the way those Scriptures have been consistently interpreted in the Holy Tradition which produced them. As
noted above, all of the questions in one way or another are related to
belief in the Holy Trinity and our knowledge of this revelatory truth.
To ask, then "Is God more important than Jesus Christ," is to ask

"What does the word 'God' refer to?" Or to ask, "Who created God?" is to be speaking of the very nature of God Himself. Or, to ask about why the Church teaches that "Jesus Christ is of the 'same substance' with the Father" is to address the question of the second person of the Holy Trinity, None of these questions can be even taken up for discussion without reference to Divine Revelation. No other access to knowledge can even begin to address them.

God and Christ

"In our Greek Orthodox Religion, is God more important than Jesus Christ, or is the reverse true?" There is a confusion evident in this question because the word "God" is used in two distinct ways in the tradition of the Church. Both Scripture and Holy Tradition speak of the Father, the first person of the Holy Trinity as "God." They also use the same word (God) to refer to the one divine being. God as the Father in the relationship of the persons of the Holy Trinity is the source of both the Son and the Holy Spirit. The second person of the Holy Trinity, the Son, took on human nature (body and soul) in the concrete historical person, Jesus Christ. Now, it becomes very difficult to determine who-the One God who is a Trinity of Persons,-or the Father,-or the Son of God in the Trinity,-or Jesus Christ (the incarnate Son of God) is "most important"! The criterion, I suppose, would be "most important in which circumstance?"

When we are thinking about the relationship of the three persons of the Holy Trinity (which are the one God), it would seem that since the Father is the source of the Son (the Son is "forever born of the Father"), the Father is the "most important." Thus, Jesus Himself said, that He did His works "in his Father's name" (John 10:24-25), and that His Father "is greater than all" (John 10:29), but also that "I and the Father are one" (John 10:30).

If, however, we think of our salvation and our life in communion with God, we are taught by what Jesus said, "I am the way, and the truth, and the life; no one comes to the Father, but by me" (John 14:

6). In the end, it seems to me that if we understand a little about the Holy Trinity and the incarnation of the second person of the Holy Trinity in Jesus Christ, it is not a very important question to ask which is more important.

God Is Uncreated

"Who created God? (Interesting article: "How Man Created God," *Time* magazine, September 27, 1993, based on the book *A History of God*, by Karen Armstrong."

From the point of view of the Church, the article is either a question based on a total misuse of terms, or it is blasphemous. A fundamental teaching of the Church is that only God is "uncreated," and all the rest of us and everything else, including *Time* magazine and Karen Armstrong, are "created."

Rather, both the article and the book are attempts to describe how different peoples have come to think about God. They come from a perspective that ignores the reality of Divine Revelation. They are two very different things.

You can describe, or even try to explain, why and how people's ideas have been formed through the ages in reference to a, or many, divine-like beings. You can never write a history of God in any technical sense of that word since "No one has ever seen God; the only Son, who is in the bosom of the Father, he has made him known" (John 1:18). What the historian has not seen, nor has any witness seen in the eternity before creation, simply cannot be described technically as "history." That which has no beginning has no "history" in any meaningful human understanding of that term. So, God is "beyond history" as God. Only when God enters human experience can we talk about the history of the human encounter with God.

The Same Substance

"As regards the seven Ecumenical Councils accepted by the Eastern and Western Churches, why and how should 318 MAN Bishops (1st

Ecumenical Council) profess the view that Jesus Christ was of the "same substance" with the FATHER considered Orthodox?"

We have previously pointed out that human beings, by God's own choice are directly involved with "revelation," that is, God revealed Himself to Moses, the Prophets, and through Jesus Christ to the Disciples. I would ask, "How could God reveal himself, except through people for people?"

It is precisely the multiple misinterpretations of the revelation of God about the person of Jesus Christ that provoke the Church to formulate its doctrinal truths. The Church, through its chief teachers, the Bishops in Councils, is the guardian and interpreter of the revelation. The Bible is very clear about this: it refers to "the household of God, which is the church of the living God, the pillar and bulwark of the truth" (1 Timothy 3:15). The Church under the inspiration of the Holy Spirit, and guided by Holy Tradition, produced the Holy Scriptures. Consequently, the Church itself is the most competent to interpret them. Hence, the Ecumenical Councils, representing the full mind and understanding of the Church, are the only earthly authority that can express its truth accurately so as to assure true faith on our part, and clear the way for living the life of salvation.

6. HOLY TRADITION: CAN IT CHANGE?

Q. It seems to me that many of our Orthodox Church members wonder about the Tradition of the Church being static and that it seems to them that the Church is no longer being inspired by the Holy Spirit. If the Holy Spirit is inspiring the Church, then Tradition understood as the life of the Holy Spirit in the Church can evolve. If the Church denies the inspiration of the Holy Spirit, isn't that blasphemy? — *Name and city withheld*

A. Many factors -both positive and negative- contribute to change in the life of the Church. But the assumption is for the Orthodox, that there is a core of unchanging Tradition in the life of the Church that keeps the Church "on track" as the "One, Holy, Catholic and Apostolic Church of Christ" and provides the opportunity for authentic growth in teaching, understanding and life.

Today's question takes the issue a step beyond understanding change in the Church. It is a question about the relationship of the Holy Spirit as the illuminator and guide of the Church. It addresses the development of Church teaching and practice under the guidance of the Holy Spirit.

Clearly, the last part of the question, "If the Church denies the inspiration of the Holy Spirit, isn't that blasphemy?" has to be totally hypothetical. The Church can't deny the ongoing inspiration of the Holy Spirit in its life and remain true to its identity. The issue is not change and development, but authentic change and development.

The Holy Spirit, The Church, The Christian Truth

First, some background. In His teaching to the Disciples just prior to His Passion, Death and Resurrection, Jesus promised them that He would send them the Holy Spirit, described as the "Comforter," and the "Counselor" (Greek = *Parakletos*) to guide them so that they, in turn, could be guides to all who follow them in the Faith.

Jesus said, "I will pray the Father, and he will give you another Counselor, to be with you for ever, even the Spirit of truth, whom the world cannot receive, because it neither sees him nor knows him; you know him, for he dwells with you, and will be in you" (John 14:16-17).

In that same situation, Jesus reaffirmed this promise a second time: "These things I have spoken to you, while I am still with you. But the Counselor, the Holy Spirit, whom the Father will send in my name, he will teach you all things, and bring to your remembrance all that I have said to you" (John 14:25-26).

And finally, a third time Jesus confirmed his promise to the Disciples: "When the Counselor comes, whom I shall send to you from the Father, even the Spirit of truth, who proceeds from the Father, he will bear witness to me; and you also are witnesses, because you have been with me from the beginning" (John 15:26-27).

Those words were realized at Pentecost, fifty days after Christ's Resurrection, when the Holy Spirit was sent to the Disciples in mighty power and the Church came into functioning existence (Acts 2). That is why St. Basil said in his *Treatise on the Holy Spirit*, "The Church itself is the work of the Spirit" and why St. Augustine said "What the soul is to the body of a human being, the Holy Spirit is to the Body of Christ, the Church" (Sermon 267). Thus, in the Creed we say that we "believe in the Holy Spirit, the Lord, the Giver of life, who proceeds from the Father, who with the Father and the Son together is worshipped and glorified, who spoke by the Prophets" and immediately following, "And I believe in One Holy, Catholic and Apostolic Church."

Conflicting Traditions

The truth and the life of God reside in the Church through the Holy Spirit. It is through the Holy Tradition of the Church that this presence is made manifest historically. That is what St. Paul was talking about when he said to the Christians of Corinth, "I commend you because you remember me in everything and maintain the traditions even as I have delivered them to you" (1 Corinthians 11: 2).

But there are other kinds of tradition. These are drawn not from the Holy Spirit, nor from Holy Tradition, but from false ideas and distorted conceptions about life and truth. St. Paul spoke about these false traditions, saying, "See to it that no one makes a prey of you by philosophy and empty deceit, according to human tradition, according to the elemental spirits of the universe, and not according to Christ" (Colossians 2:8).

So, in principle there can be empirically present in the life of the Church two basic kinds of tradition. One is inspired and guided by the Holy Spirit. The other is guided by "philosophy and empty deceit . . . and not according to Christ."

The critical issue, of course, is how to discern between them. When is development or change a result of the guiding of the Holy Spirit in the Church? When is change in the traditions of the Church a result of "empty deceit" and "not according to Christ"?

So when we look at the meaning of the presence of the Holy Spirit in the Tradition of the Church we can affirm many things. One of the hymns of the Vespers of Pentecost puts it this way, speaking about the living presence of the Holy Spirit in the Church:

"Light, Life and a living supersenuous Fountain is the Holy Spirit, good, upright, supersenuous Spirit of understanding, presiding and purifying offenses, God and deifying, Fire projecting from Fire, speaking, active, Distributor of gifts, through whom all the prophets, the apostles of God and the martyrs are crowned, a strange report, a strange sight, a Fire divided for the distribution of gifts."

How does such a vibrant understanding of the Holy Spirit relate to Holy Tradition and "the traditions of men" in the life of the Church? We'll begin an answer to this question in the second part of this response.

7. TRADITION: DIFFERENT KINDS

Q. It seems to me that many of our Orthodox Church members wonder about the Tradition of the Church being static and that it seems to them that the Church is no longer being inspired by the Holy Spirit. If the Holy Spirit is inspiring the Church, then Tradition understood as the life of the Holy Spirit in the Church can evolve. If the Church denies the inspiration of the Holy Spirit, isn't that blasphemy?
                                                    – *Name and city withheld*

A. In the previous column we saw a beginning of an answer to this question. The presence of the Holy Spirit in the Church was affirmed, but it was also acknowledged that it was possible also for there to be "traditions of men" in the empirical life of Christians, that were not "according to Christ." The key question is discerning between the developments arising from the creative activity of the Holy Spirit in the Church and the changes that come from other sources.

The Church understands the presence of the Holy Spirit in the authentic life of the Church as living, dynamic, stimulating, evocative and effective Divine presence in the Church's life. In the preceding response we concluded: "How does such a vibrant understanding of the Holy Spirit relate to Holy Tradition and 'the traditions of men' in the life of the Church"

Holy Tradition and traditions

We can speak about three kinds of "tradition" in the Church: "Big T" Tradition; "Little t" tradition; and "minuscule t" tradition. The first is authentic Holy Tradition as the manifestation of Divine Revelation. The second are practices and perspectives authentically harmonious with the Scriptures and Holy Tradition which developed in the long centuries of the life of the Church. The last of these are inventions of the past and present that are unrelated to, or even opposed to authentic Holy Tradition. An example of the latter is the belief that it is more pious and Christian to restrict receiving Holy Communion to only a few times a year.

In this column I'm going to suggest that these three categories can be analyzed in more detail, so that we can actually speak about seven distinct kinds of tradition in the experience of Church life.

Seven Kinds of Tradition

The names I have given these various forms are Dead tradition, Dying tradition, Static tradition, Reviving tradition, Living tradition, Creative tradition and Faithful tradition. Here are a few thoughts on each.

Dead tradition: Throughout the history of the Church there have been two kinds of "Dead traditions." On the one hand there have been what we've called "minuscule t" practices. These are behaviors that are passed on from one generation to another, that violate the spirit and letter of the Orthodox Faith. The practice of Orthodox Christians consistently arriving late for Church is a "dead tradition" violating the very spirit of worship.

On the other had, we can speak of valid and authentic traditions that for vast numbers of Orthodox are "dead," that is, no longer practiced. An example of this from the Bible is cutting one's hair, which was customarily maintained long, as a sign of a vow. We read in Acts about St. Paul that "At Cenchreae he cut his hair, for he had a vow" (Acts 18:18). In fact, in this case, monks do just opposite, leaving their beards and hair uncut as a sign of their monastic calling and vows.

Another example of a valid tradition that has almost died for many members of the Orthodox Church is the refusal of numerous Orthodox Christians to fast on Wednesdays or Fridays, even though this is one of the most ancient "little t" traditions in the Church. It was ordered in the first century book of *The Teaching of the Twelve Apostles* which was written about the same time that the last books of the New Testament were written.

So some traditions are "dead" in the sense that they are the opposite of authentic tradition. Others are valid and good traditions, but are "dead" for many people because they refuse to follow them.

Dying traditions: This term refers to valid and authentic "Big T" or "Little t" traditions that are apparently in the process of being forgotten because they are not being widely practiced. A beautiful "little t" tradition is the procession of the "Epitaphion" (the flower decorated funeral bier of Christ) in the streets around the Church building on Great Friday. In many places this tradition is dying. Elsewhere, it is just a memory.

There are many practices that have similarly reached a low point. The Sacrament of Holy Confession in the Greek Orthodox Church in America is an example of a "Big T tradition" that has reached a low point in practice, even though it is one of the most important Sacraments of the Church.

Similarly, "Little t" Byzantine traditional iconography in the 18th and 19th centuries was not being practiced by iconographers and was close to disappearing. For centuries in Russia and even on the Holy Mountain Athos, a style of painting was adopted that reflected not the earlier tradition of Byzantium, but the more recent style of the Italian Renaissance. Authentic Byzantine Iconography was dying.

Static traditions: Many non-Orthodox condemn our Church for maintaining "static traditions." Some say this to criticize our Church precisely because it struggles to "maintain the Tradition." For them the Church of a generation ago, of a century ago, or a thousand years ago, or even two thousand years ago, is literally, objectively and historically no longer in existence. Only the Church made up of people living today exists. So they understand the maintenance of Orthodox traditions as a museum-like existence -no life, no relevance, no vitality. They criticize the Orthodox as adhering to "static tradition."

Yet, we Orthodox people see the picture very differently. We are the Church of the Apostles maintaining basically unchanged the authentic Christian Tradition for two millennia. What others call "static" we affirm as faithfulness.

We can, however, recognize a certain validity to this charge if we maintain these authentic traditions without understanding or spiritual vitality, or consciousness of why we maintain the traditions. In this case, we are guilty of formalism. We keep the form of the truth, but we do not live it spiritually. The New Testament describes this approach to maintaining the valid traditions of the Church as "holding the form of religion but denying the power of it" (2 Timothy 3:5), and it adds "avoid such people."

If we do not allow the Holy Spirit to illuminate our thinking and living in creative ways that are consistent with the authentic Holy Tradition, then we can be justifiably charged as participating in a "static tradition." Needless to say, formalistic Orthodoxy is a violation of the authentic "Big T" and "Little t" tradition of belief and practice of the Orthodox Church!

8. MORE KINDS OF TRADITION

Q. It seems to me that many of our Orthodox Church members wonder about the Tradition of the Church being static and that it seems to them that the Church is no longer being inspired by the Holy Spirit. If the Holy Spirit is inspiring the Church, then Tradition understood as the life of the Holy Spirit in the Church can evolve. If the Church denies the inspiration of the Holy Spirit, isn't that blasphemy?
– Name and city withheld

A. Last week, in the second response to this question, we discussed the familiar three-fold "Big T," "Little t" and "minuscule t" traditions and began an expansion of the meanings of them, suggesting that there are forms of them that could be called Dead tradition, Dying tradition, Static tradition, Reviving tradition, Living tradition, Creative tradition and Faithful tradition. The first three of these were discussed last week.

More Kinds of Traditions

Reviving traditions: For the Greek Orthodox in the United States, one of the almost dead traditions of our faith that has received widespread attention has been singing liturgical hymns by the congregation (for example, see Acts 2:47, Acts 16:25, 1 Corinthians 14:15 and 14:26, Ephesians 5:19, Colossians 3:16).

A number of years ago the Hierarchs of the "Standing Conference of Canonical Orthodox Bishops" (SCOBA) issued an encyclical encouraging congregational singing during the Divine Liturgy and other services. In many Greek Orthodox parishes this practice is reviving. So valid "Dead traditions" and "Dying traditions" can be resuscitated!

Similar efforts were made by Archbishop Michael to renew the practice of Holy Confession, with some results. More recently, we have seen the renewal of the monastic tradition in the Greek Orthodox Archdiocese, which had been essentially absent from its life.

Such "Reviving traditions" are a valuable contribution to the life of our Church.

Living traditions: There are of course, "Living traditions" in the Church. These reach back to the earliest periods of the Church. All of the Sacraments, for example, are "Living traditions," first and foremost of which are Baptism and the Holy Eucharist. The Wednesday and Friday tradition of fasting can be traced to the *Teaching of the Twelve Apostles*, written sometime around 100 A.D. Many faithful Orthodox Christians maintain this fast, and the Church admonishes all of its members to do so. The Creed and its teaching are as alive today as they were when first written.

In the early Church there were two very important dimensions of Christian life, what we call today missions and social concern. Yet, because of almost 500 years of life under the Ottomans, circumstances served to eliminate these from the practical consciousness of Orthodox Church members. For the Greek Orthodox, these two authentic almost "Dead traditions" have not only revived, but are now "Living traditions," with a strong mission program in the United States and a developing social consciousness in the form of healthy Ecological awareness (Patriarch Bartholomew leading the way), the repudiation of racism (Archbishop Iakovos in Selma), and even Orthodox sponsored AIDS prevention and education programs (Diocese of Chicago). All these are "Living traditions."

While it is possible to criticize the contemporary empirical

Orthodox Church for many failings, we can honestly emphasize that more and more, it is Orthodox Christianity that reflects the faith and practice of the One, Holy, Catholic and Apostolic Church of the earliest centuries of Christianity.

Creative tradition: The chief point that the letter writer makes is that the Holy Spirit must be understood as being a creative force in the life of the Church. The letter says, "Tradition understood as the life of the Holy Spirit in the Church can evolve." In the section below, I want to speak about what is meant by Tradition "evolving." Here, we need to see in what way we can speak about "Creative Tradition." An area of great concern is the moral challenge of the new biology. We usually refer to such concerns as "issues of bioethics."

With the development of medical technology, issues such as artificial insemination, cloning and even ecology, just to name a few, our Orthodox faith has been challenged to say things about our beliefs on such issues that have never been addressed before.

The main question regarding this challenge is: "On what basis are such answers to be developed?" Well, certainly we can number some sources: the Bible, the Holy Tradition (both "Big T," and "Little t" Tradition) including the Teachings of the Church Fathers, Canon Law and the liturgical and sacramental life of the Church.

Competent Orthodox Church thinkers will try to show the way by offering assessments of the issues and proposing responses. Church bodies will try to develop answers that are coherent with the rest of the Church's teaching in a responsible way. All of this will be done in an effort to be in accordance with the "mind of the Church."

To be successful, such efforts will be conducted with prayer for the guidance of the Holy Spirit. We can assume that if in the minds and hearts of faithful Orthodox Christians there is a consensus, it eventually may be affirmed in Church Councils by Orthodox Hierarchs at various levels. *Should this kind of creative effort happen, we can be confident that the Holy Spirit is guiding the teaching of the Church today, just as it has from the beginning and throughout the ages.*

But "Creative tradition" will never be just private opinion. It will always be a process in the consciousness of the whole body of the Church.

Faithful tradition: What needs to be looked at is the precise meaning of "evolving tradition." Without question, for something to "evolve" means that there is change in it. So a teaching or practice in one period and situation may develop into new forms.

An example is the evolution of the Sacrament of the Holy Eucharist. At first, with the "Last Supper," it was associated with a meal. We know that in the time of St. Paul this practice was creating problems (1 Corinthians 11:20). Little by little the Eucharist was separated from these meals and in different parts of the Church distinct liturgical services having at their core the same essential elements, began to be formed. We have descriptions of these in writings of the second and third centuries of the Christian era. By the fifth century there were several different Divine Liturgies, all having the same basic substance. In the Orthodox Church we know them as the Liturgies of St. John Chrysostom, St. Basil, St. Iakovos and the Presanctified Liturgy. This development is consistent and coherent. We could call this the evolving of our Eucharistic liturgical tradition.

While there is development and evolving, nothing is violated regarding the core of the tradition. Only its expression changes. This is "Faithful tradition." But how do we know that an "evolving" belief is authentically Orthodox? That's the heart of the matter.

9. LIVING TRADITION

Q. It seems to me that many of our Orthodox Church members wonder about the Tradition of the Church being static and that it seems to them that the Church is no longer being inspired by the Holy Spirit. If the Holy Spirit is inspiring the Church, then Tradition understood as the life of the Holy Spirit in the Church can evolve. If the Church denies the inspiration of the Holy Spirit, isn't that blasphemy?
– Name and city withheld.

A. Last week we concluded with these words, "How do we know that an 'evolving' belief is authentically Orthodox? That's the heart of the matter." This series will be concluded with some thoughts on answering this crucial question.

The Holy Spirit and Holy Tradition

According to the prayer "Heavenly King" (*"Vasilef Ouranie"*) the Holy Spirit is "the Spirit of truth," "the Treasury of good things," and "the Giver of life." Nothing could be further from a static understanding of the Christian life!

As we have pointed out in the previous parts on this question, we believe that the Holy Spirit has guided the Church throughout its existence. The gift of the Holy Spirit is a response to the Psalmist's (and our) request: "Guide me, O Lord in thy way, and I will walk in thy truth" (Psalm 85:10).

The whole of Holy Tradition, including the Scriptures, the decisions of the Ecumenical Councils, and the Canons, and the writings of the Church Fathers, are embodiments of that Spirit-guided way of life that is God's. Holy Tradition represents a base line of truth.

When the culture and society in which we live holds to the same principles and norms as those of the Church, we do not feel the need for change or development. But, when circumstances surrounding us seem to challenge the traditional teachings of the Church, questions arise, and we wonder if the ancient teaching is adequate, or even true. So the idea of the Spirit's leading to new truths or new teachings comes to the fore. What guidelines do we have for such a situation?

The Holy Spirit's Guiding

If there is to be "development," or "evolution," or "progress," it must start from what has already been discerned in the teaching and the practice of the Church. The assumption has to be the continuity of the Christian truth: "Unto generation and generation will I declare thy truth with my mouth" the Psalmist says (Psalm 88:2).

But as we have seen already, that does not mean a static understanding of the Christian Faith as the circumstances of life change. There can be and must be a creative and living understanding of the Faith. The Psalmist, once again, shows the way:

> I have chosen the way of faithfulness, I set thy ordinances before me. . . . I will run in the way of thy commandments when thou enlargest my understanding! Teach me, O Lord, the way of thy statutes; and I will keep it to the end. Give me understanding, that I may keep thy law and observe it with my whole heart" (Psalm 119:30-34).

This is not an insignificant passage. It is part of the set of readings known as the "Kathismata" that are read every day in Orthodox monasteries.

If we read this passage carefully we will see that "the way of truth" and committed loyalty to it, is foundational. But it also affirms that God "enlarges" our understanding of His commandments, and that they must be approached with "understanding" given by God, so that we have an obligation to "search out" God's law.

Continuity and Newness

Here we come to a crucial point. If there are going to be new things in God's guiding of the Church, can they logically be totally discontinuous, or even the exact opposite of what we have been taught from time immemorial? Of course, God is the Lord, and anything is possible.

But, from our human perspective, the burden of proof would be on those who argue that the Holy Spirit would guide us into something that was totally discontinuous with Divine Revelation up to this point. We have affirmed repeatedly "Thy righteousness is an everlasting righteousness, and thy law is truth" (Psalm 118:142), and the frequently repeated liturgical verse, "His mercy is great toward us, and the truth of the Lord endureth forever"

What we would expect is that there would be a certain continuity between the truth as we have known it and the new embodiment of the truth. Earlier in this series, I gave the example of issues arising out of the new biological technologies.

An example is artificial insemination. In reflecting on this development, Orthodox bioethicists have recognized that this is a totally new situation, but that there are existing values and teachings that can guide us. The tradition of support for medical means of healing encourages us to accept the idea of artificial insemination. Further investigation however, points to the teaching about the unity of the spouses in marriage. So, we conclude that artificial insemination using the sperm and ovum of the married couple is acceptable. It is a way of helping a married couple to achieve one of the purposes of their marriage. But, the line would be drawn at using donors, because of the inviolable unity of the married couple. Thus, old traditions contribute to resolving new issues.

Recently, I think for the first time ever, an Orthodox Priest, Fr. Samuel Kedala, of the Orthodox Church in America, sued the United States government over biogenetically altered foods. He gives theological reasons for his objection. In his declaration to the United States District Court in the District of Columbia, he says, "I believe that the manner in which our food is being genetically reconfigured through recombinant DNA technology degrades the integrity of God's creation and conflicts with the divine plan." He adds, "My belief is grounded in basic Christian principles and in particular teachings of the Eastern Orthodox Church." This is a totally new example of a previously non-existent Orthodox position. Whether he is correct and whether the Orthodox Church will ultimately agree with him is something time will tell. But his use of Orthodox doctrine to support his views is perfectly legitimate and properly "creative."

What about total reversals of teaching? Regarding issues such as the ordination of women to the Priesthood, and the blessing of homosexual marriages, while theoretically possible (the Holy Spirit "blows where it wills"), the burden of proof is on those who advocate these views, since the Holy Tradition is unexceptionally and historically on the other side. It's no change in belief to hold that the Holy Spirit guides us in new understandings of the Tradition in new circumstances. It is a radical change to hold that the Holy Spirit obliterates past teaching and substitutes it with its opposite. Is that impossible? No. But neither is it likely.

10. HOW CHURCHES DETERMINE THEIR TEACHINGS

Q. In determining an Orthodox viewpoint, a variety of sources play in the determination (i.e., Scripture, Writings of the Fathers, Canons). Which of these, if any, takes precedence, or do any and all?

– J. K., Vero Beach, FL.

A. Your question is essentially, "What is the way that the Orthodox Church determines its faith and its teaching?" This is an important point not just for the sake of understanding the past, but also for understanding how the Church addresses new circumstances, new conditions, and new issues which it must face for the well-being of its faithful members and for the sake of Christ's Church.

It might help to answer your question if we put it in the context of the religious world in which we live. In today's column, we will see in a very cursory and inadequate way, how other Christian churches determine their teachings. Today's column will end with a few words about the Orthodox Christian approach to this question. In the next column we will show the different way by which the Orthodox Church addresses the sources of its faith teaching. In sketching out the contrast (and that is all we can do here), we hope to make clear the Orthodox difference.

The Roman Catholic Alternative

In our experience we see other church bodies address this question in various ways. Over the centuries the Roman Catholic Church developed an approach which had a basically two-pronged direction. On the one hand was the Natural Law, which was represented by philosophy. In many ways it was considered adequate to address many theological and moral questions. To it was added the saving knowledge of Divine Revelation, especially the Bible as understood by the Roman Catholic Church. The Roman Catholic Church's authority in interpreting the truth of the Christian Faith over the years came to be concentrated in the clergy and ultimately in the Pope of Rome who pronounced authoritatively on matters of faith and morals.

In spite of internal differences, the Roman Catholic Church, basing itself on the authority of the Pope of Rome, is able to maintain a wide range of official teachings which are considered binding upon members of the Roman Catholic Church. The term used by them is the "Teaching of the Magesterium" and the source of that authority and the chief spokesman for their religious truth is the Pope of Rome.

The Early Protestant Alternative

Protestants, beginning in the sixteenth century, rejected the authority of both Pope and Church to pronounce the truth of the Christian faith. They found their single authority in the Bible, both the Old and the New Testaments. They taught that every Christian should read the Bible on his/her own, and they believed that the Holy Spirit would guide the reader to the truth.

Over the years, however, this view began to create problems. From the beginning there were several different basic interpretations of the Bible as the sole authoritative source of the Christian Faith.

Three very different traditions developed in the first years of the Protestant movement. Lutheranism in Germany, kept many of the Roman Catholic liturgical traditions, though in a modified form. The emphasis was on free grace and forgiveness in Christ and the centrality of the Word of God, best expressed in preaching and the two sacraments of Baptism and Holy Communion.

Parallel to this church movement was the Reformed tradition, based in Geneva, Switzerland. The leader of this church movement was John Calvin. This tradition taught that God predestined certain people for salvation and that one showed he/she was saved by living an upright and moral life. It was easier to know what it meant to be upright and moral if there was a clear moral code of behavior, so this Protestant tradition had a strong legal character to it.

In addition to these major Protestant church groups were numerous Radical and Free Church movements which emphasized personal holiness and piety. They demanded less in terms of doctrinal belief than did the Lutherans and the Calvinists, but more in terms of the close bond of individual believers. Among the groups to come from this trend were church bodies such as the Baptists, who while insisting on some doctrines, allow a great deal of interpretation.

From an Orthodox point of view, "the Bible alone" approach could not be an adequate approach, since all these varied traditions appealed to the same Bible, yet they interpreted it in so many different and contrary ways, it was not possible that they could all be accurate witnesses to the Christian truth.

Later Protestant Alternatives

Later, these groups split on different lines. Some were influenced by new philosophers such as Emmanuel Kant, by philosophical rationalism, and other intellectual schools of thought and became closely identified with social and political activism. They have also committed themselves to an understanding of the Bible in historical terms, with a critical and more diffuse understanding of the message of Divine Revelation in the Scriptures. These trajectories within classic Protestant denominations often times are referred to as the "Mainline Protestants."

Others, still influenced by classical Protestant theologies and traditions, are much more conservative. They focus on the personal commitment dimension of the Christian faith, and are often very individualistic. Those who understand the Bible more or less literally, often identify themselves as Fundamentalists, based on an agreed list of "Fundamentals" that some nineteenth century Protestants propounded as the essential teaching of the Bible. Their theology holds that salvation comes to a person by a confession of personal faith in Jesus Christ. So they are very much committed to evangelism. Much less attention is given to the sacraments, even as they understand them. Even less attention is given to social concern.

More moderate, though very committed to the Bible as the sole source of knowledge regarding the Christian faith, are those who call themselves Evangelicals. As their name implies they are committed to evangelizing non-believers as they define them. A well-known example of this thread of belief and church life in Protestantism is Billy Graham. Not so long ago, their teachings reflected strong individualism, but in recent years, they have sought to become more "ecclesial" or "church-minded" on the one hand, and more out-reaching in terms of social concern, on the other.

Alternatives: A Cautious Reservation

I hope that you understand that this description is an inadequate description of the trends of understanding in both the Roman Catholic and the Protestant church traditions about the sources of the Christian faith. It is almost a caricature, since life and thought is so much more complex than a few paragraphs can describe.

But if we were to sum up what we have said so far, we would say that the Roman Catholic Church has a more unified sense of the sources of the Christian faith and teaching, since it is seen to be subject to the teachings of the natural moral law and the revelation of God in Jesus Christ as found in the Bible and as interpreted by the Church, and ultimately by the Pope of Rome, who is understood to be the Vicar of Christ on Earth.

In contrast, Protestants tend to focus on the Bible alone, but in all the variety described above. The issue of how divine grace and nature work together to let us know about the truth of God for us is answered in a wide range of potential responses. Perhaps that is why in the United States today there are almost three hundred recognized Protestant church bodies. Since the private interpretation of Scripture is a basic Protestant teaching, it means that the differences are often even deeper, since each minister and each Christian determines for him or herself what that truth is.

Toward the Orthodox Alternative

The Roman Catholic and Protestant churches share much in common. The Protestants rebelled against what they perceived to be errors in the Roman Catholic Church about five hundred years ago. In many ways the present state of each Church is formed by the differences between them.

The Orthodox Church is more strongly rooted in the ongoing tradition of faith in the early Christian Church. As the question above implies, the Orthodox viewpoint has what appears to be many sources (the writer mentions Scripture, the writings of the Church Fathers and the Canons). These clearly lend richness and complexity to the formation of the Orthodox viewpoint. Yet, at the same time, there is a sense that all these sources in the ongoing tradition of the Church have a single source for the truths of the Christian faith.

The Orthodox Church's approach to this question is at once rich in variety, but in the end, essentially united. Further, within this complex/simple source of the truth of the Christian faith, there is a belief in the ongoing presence of the Holy Spirit that keeps the Orthodox faith alive and able to address the new issues of each age. It comes with a freedom built upon the truth of the Christian faith which is ultimately rooted in the experience of the Holy Spirit in its life.

11. DETERMINING THE ORTHODOX VIEWPOINT

Q. In determining an Orthodox viewpoint, a variety of sources play in the determination (i.e., Scripture, Writings of the Fathers, Canons). Which of these, if any, takes precedence, or do any and all?
                                                    – J. K., Vero Beach, FL.

A. Last week we spoke about how other church bodies go about clarifying their teachings and viewpoints on various issues. Today we will try to make clear how the Orthodox Church has done this.

Natural Knowledge About Divine Things

It is the belief of the Orthodox Church that we can have some limited knowledge about God through ordinary human thought and experience. An example is the "watchmaker" argument. Suppose you found a watch on the beach of an abandoned island. Logic would tell you that it didn't come together accidentally or by chance. The likelihood of that happening is so minuscule, that reason forces you to assume the existence of a watchmaker. So, one could reason that the complex world could not have come into existence without a Creator who must be intelligent enough and wise enough and capable enough to make the physical world in which we live.

The Orthodox recognize that such efforts to understand the divine in the past have had some measure of success. St. Paul, in his letter to the Romans (chapters 1 and 2) points to this kind of natural knowledge of God and His will for us regarding moral behavior. The Church Fathers identified the content of the Ten Commandments as presented in the Old Testament with a natural moral law common to every culture and society. But it is clear that this could not be taken too far.

Two factors work against expecting too much from this natural knowledge: human limitedness and human sinfulness. The variety of cultures, religions, customs, traditions, styles of life speak too loudly against assuming deep agreement on too many aspects of life and thought. Each of us personally and every culture is too limited in its experience to be able to fully understand itself, much less all of reality. This is even truer about beliefs regarding the divine.

Further, little is to be known about God because of our fallen, darkened and sinful condition. Too much subjectivity, too many ways of interpreting events and experiences, too many possibilities of seeing things under the light of our selfish interests mean that we could not know much about the reality of God and His expectations of us with our unaided human experience, reason or intuitions.

God's Self-Revelation

The only way we could know about God and His will for us, was for Him to tell us; that is, to reveal Himself to humanity. It is the contention of the Judeo-Christian tradition, that God has done that. He revealed Himself first to the Hebrew people through the great prophets and during the later history of the Jews. The record of that revelation is the Old Testament.

Christians believe that God revealed Himself fully in Jesus Christ. And Jesus revealed Himself most fully to His Apostles. Before a word of this revelation was written down, the message about God and the Son and the Holy Spirit was revealed by Christ through His public preaching and His private teaching to the Apostles. He taught them, also, about the creation of humanity in God's image and likeness; about the fall of humanity into separation from God; about His saving work offered for the "life of the world"; about how one should live in love for God and neighbor; He offered moral and spiritual guidance; and He foretold His victory over sin through His Death and Resurrection. All these things and much more were conveyed to the world. Our Church's language for this living experience of the truth of God is "Holy Tradition."

Subsequently, under the guidance of the Holy Spirit much of that teaching was written down in what the Church calls the New

Testament. The Church produced it with God's guidance and inspiration; the Church understands it within the framework of Holy Tradition; and, finally, the Church interprets Holy Tradition and the Holy Scriptures to respond to new issues, new questions and new problems.

The Mind of the Church

Often a long time is needed to clarify the meaning of the revelation of God in reference to a newly raised question or issue. For instance, it wasn't until the Fourth Ecumenical Council that the Church finalized its basic understanding about the person of Jesus Christ as both Son of God and a fully human being in one Person. The teaching was there in Holy Tradition and Holy Scripture, but it had to be formulated just right, to reflect the mind of the Church regarding its interpretation of revelation about just who Jesus Christ was.

It is precisely the "mind of the Church" which addresses new issues and new problems as they appear. Holy Tradition is embodied now in many different sources in a loosely coherent way. Certainly, at the heart of the sources of our knowledge about God are the *Holy Scriptures*, that is the Bible. But, as we have seen, the Bible must be understood from within its churchly context in Holy Tradition. Some of the most important embodiments of Holy Tradition other than Holy Scripture, which express the mind of the Church are the following: the decisions of the *Ecumenical Councils* and other *Church Councils*; the writings of the *Church Fathers*; the Church's rules and regulations known as *Canons*; the expression of the faith in the *Worship of the Church* its sacraments, prayer life and hymns; the received *ethical and moral teachings* of the Church; the holy *monastic and ascetical* tradition; and in general, the style or "ethos of life" which we could call the "churchly mindset."

Determining the Stance of the Church

All these elements interpenetrate, mutually inform, and alternately illuminate each other in the mind of the Church. The process of identifying a new problem or issue can begin anywhere. The laity may raise the issue; theologians may seek deeper understanding; false teachings may provoke the search, and so on. Often, the issue is not so new at all.

Resources exist in the living tradition of the Church which speak directly or provide clear parallels so as to make the view of the Church quite clear. An example is a recent column question which dealt with Cremation. The Church's practice and teaching need only to be rediscovered and articulated to respond negatively to the renewed question of whether Orthodox Christians should choose cremation. The tradition affirms only burial.

The more knowledgeable we are about the early tradition of the Church, through understanding the Bible, the writings of the Church Fathers, the history of the Church, and all those other sources mentioned above, the more likely we are to come to a correct assessment of the Church's understanding of a new issue.

Guidelines

That is why this work must be done 1) in a disciplined and orderly way, 2) exercised with care and knowledge, 3) collegially, and, 4) under the guidance of the Holy Spirit. A current example consists of the ethical understanding of gene and stem cell research. Since the determining of the Church's teaching on a new issue is the work of the whole Church, it normally takes place from within its normal life. At the head of the life of the Church are the Bishops. In their reflection on the sense of the appropriateness of any given response to a new question or issue they are ultimately the guides, "teaching aright the word of (God's) truth." In the process, the Church's scholars and teachers help the Church understand its tradition, seeking to provide guidance on the issues. While the process may seem undirected, the fact that the Bishops meeting as a council of the Church are its highest earthly authority, leads the process eventually to decisions. In addition to this structure and order and the cultivation of knowledge of the tradition, collegiality means that the voice of the people of God, the laity, is also important and is listened to by the "official" Church. Above all, the Church which is founded on the gift of the Holy Spirit, prays for the Spirit's guidance in forming its responses.

A Contemporary Example

A brief example of this process was the discussion that has taken place in the Orthodox Church about organ donation, and in particular the donation of one's eyes after death. The technology was developed several decades ago by scientists. In Greece, the rightness or wrongness of it was discussed by bishops, priests, scholars, and laypeople -some arguing it was wrong, some that it was in harmony with the Orthodox faith. A consensus formed. In the mid-1980s, the Archbishop of Athens endorsed the lay organization sponsoring the eye donations for transplantation and announced in an encyclical that he, himself, had willed his eyes for transplantation after his death. It now is at the stage where there is a positive climate, supported by theological reflection, and the practice is considered to be in harmony with the Orthodox Christian faith.

12. CREED AND CONFESSIONS IN THE ORTHODOX CHURCH

Q. I am interested in the "Synod of Jerusalem" held in the 17th century and in a book called the "Diocletian Confession," I think. It was the Orthodox response to the Protestant Reformation and discussed where Orthodoxy stood on the doctrines of the Reformation. I can't find anything in print. Can you provide any information?

– J. C., Charlotte, NC.

A. The document you are referring to is the *Confession of Dositheos* (Dositheus). We need first, to understand the background of "Creed and Confessions in the Orthodox Church."

Creed and Confessions

In Orthodoxy the term "Creed" ("*Pistevo*") refers to a fully authorized, formal statement of the faith of the Church deriving from an Ecumenical Council. So, there is strictly only one Creed, or, by an extension of the term, two additional Creeds. "Confessions" are widely accepted decisions of local councils or writings of illustrious hierarchs or theologians.

1) *Creeds*: Broadly, these are the doctrinal decisions of the first seven ecumenical councils. Specifically, "The Creed" is the **Nicene-Constantinopolitan Creed**, the only Creed used in Orthodox worship and instruction.

    The so-called "Apostolic Creed" and the "Athanasian Creed" are considered at one and the same time of intrinsic historic value and in harmony with the deposit of faith, yet basically irrelevant to the present worship life of the Orthodox Church.

2) *Confessions of Faith*: These "Confessions" or "Symbolic Books" arose particularly after the Great Schism and the rise of Protestantism, often with the purpose of counteracting either Roman or Protestant teaching. They have less authority than the Creed but have great value as authentic witnesses of the Church's belief. Among those commonly accepted are:

a) *General Orthodox Confessions of Faith*: These include the *Confession of Faith* by Patriarch Gennadios (1455-6), the *Confession of Faith* of Mitrophanes Kritopoulos (1827), and the *Orthodox Confession* of Bishop Peter Moghila (1643).

b) *Confessions Dealing with Roman Catholicism*: There are eleven of these, dating from 866 to 1948, detailing deviations of the Roman Church from Orthodox doctrine and practice.

c) *Confessions Dealing with Protestantism*: There are nine such "Confessions" dated from the 1573-1581 discussions between Lutherans and Patriarch Jeremiah to the encyclical of the Council of Constance in 1836.

Modern documents of a confessional character derive chiefly from official statements related to the ecumenical movement.

The Confession of Cyril Loukaris

The *Confession of Dositheos* is one of the responses to an unusual and very controversial document, the 1629 confession of faith of Cyril Loukaris, Patriarch of Constantinople. This document is Calvinistic in content and was repudiated and condemned by the Orthodox Church. Calvinism is the form of Protestantism that arose in Switzerland. In the U.S.A. the Presbyterian Churches, Reformed Churches, and Southern Baptists are Calvinistic in doctrine and practice.

The Orthodox Confessions dealing with the Calvinist Protestant tradition were all acts of local councils which took place between 1638 and 1691. All were responses to the unorthodox confession of faith of Patriarch Cyril Loukaris (1571-1638). Cyril was strongly anti-Roman, and in struggling to combat Roman Catholic influence among the Orthodox, he depended heavily on the political support of the Protestant embassies in Constantinople. Thus obliged, he apparently signed a confession of faith which was almost completely Calvinist in content. The *Confession* of Loukaris is clearly based on the *Institutes* of John Calvin.

This so-called "Orthodox" confession of faith was published in Geneva in 1629 and became the basis of Calvinist proselytizing among the Orthodox, and, paradoxically also, a tool in the hands of the Roman Catholic missionaries at the expense of the Orthodox Church.

The consternation within the Orthodox Church caused by such a document cannot be overestimated. The Patriarch of the leading

Orthodox Church was presented as espousing doctrines and beliefs of a Protestant movement in the West! Loukaris never repudiated his *Eastern Confession of the Christian Faith*. But also, he never publicly referred to it, nor defended it when attacked, nor attacked it, nor explained its existence. He died violently when in 1638, he was strangled by Turkish janissaries who cast his body into the Bosporus.

The Council of Jerusalem

Three months after his death in September of 1638, a Council met in Constantinople, condemning Cyril's *Confession* as heretical. Since the confusion over the *"Confession"* of Cyril was not abating but was being complicated by his memory as a national martyr, two councils met, one in Constantinople in May of 1641 and another in Jassy in September of 1642. The results became known as *The Acts of the Council of Constantinople and Jassy—1642*. Finally, both Roman Catholics and Protestants asked the Orthodox to clarify their position. To do this two councils were held in 1672, one in Constantinople and one in Jerusalem in which authoritative answers were given. The council in Constantinople issued a succinct *Synodical Tome* of about five pages.

More important was the Jerusalem Council. Patriarch Dositheos, on the occasion of the consecration of the Church of the Nativity in Jerusalem called a council in which we have a final and complete refutation of the issue of the validity of the confession of Cyril, especially for the benefit of the non-Orthodox. Included in it was the first draft of an extremely important *Orthodox Confession of Faith* by Patriarch Dositheos. *The Acts of the Jerusalem Council of 1672* are about 32 pages long.

Confession of Dositheos

The *Confession of Faith by Dositheos*, which was part of the *Acts of the Jerusalem Council of 1672*, has become one of the most important confessional documents of the period. Written carefully on the exact plan of the confession of Cyril it presented the Orthodox position on every issue touched upon by Cyril's work. Thus externally it was very much like the former, but in content it expressed the Orthodox faith. In eighteen *"Oroi"* (Definitions) and four "Questions" the whole range of theological topics is treated. Repeatedly approved by Orthodox hierarchs and councils, the *Confession of Dositheos* is one of the most authoritative documents in the history of Orthodox-Protestant relationships.

The first edition, however, was partially dependent on Roman Catholic sources. By the third edition, published in 1690, nearly all of these influences were neutralized and a more patristic character was added. An Orthodox scholar, John Karmiris, characterizes it "as one of the most complete Orthodox expositions of the faith of that period, as well as an historic document of supreme significance." It has been published in thirteen editions to date in its original Greek form. The *Confession of Dositheos* is a document of about twenty-five pages.

To my knowledge there is only one English translation: *The Acts and Decrees of the Synod of Jerusalem*, New York: AMS Press, 1969. Most of this response is excerpted and revised in: Stanley S. Harakas, "Creed and Confession in the Orthodox Church." *Journal of Ecumenical Studies*, vol. 7, no. 4, 1970, pp. 721-743.

One God: A Trinity of Divine Persons

13. THE HOLY TRINITY: A MYSTERY

Q. I was informed by my father that you would be the best person to ask about the Trinity. My question has many parts. *– S. F., Peoria, IL.*

A. Please thank your father for me for his confidence, but the fact is that no one is fully capable of answering completely all of your questions which you have included in your letter. I will not present these in the same order as you have written them, so that all the readers will be able to follow the course of the response in a more or less logical fashion.

Because you have many questions about the Holy Trinity, this week's and next week's columns will be devoted to responding to them. Readers may want to save this week's column in order to refer back to it when next week's column appears.

The Mystery of the Holy Trinity

The doctrine of the Holy Trinity seems to be filled with contradictions, but I know there are no concrete answers to this awesome mystery and that faith alone should suffice, but I do wish to know where our Church stands.

You ended your question with this statement. I would like to begin with it. When we try to talk about God, we need to remember something very important. You and I and everything that we know and experience are "created." All the rules, including the logic of our experience and reality belong to the realm of the created universe. When we think about the things of the created world, we normally (and correctly) expect them to follow a certain rational pattern. If something doesn't quite fit, it usually means that our understanding of the created world needs refining and development. As a result, our knowledge of this world constantly grows and develops, becoming more and more complex, but still, we see it as forming a coherent description of reality. This is why we can speak of the development of scientific knowledge.

But God, in His very being, is not created; He is the Creator. He is the only "uncreated one." His very being and nature cannot be subjected to the rules of logic and knowledge that describe created reality. Since the way we think cannot help but be conditioned by our creaturely experience and knowledge, it is very possible that, while some things about God may seem to fit our reasoning, others will not. The only way we can know about these things, which don't fit our reasoning and knowledge pattern as created beings, is if God makes them known to us by revealing them to us. When this happens, if we compare them with our ordinary experience and knowledge from the created world, they seem not to fit; they are "mysteries" or "paradoxes" or, literally truths "not of this world."

There is nothing in this created world which can compare to the inner nature of God. One of the aspects of this divine reality is the reality that God is a community of persons, sharing the one divine nature: Father, Son and Holy Spirit. The paradox, or mystery is, precisely, that there is one God, who is in His very being and nature, three persons in relationship and communion with each other. With this background we can go to your queries.

Christ as God

The Church says that Christ was all-God and all-man, simultaneously. Firstly, when the Church says Christ was all-God, does it mean that He was all-divine, all-powerful, all-loving, and simply, of a Godly nature, or does the Church mean all of the entire Godhead - the Father, Son and Holy Spirit?

The revelation of God about Jesus Christ is that in the Incarnation we have a unique reality never before and never after duplicated in the created world. We have in Jesus Christ a single person who is fully God and fully human being. Your question is about how Jesus could be fully God and how that fullness of divinity relates to the other persons of the Holy Trinity.

Next, we must point out that the revelation of God in the Holy Bible and Holy Tradition shows that the fully divine nature of Jesus Christ was the second person of the Holy Trinity, the Son. As the Son, He shares fully in the single divine nature. Therefore He has all the characteristics and attributes of the one God: all-powerful, all-knowing, all-loving, etc. The only thing about the Son which differentiates Him from the Father, is that the Father eternally "gives birth" to His Son. What exactly this language describes is beyond human understanding. It is one of the "mysteries" of the doctrine of the Holy Trinity. "Eternally giving birth" is a concept that does not fit any of the created realities that we know from our experience in this world.

To say that the Son (and not the Father and not the Holy Spirit) took on human nature means that only the second person of the Holy Trinity took on human nature. But that does not mean that the Son was separated from the commonly shared divinity of the three persons. Hence, we have the responses to your next questions.

Was the Trinity Divided in the Incarnation?

If it is the first statement that holds true, then doesn't it imply that the Trinity was "divided" during Christ's earthly stay.

No, the Holy Trinity was not "divided" since all three persons of the Holy Trinity share in the one divine reality. In this they were and are eternally "one."

However, if it is the second statement which holds true (which it must since we say the Trinity is undivided) and if we say the Trinity was present in Christ, two questions arise. Firstly, it would mean that in one nature (Jesus-the Son) there was present two other natures.

Here, I must correct the use of your language. The word "nature" in the theology of the Trinity refers only to the one divine reality which is equally that of the Father, the Son and the Holy Spirit. As this part of your question stands, it talks about "three" natures. Technically, that would mean three gods! I'm sure you don't mean that. The right word to use here is "persons" or "hypostases." In God there is one divine nature, but three "hypostases" or "persons." If we then say, "...with the *one person* there were present two other persons, we would be correct in the sense that all three persons "indwell" in each other. The technical theological term for this is *"perichoresis."* Yet, the three persons continue to be distinguished from each other by the way they relate to each other.

14. THE PERSONS OF THE HOLY TRINITY

Q. I was informed by my father that you would be the best person to ask about the Trinity. My question has many parts. – *S. F., of Peoria, IL.*

A. Last week we pointed out how all truths about the Holy Trinity by necessity are "mysteries" or "paradoxes" because of our understanding is limited to the "created" world, while God is "uncreated." We pointed out that Jesus Christ is the only person who was ever both fully divine and fully human. As divine, He was the second person of the Holy Trinity, the Son. His is the divine nature, which also belongs to the Father and the Holy Spirit; but because He is the Son, he is differentiated from them as well. This means that the Trinity was not "divided" when the second person, the Son, took on human nature in the Incarnation. This is so, because the one nature of God was present in the Incarnation, and because all three persons of the Holy Trinity "indwell" in each other. But if this be the case, S.F. then raises another question.

How Did Christ Then "Return to the Father"?

Why then did Jesus tell His disciples that He was going to return to His Father, if the entire Godhead was present in Him? The mere fact that Christ said He would return to His Father clearly indicated separation of some sort.

The only "separation" which we can speak of, is the presence of the Son as Son in the divine-human reality of Jesus Christ. This is not either a separation of the Son from the divine nature, nor from the shared indwelling ("*perichoresis*") of the three persons of the Holy Trinity. The mistake in thinking this way comes from the almost necessary need you and I have to think of these things in terms of space: the Father "up there," and the Son "down here." But since God is everywhere present, even in His Incarnation the Son is in relationship and communion with the Father.

"Returning to the Father" is not talking about space categories, but about the plan of salvation. Jesus Christ completed His work of redemption with His Death on the Cross and His Resurrection from the grave. The next step in the plan of salvation was for the Holy Spirit to relate the saving work of Jesus Christ to the fallen world and every human being in it. In this sense–to use spatial terms again- the Son left "center stage" and the Holy Spirit came to the fore so that in the Church human beings might appropriate for themselves on a personal basis the work which Christ did for the salvation of the whole world.

The "Equality" of the Persons of the Holy Trinity

Furthermore, if we say that Trinity is equal, then how is it that our Church claims the Holy Spirit proceeds from the Father and not the Son when the Father and Son are equal and of the same essence.

The persons of the "Trinity are equal" in the sense that all three persons of the Holy Trinity are divine, that is, the revelation shows that all three persons are equally divine, since they share the same, single, unique divine nature. Consequently, the divinity of the Son is not a "lesser divinity" than that of the Father. Also, the divinity of the Holy Spirit is not a divinity that is "inferior" to the divinity of the other persons of the Holy Trinity. The divinity of the three persons is one. They are therefore equal.

Also, when the Church says that the Holy Spirit proceeds from the Father and that the Son is generated, it indicates the seniority, or superiority of the Father.

This is also part of the mystery or paradox. It seems so because we cannot help thinking, as beings who are part of the created world, in space and time categories. But the revelation of God indicates that the Son is forever and eternally "born of the Father." This means that the Father is forever and eternally the "source" of the Son. The revelation of God also indicates that the third person of the Holy Trinity, the Holy Spirit, forever and eternally "proceeds from the Father." This means that the Father is forever and eternally also the "source" of the Holy Spirit. In the plan of salvation, the Son "sends" the Holy Spirit into the world for its sanctification, but "within the Trinity" the Son is not the "source" of the Holy Spirit -the Father is.

So, each person of the Holy Trinity relates to the others in a special and unique way. The Father is the "source" of the Son and the Holy Spirit. The Son is forever "born" of the Father. The Holy Spirit forever "proceeds" from the Father. All three persons "indwell" in each other. Only in the sense of the Father as the eternal source of the other two persons could we use the word "seniority" to refer to the Father. He would not be "superior" in nature since all three share the one Godhead. He would be "senior" only in the sense that the Father is eternally the "source" of the other two persons. But since this takes place eternally, there was never a time when the Father "pre-existed" the Son and the Holy Spirit. "Time categories" however belong only to created reality. Therefore, in reality, the Father does not have "seniority" time-wise over the Son or the Holy Spirit, since God is beyond categories of time.

In regard to the created world (that which is not God), the revelation teaches that the Father created it (but through the Son and in the Holy Spirit); the Son, having been incarnated as Jesus Christ, redeemed and saved it (in the Father and with the Holy Spirit); and that the Holy Spirit sanctifies the world (as sent by Christ, and in and for the Father). So, all actions of each of the persons of the Holy Trinity in reference to the created world also include the other two divine persons. In the final analysis all actions of the Holy Trinity toward, in, and for the world are actions of the one God.

Inadequate Examples and Living Faith

Many efforts have been made to illustrate the revealed truth of the Holy Trinity through examples taken from the created world. For example, the one tree which is at the same time roots, trunk and branches; or, water which at times is liquid, solid (ice) or steam, depending on circumstances. All these examples may help us a little, but none of them can be an adequate interpretation of the Holy Trinity, precisely because they come from the "created world" and cannot illustrate fully the relationships and realities of the "uncreated divine reality," which is only God in Himself.

Fortunately, our salvation is not dependent on the intellectual comprehension of the doctrine of the Holy Trinity, but on our commitment, love, devotion and service to God. What is required is faith, worship, obedience and love, not theological acumen. How we behave is much more important than whether we intellectualize about God or not. Nevertheless, we also need to have a fairly clear idea about these things, for the truth about God is important for our faith commitment. As the Scriptures say, "the truth...abides in us and will be with us for ever: Grace, mercy, and peace will be with us, from God the Father and from Jesus Christ the Father's Son...Any one who goes ahead and does not abide in the doctrine of Christ does not have God; he who abides in the doctrine has both the Father and the Son. (2 John 2-3, 9).

The understanding which we have is of Christ, the Son of God as our savior and redeemer, of Christ through whom we receive the redemption of our sins, of Christ in whom we are brought to communion with God, of Christ the one in whom we find the quality of life which we know and experience even in this life as eternal. "And we know that the Son of God has come and has given us understanding, to know him who is true; and we are in him who is true, in his Son Jesus Christ. This is the true God and eternal life. Little children, keep yourselves from idols" (1 John 5:20).

15. NEW NAMES FOR THE HOLY TRINITY?

Q. Some Protestant Feminist theologians have taken their agenda to the next step (after ordination and gender free Bibles), which is to take the gender out of the names of the persons of the Holy Trinity. For example, instead of saying "Father, Son and Holy Spirit," they say "Power, Light and Warmth." Could the Orthodox ever be open to considering this terminology?   *– H.K., Livonia, MI.*

A. At the heart of this question is the change that has taken place in some people's thinking about how we are to reflect about God. So, before answering the question itself, it is important that we understand the extent and the limits of what we can know about God.

What Can We Know About God?

The traditional way of answering this question is to affirm that we can know little about God and things divine through our own experience. We affirm that God is active in the world and our lives, but our knowledge about God is filtered through our human experience and human categories of understanding.

The traditional Christian faith (rooted in the practice of faith found in the Bible and the Patristic tradition), however, affirms the transcendence of God. This big word means the "otherness" of God that can never be fully understood and captured in human thought categories. Hence, the Orthodox Church teaches that God's "essence" (that is, God's very *Being*) is absolutely unknowable to the human mind.

But God can be known in some limited way because God has revealed His existence and being in some measure through His "energies." The term "Divine Energies" refers to all the ways God has *acted* and now *acts* in the created world. From these Divine Energies we are able to obtain some knowledge of God. In fact, what God has revealed is what we *need to know* to achieve salvation and to fulfill God's intention for us. But what God has revealed through His energies doesn't address every possible question our curiosity can devise.

One of the most important sources of our understanding of God's Energies (that is, God's action among us) is the Bible, coupled with the Church's understanding of this inspired written record of God's activities among us in history.

Naming God

On the basis what has just been said, the language of the Bible would then serve us in understanding who God is, but in a limited and restricted way. The Bible affirms that there is one God, who can be called by many different names, such as "All-powerful," "Merciful," "Love" and "Just," etc. It also affirms (in the New Testament, especially) that God is also a trinity of persons who make up the one God. The three persons of the Holy Trinity are most often (but not exclusively) referred to as "Father, Son and Holy Spirit." We have no other revealed terms or concepts that measure up to the frequency and theological interconnectedness of these terms in the Bible.

An Erroneous Modern Approach

An erroneous modern theological approach to these questions is to "do theology from below." The idea is that we can and should seek to understand God from our own human experience. In the past, this had all the makings of idolatry and false religion. When introduced into Christian Theology, it means that God is made in the image of humanity, and not the other way around.

So, in this case, some people decide to interpret all of existence as a struggle between "male oppression" and "female victimization." This claimed human experience is then used to think about God and extended to an effort to understand who God is on the basis of human sexual and gender experiences. Hence, they have the desire to change the biblically given names of the persons of the Holy Trinity.

No Renaming of the Holy Trinity

Whether or not this is true in the human realm is, from the Orthodox perspective, irrelevant to how we seek to understand who God is and how God exists. No one claims that the specific words used are to be understood as referring to sexual or gender dimensions in God. God is beyond gender. What it says is that the Father is the source of the divinity, the Son is forever born of the first person of the Trinity, and the Holy Spirit forever proceeds from the Father. Beyond this, we know little; it is a mystery.

What is wrong with changing the words describing the first, second and third persons of the Holy Trinity? Long experience in the Church has shown that every substitute carries with it serious dangers in distorting the revealed truth about God. For example, do you see what is wrong with "Power, Light and Warmth"? All these words are impersonal categories. As such, they do not reflect the most important thing about the revealed truth regarding the Holy Trinity. That truth is that God has revealed that divine reality is a *community of inter-related divine persons.* "Power, Light and Warmth" doesn't do that.

We Have No Other Name

As inadequate as they may be for curious minds, "Father, Son and Holy Spirit" are the only terms the Bible and Holy Tradition give us for the persons of the Holy Trinity. While God is referred to in the Bible and the Tradition with many different words and characteristics, the only formula referring to the Holy Trinity in the faith tradition of Christianity is "Father, Son and Holy Spirit."

We introduce terrible misunderstandings of the revelation of God when we discount these biblical words and substitute names that express one or another aspect of our experience. Our experience certainly **illuminates** the message of divine revelation; it cannot **substitute** for divine revelation.

We have no other names given us for Holy Trinity in the Bible other than "Father, Son and Holy Spirit." They will have to do for us.

Jesus Christ

16. WAS JESUS CHRIST REALLY HUMAN?

Q. Orthodoxy and Roman Catholicism both teach that the Second Person of the Trinity, Jesus Christ, was incarnate (by the Holy Spirit, of the Virgin Mary) and became truly and fully man. Both teach the Logos, the God-Man Christ is one Person in/of two natures, human and divine. What "kind of person" is Jesus Christ? That is, is He a human person or not, and why?　　　　　– *K.L., Chicago, IL.*

A. Your question has a certain complexity to it, so I will try to be as plain as possible in my response. I do this because it is very important that the readers of this column–who are interested in the Orthodox faith not out of mere curiosity, but because they desire to come to a deeper living experience of the Faith–should have a crystal clear perception of who Christ is, and what that means for us personally. I will try, in short steps, to answer your question, but it should be understood that as we seek to do so, we stand before an awesome mystery, which can be described in part, but which cannot be "explained" in some totally rational manner.

The Holy Trinity

The beginning of all Christian teaching is God. God is known to us not as an abstraction, but as Father, as Son, as Holy Spirit. Since God is one, we do not speak of three Gods, but of three persons who share divinity in common. The Father is the "Source" of the other two persons of the Holy Trinity. The Son is eternally "born" of the Father. The Holy Spirit eternally "proceeds" from the Father. In all other things regarding divinity, the three persons of the Holy Trinity are the same.

So, when we speak of the Holy Trinity, we name the second person the "Son," -not, as you say in your question, "Jesus Christ."

Humanity

The Holy Trinity, the One God, is without beginning. God is uncreated. But, at a particular point in time, God created that which is other than Himself. Everything that now exists, except for evil, has been created out of nothing by God. God, then, is *uncreated*; everything else is *created*.

Humanity, thus, is a creation of God; but humanity differs from everything else in creation. This is so because human beings are created "in the image and likeness of God." Our Church understands the word "image" to mean all of those characteristics that separate us from the rest of creation, animate and inanimate. These are things such as our minds, our freedom of choice, our moral sense, our creativity, our sense of beauty, our ability to act ethically, our ability to commune with God, our spirituality, etc. We understand the "likeness" to mean our potential to fulfill in practice and reality this limited, though real, "God-likeness."

Our Sin

But this potential has not been fulfilled in human existence because we have separated ourselves from the source and power which would have made our human "God-likeness" potential into a reality. This separation from life in God we call "sin."

The story of Adam and Eve in the Bible describes our situation as we find ourselves, at various stages and degrees of separation from God. The result of this separation is that humanity has lost the possibility of realizing our full human potential (the "likeness" has been lost). It also means that our minds, our wills, our sense of right and wrong, even our sense of beauty are distorted and darkened and lacking in completeness (the "image" has been distorted.) Though "human beings," we are really less than fully human because of sin.

Our Redemption and Salvation

But God loves us, even in our sinful condition. He began a process to lift us out of it, by first choosing a people, Israel, to be the means of salvation for all humanity. Through the Old Testament Patriarchs and Prophets He prepared His people to receive the "One" who would redeem and save sinful humanity from its fallen, "less than human," condition.

To do this, God would have to be involved, because it was He who was sinned against. But to do this, a human being would have to be involved, also-but a human being without sin. Only in that way would the human and divine be able to come together once again. The separation would then be overcome; the unity of the divine and the human would also be realized; what it means to be fully human would then become possible again for us.

Christmas-Jesus' Birth

This is why the Second Person of the Holy Trinity had to take on human nature and "dwell amongst us" (John 1:14). As the questioner says, the Son of God, the Second Person of the Holy Trinity, "was incarnated (by the Holy Spirit, of the Virgin Mary)." Him we call "Jesus Christ."

The Incarnation meant that God took on full human nature (body and spirit). The Divine and the human were united without division and without confusion in one person. This "unconfused union" of the divine and the human in one person is the model for the rest of humanity. Human beings, to be fully and truly human, must be as much as is possible for us creatures, in communion and union with God. That is why the Incarnation, which the Church celebrates at the feast of Christmas, is the first step in the salvation of humanity and the restoration of our fallen and distorted nature.

Easter-Christ's Resurrection

But Jesus Christ also brought about the salvation of humanity in other ways as well. None of these can be separated from the others: Jesus Christ is our teacher, addressing our minds; He is our Master and Lord, addressing our wills; He is the High Priest who offered Himself as a sacrifice for our sins on the Cross.

But, above all, through His Resurrection from the dead, He conquered and defeated all of the diabolical forces that controlled us and limited our humanity. His Resurrection is the fundamental victory over sin, evil, unrighteousness, false values, and our inauthentic human life. The Bible and the Fathers refer to all these as "death."

The resurrection gives us "life." That is why Easter, which celebrates the Resurrection of Jesus Christ, is so important in our Church. We share in this new life through our Baptism, Holy Communion, the sacramental life in the Church, and our growth in prayer and Christian behavior.

Jesus Christ: A Human Person So We Can be Truly Human

"God became human, so that humans could become God-like," is the way the Church Fathers put it. Christ is a fully human person, precisely because His human nature came into intimate and full communion with His divine nature. How could it be otherwise, since to be a genuine human being *means* being the image and the likeness of God?   As a fully human being, Jesus Christ lived His life expressing in all He did, the love, goodness, gentleness, compassion, power, purity, justice and forgiveness of God. Thus, Jesus Christ in all ways is THE human being, to whom all the rest of us turn to comprehend what it means to be truly human.

17. CHRIST'S DIVINITY

Q. In a conversation I had with a non-Greek person studying with me in a Modern Greek class, the question arose about the divinity of

Christ. I quoted Genesis "Let us..." and later gave her more quotes from the Bible that stated or implied that Jesus and God and the Holy Spirit are one. What I seek from you are some references and sources on the Holy Trinity to give to her, including some "fairly light" reading, that is, non-academic material.

– *Name withheld. East Brisbane, Queensland, Australia.*

A. I am sure that you and the readers of "The Religious Question Box" understand that you are asking one of the most comprehensive questions that could be asked about Christianity. To answer your question fully would take many columns, and even volumes! So my response has to be cursory and all too brief.

The most important point in addressing this question is to be careful not to succumb to the attitude that sees the New Testament as standing alone as a source of the Christian faith. As you know, the early Church and the New Testament itself understand that the Christian teaching as the Tradition of Faith came before the writing down of the books of the New Testament.

Fr. Emmanuel Clapsis, who teaches Systematic Theology at Holy Cross Seminary, Brookline, MA, put it this way in an article recently: "St. Paul understands Tradition as the Christian teaching and he asks the Church to keep to it, since salvation depends on it. He conceptualizes Tradition in a three-fold act that can be uttered in three verbs he uses: I received from the Lord, (1 Corinthians 11:23), I gave to you (v.23) and Keep! (1 Corinthians 11:2) ... He exhorts 'Stand firm and hold to the traditions which you were taught by us, either by word of mouth or by letter' (2 Thessalonians 2:15)."

Though the teaching that Christ is a divine-human person is rooted in the New Testament, the different passages that refer to the person of Christ have to be interpreted and understood within the ongoing historical deposit of faith, which is Holy Tradition. What is central about this tradition is that it has consistently taught that God is a trinity of persons, yet, God is one. The teaching continuously proclaims the Christian truth that in God, the source of divinity is the Father; that the Son is forever born of the Father; that the Holy Spirit proceeds eternally from the Father. One could say that this describes the "inner life" of the one God. The second person of the Holy Trinity is the Son. At a specific moment in history, the Son took on human nature and "dwelt among us" (John 1:14) as the concrete divine-human person, Jesus Christ.

Space does not allow us to quote every possible passage in the New Testament, which refers to the divinity of Jesus. In this column, I will limit myself to presenting passages from just the first three chapters of one Gospel, John.

In the beginning of the Gospel of John, Jesus is referred to as "the Word," or in Greek, the *Logos* of the Father. In that passage, we read "In the beginning was the Word, and the Word was with God, and the Word was God. He was in the beginning with God; all things were made through him, and without him was not anything made that was made (John 1:1-3). Here the word "God" is used in two ways: "with God" means "with God the Father" and "the Word was God" refers to the second person of the Holy Trinity, the Son. It also ascribes to the Son a divine activity, creation.

In the same passage the Logos is described as taking on human nature and he is explicitly identified as the Son of the Father. "And the Word became flesh and dwelt among us, full of grace and truth; we have beheld his glory, glory as of the only Son from the Father" (John 1:14). The Gospel also teaches that the Son of God reveals God the Father to us: "No one has ever seen God; the only Son, who is in the bosom of the Father, he has made him known" (John 1:18).

There are other passages as well. In John 1:34, John the Baptist, God's Prophet, says, "And I have seen and have borne witness that this is the Son of God." In the description of Jesus' first meeting with Nathaniel and Philip we read that "Nathaniel answered him, 'Rabbi, you are the Son of God! You are the King of Israel!'" (John 1:49), a name which Jesus accepted. Elsewhere in this same Gospel, we read a report of Jesus' own words where He speaks of His mission as the Son of God: "For God so loved the world that he gave his only Son, that whoever believes in him should not perish but have eternal life. For God sent the Son into the world, not to condemn the world, but that the world might be saved through him. He who believes in him is not condemned; he who does not believe is condemned already, because he has not believed in the name of the only Son of God" (John 3:16-18).

In another passage Jesus speaks of His person and work as Trinitarian, because a Gospel verse speaks of the Father, the Son and the Holy Spirit. This passage also indicates the importance of belief in His divinity:

> For he whom God has sent utters the words of God, for it is not by measure that he gives the Spirit; the Father loves the Son, and has given all things into his hand. He who believes in the Son has eternal life; he who does not obey the Son shall not see life, but the wrath of God rests upon him (John 3:34-36).

The divinity of Jesus Christ has been affirmed repeatedly in the Tradition of the Church in the writings of the early Church Fathers, in the Creeds, in the hymns and worship of the Church and in decisions of the Ecumenical Councils. I conclude this column with portions from the decision of the Fourth Ecumenical Council, held in Chalcedon of Asia Minor in 451 A.D.

> Wherefore, following the holy Fathers, we all with one voice confess our Lord Jesus Christ one and the same Son, who is perfect in Godhead, also perfect in humanity, truly God and truly man, Himself at once consisting of a rational soul and a body; of one substance with the Father as regards the Godhead, and of one substance with us as regards the humanity and like us in all things apart from sin; begotten

of the Father before the ages in regard to the Godhead, who was Himself in these last days, for us and for our salvation, born of the Virgin Mary, the Theotokos, as regards the humanity; one and the same Christ, Son, Lord, Only-begotten; to be acknowledged in two natures, without confusion, without change, without division, without separation...one Person...

If you would like to read a short description of the Orthodox faith and the Ecumenical Councils, including the Fourth, I suggest you read the relevant passages in Timothy Ware's *The Orthodox Church*. For a chapter-length explanation of Orthodox doctrine, read Bishop (now Metropolitan) Maximos Aghiorgousis' article about Church doctrine in *A Companion to the Greek Orthodox Church* and Fr. Thomas Hopko's set of four small books on *Church Doctrine*. For a readable, but thorough description of the first seven Ecumenical Councils, read Leo Donald Davis' *The First Seven Ecumenical Councils (325-787): Their History and Theology*.

18. A FALSE TEACHING ABOUT CHRIST

Q. I am not an Orthodox Christian, but I'm very interested in what the Orthodox Church teaches. Recently someone gave me an article that holds that Jesus was not the Son of God and that the early Church made it up so that they could be better than the other religions of the day. I do find myself agreeing with the author that there may be other ways for people to come to know God and the final judgment on that issue will be God Himself, but I find myself struggling to find words that would best refute the main theme of the article. — *S.F.B., Pawtucket, RI.*

A. The article, by a liberal Protestant clergyman is titled "If Jesus Said He Was the Only Way to God, Why Don't I Believe It?" It is too long to summarize here but the bottom line is your summary: "Jesus was not the Son of God and that the early Church made it up so that they could be better than the other religions of the day." There can be three answers from an Eastern Orthodox perspective. I will call them "Reading the Bible;" "The Bible As Revelation," "Only the Church."

Reading the Bible

This article and many like it are the end result of a process of studying the text of the Bible as an exclusively human text. This method examines the text in its social environment, its language consistency, and eventually often interprets it with the secular values of the scholar. For example, since rationalistic thought does not believe in miracles, miracle stories in the Bible are rejected as fabrications. This method can teach us some important things about the Bible, but in the end, it reaches absurd the conclusions of the "Bible Seminar" which reduces even the Lord's Prayer to a third of its length.

In this article, the author sharply distinguishes the Gospels of Matthew, Mark and Luke from the Gospel of John, holding that only in the latter does Jesus identify Himself as the Son of God. It is true that the Gospel of John emphasizes the divinity of Christ more than the other three Gospels and that only in it is Jesus presented as identifying Himself as the Son of God. But it is not true that Jesus is never referred to as the Son of God in the Gospels of Matthew, Mark, and Luke.

For instance, when Mark tells the story of Jesus' Baptism, we read: "In those days Jesus . . . was baptized by John in the Jordan. And when he came up out of the water, immediately he saw the heavens opened and the Spirit descending upon him like a dove; and a voice came from heaven, 'Thou art my beloved Son; with thee I am well pleased'" (Mark 1:9-11). You read the same thing in Luke 3:21-23 and Matthew 3:15-17.

Also, in the description of the Transfiguration of Jesus in the presence of three of His disciples, Mark reports, "And a cloud overshadowed them, and a voice came out of the cloud, 'This is my beloved Son; listen to him'" (Mark 9:7; see also Matthew 17:3-9 and 2 Peter 1:17-18).

It might be objected that these are statements *about* Jesus but not *by* Jesus. But in the parable about the householder who rented out his vineyard to some wicked men, the story told by Jesus in a barely veiled way refers to Himself as God's "beloved Son." "He had still one other, a beloved son; finally he sent him to them, saying, 'They will respect my son.' But those tenants said to one another, 'This is the heir; come, let us kill him, and the inheritance will be ours'" (Mark 12:6-8).

New Testament writings much earlier than the Gospels also speak of the Divinity of Christ. There is not enough space to present all these passages from Acts, Romans, 1st and 2nd Corinthians, Galatians and Colossians. I will mention just one. For example, in Galatians we read "But when the time had fully come, God sent forth his Son, born of a woman, born under the law, to redeem those who were under the law, so that we might receive adoption as sons" (Galatians 4:4-5).

The Bible As Revelation

A big mistake, of course, is to conduct one's study of the Bible as though it is only a human book. There is one sense in which the Bible *is* a human book. Human beings recorded God's revelation as it was expressed in events, actions, spiritual experience, teachings, prayers, miracles, and understandings. Consequently, the Bible is a witness to Divine Revelation experienced by human beings. Saint Paul summarized the "Good News" of God's revelation this way: "But when he who had set me apart before I was born, and had called me through his grace, he was pleased to reveal his Son to me, in order that I might preach him among the Gentiles, I did not confer with flesh and blood" (Galatians 1:15-16). Without this belief, then you can easily come to the conclusions of the Protestant pastor who sees the Bible as just one of many human efforts to reach God.

This too needs comment. Nice and friendly as this view sounds, it overlooks the real differences among the beliefs and teachings of the various religions. There is much variety in the New Testament, even about the person of Jesus Christ. But that variety is limited. There are things that you can say about Jesus that are beyond the boundaries. One of them would be to say that Jesus was not the Son of God.

The belief in the divinity of Jesus Christ led, together with the Church's reflection on the Holy Spirit, to Christian belief in the Holy Trinity. This belief is central to the Christian understanding of God. No one would have made up such a belief if they wanted to make the Christian religion "better than other religions." In fact, Islam consciously rejects it, misunderstanding it as a teaching that there are three gods, not one. How can one argue that the teaching about the Trinity and the teaching about Allah are equally true ways to approaching God in His fullness? What about Buddhism which teaches that there is no God?

Nevertheless, the Christian Church remains faithful to a hard to understand, yet profound teaching about God, because that is the witness of Divine Revelation. The result is that the Bible is also a book that reveals the reality of God in a unique way. Most importantly, it serves God's purposes and is not propaganda writing with an eye to being better than other religions. St. Paul put it this way: "For Jews demand signs and Greeks seek wisdom, but we preach Christ crucified a stumbling block to Jews and folly to Gentiles, but to those who are called, both Jews and Greeks, Christ the power of God and the wisdom of God. For the foolishness of God is wiser than men, and the weakness of God is stronger than men" (1 Corinthians 1:22-25).

Only The Church

What Jesus was and what Jesus thought about Himself cannot be separated out from the rest of the biblical text. The New Testament letters and the four Gospels were all written after the Church was proclaiming the Gospel for decades. It was preaching the Gospel, baptizing people into membership in the Church, conducting the Sacrament of the Body and Blood of Christ, teaching about the Father, the Son and the Holy Spirit, about what was true about the human condition, and so forth, before it produced the writings in the New Testament. It also discerned which of these writings reflected its already existing faith, rejecting as unauthentic many other writings. In Orthodox language, we refer to this process as Holy Tradition. Holy Tradition consistently taught and believed as Apostolic teaching that Jesus was God. It was this same Holy Tradition that produced the four Gospels. Consequently, it is the Church's Holy Tradition that is in the best position to describe what the Bible teaches about Jesus Christ.

We have an example of that Holy Tradition in something familiar to every Orthodox Christian–the Creed. "I believe . . . in one Lord Jesus Christ, the Son of God, the Only-begotten, begotten of the Father before all worlds, Light of Light, very God of very God, begotten not made, of one essence with the Father, by whom all things were made."

19. CHRIST AND THE DEVIL

Q. Does Christ love the Devil?

– C. S. Strongsville, OH.

A. This is an interesting question, because there are at least two ways that we can answer it, and both are correct, depending upon the meaning that we give to the words in this question.

Since Christ is the Son of God, sent into the world for the salvation of humanity by taking on human nature, He has identified Himself with humankind. Since God is the source of all good and the Devil is identified with all that is evil, the Bible identifies the relationship between good and evil, humanity and the Devil as one of "enmity" (Genesis 3:14-15). Enmity is a state of deep-felt hatred that seeks to eliminate the other. "The world" is another word used in a special sense to describe the evil in the world (of course, used to describe creation in general, it also has a positive meaning). James says, "Unfaithful creatures! Do you not know that friendship with the world is enmity with God? Therefore whoever wishes to be a friend of the world makes himself an enemy of God" (James 12:4).

In this sense, Christ could not "love" the Devil or "the world," understood as "liking" the Devil or "the world." The whole biblical and patristic tradition teaches that we are to hate and abhor evil and sin, which is precisely what the Devil stands for and embodies.

On the other hand, the Bible usually describes enmity among people, when it describes personal antagonisms and conflict, as something bad. It is described as one of the "works of the flesh" (Galatians 5:19-21). One of the many meanings of Christian love is concern for the welfare of another, without seeking to gain anything out of it for one's self. In this sense, Christ could love the Devil. He is, thus, seeking the repentance of the Devil, if that were possible. Most theologians of the Orthodox Church hold that the Devil has fallen so deeply into evil that the hope of the Devil's repentance is so slim that it is nonexistent. Nevertheless, if we assume that Christ still hopes for the conversion of the Devil, in this sense, He can be said to love even the devil.

20. THE TRANSFIGURATION OF CHRIST

Q. I have many questions to do with the Transfiguration of Jesus Christ.   – R. D., Haverhill, MA

A. Your letter has, indeed, many questions about the Transfiguration of our Lord. I will group these together and give answers to them, as best I can. The Transfiguration of our Lord is described in the Gospels of Matthew (17:1-8), Mark (9:2-8) and Luke (9:28-36). The event is summarized by this hymn (*"Doxastikon"*) from the Orthros service of the feast: "Christ took Peter, James and John up into a high mountain apart, and was transfigured before them. His face shone as the sun and His raiment became white as the light. There appeared Moses and Elijah talking with Him; a bright cloud overshadowed them, and behold, a voice out of the cloud saying: 'This is My beloved Son in whom I am well pleased: hear ye Him.'" Some understand the event as symbolic, or a vision, or as a transference of one of the resurrection appearances to this place. These views are not accepted in the Orthodox Church.

What is the opinion of our Orthodox Church Fathers as to which mountain the Transfiguration occurred on?

It is generally accepted that the mountain is the ancient Mt. Hebron also known as Mt. Tabor, the name by which it is generally described in the Church. Tabor is 9,200 feet high, and located 12 miles northeast of Caesaria Philippi which is in the northernmost part of the Holy Land.

How do we interpret the Transfiguration of Jesus, that is, what is meant when it is said, His face began to shine like the sun and His clothes turned dazzling white?

The tradition of our Church generally understands that the illumination of Jesus Christ in this event is a disclosure of His divinity. In all three Gospel accounts the Transfiguration follows Peter's confession of faith that Jesus is the Son of God. Other views exist, but for the Orthodox Church this is the main meaning. It is primarily described as Christ "shining as lightning with divine splendor," with "divine glory," and showing to the Disciples "the splendor of His Godhead."

But additionally, the Transfiguration is also described as showing the brightness of the Gospel as compared to the Old Testament Law; the darkness of human nature before Christ, compared with its brightness in Christ; as giving courage to the Disciples as they were to soon face the Lord's Crucifixion; that a good and virtuous life shines with divine light; as the revelation of the mystery of God; as a witness to the forthcoming Resurrection of Christ; as the power and might of the holy divine nature of Christ; as the mission of Christ to enlighten us with His knowledge; and clearly, the Transfiguration is a revelation of the Holy Trinity. Further, the Transfiguration is a visible call to our own human transfiguration from sin to God-likeness. One vesper hymn puts it this way: "let us be transformed this day to a better state and direct our minds to heavenly things, being shaped anew in piety according to the form of Christ."

Did Jesus remain in His physical state or become spirit only?

It is very clear that this is a bodily transfiguration, showing the divine nature of Christ, "as much as the disciples were able to bear it," through His human nature which, of course, includes the body. One of the hymns of the Orthros puts it this way: "Thou hast shown...Thy nature and of Thy divine beauty beneath the flesh."

What is the significance of Moses and Elijah appearing with Jesus as witnessed by His disciples Peter, James and John? Did Moses and Elijah appear in their physical bodies or spirits? Does this mean that Moses was raised (resurrected?) to life before Jesus Crucifixion and Resurrection? Likewise does this mean that Elijah had not experienced death from the time he was taken up to heaven?

The details of the appearance of Moses and Elijah are not fully clear to us. One of the hymns sung on this day provides a possible answer: "Moses and Elijah stood at thy side, for the Law and the Prophets minister to Thee as God." In this understanding, Moses and Elijah are seen as Old Testament witnesses to the coming of Christ for the salvation of all humanity. When connected with the presence of the disciples, it allows for a slightly different interpretation: One hymn from the Orthros thus sings "Because Thou art Master of heaven and Lord of the earth, and hast dominion over the things under the earth, there stood beside Thee, O Christ, the apostles from the earth, and Elijah the Tishbite as if from heaven, and Moses from the dead..."

It is unlikely that we are speaking of a pre-resurrection of Moses and Elijah. Rather, it is more likely that we are talking here of an "appearance" of these persons. It is also interesting that Moses was married, while Elijah was not. Both shared in the wondrous experience of the divine transfiguration of Christ.

What do other early Christian writings besides the Holy Bible have to say about the Transfiguration?

In this column I have quoted mostly from the Bible and from the Church's services for the Feast of the Transfiguration. These hymns summarize the teachings of the Fathers of the Church on the Transfiguration. We do not have space here to describe all that has been written on this theme in the Church's tradition.

Since what year has it been celebrated on August 6?

Evidence indicates that the feast of the Transfiguration was first introduced in Jerusalem, perhaps in the 5th century. We have sermons by St. Cyril of Alexandria (+444), St. Proclos of Constantinople (+446), and Basileios of Seleucia (+459) that imply some sort of celebration of the Transfiguration. There is also a Jerusalem liturgical document known as the "Typikon of Patriarch Sophronios" (634-644) that says for August 6, "Synaxis...in Tabor, Transfiguration of the Savior." So, we can say that from the mid-fifth century some sort of official observance of the Transfiguration began to take place and that by the first of the seventh century, a feast had been designated for August 6.

On August 6, 1945, the United States dropped the atom bomb on Japan. Was this just a coincidence or is there some meaning to it?

The decision to use the atomic bomb was made in the context of a terrible and savage war. The motivation to use it was to end the war as soon as possible and to save the lives of our armed forces. But the dropping of those bombs on Hiroshima and Nagasaki moved the world into a new and many times more terrible age: the nuclear age. As we all know, the subsequent proliferation of nuclear weapons brought the world to the brink of destruction. It is transformation, tragically, from life to death. If this judgment is correct, the date of August 6 for the beginning of the nuclear age is a tragic, if not demonic coincidence. The Lord's Transfiguration is a promise of true and genuine life, not death.

21. COULD JESUS HAVE SINNED?

Q. Was it possible for Jesus Christ to have committed sin, even though He never did?   *– C. G. Carthage, MS*

A. Your question helps us understand better who Jesus Christ is according to the teaching of the Orthodox Church. It forces us to "go back to basics" about the person of Jesus. Only then can the answer be given to your question.

Understanding Who Jesus Christ Is
    In order to understand who Jesus Christ is, we must begin with the teaching of the Church about God and the teaching of the Church about human nature. For, in the teaching of the Scripture and the Holy Tradition of the Church, Jesus Christ is "perfect (=complete, total, fully) God" and "perfect (complete, total, fully) human." God is a Holy Trinity: Father, Son and Holy Spirit. According to the Bible and the living Apostolic Tradition, the second person of the Holy Trinity, the Son, at a specific point in time, took on human nature. This is what we mean by the word "Incarnation," and it is what we celebrate at Christmas time. The human nature He took on through the Theotokos Mary, was "complete," that is, it consisted of a real body and a real human soul. The Church has understood this to mean that the divine and human in Christ were united in one person (or, "hypostasis"), yet, the human was not absorbed by the divine nor was the divine lost in the human. This goes beyond our ability to fully comprehend, since it does not fit the categories of understanding that we have about the things of this world. But since the Incarnation

expresses a unique divine-human reality, this does not surprise us. It was necessary for both the divine and the human to be directly involved in the work of salvation. Because the work of Jesus Christ was the salvation of the world, He was both divine and human in One Person.

Each Sunday, in many ways, we take note of the Incarnation. One of the best expressions of this belief about Jesus Christ and His saving work is found in the "Second Antiphon," which begins in Greek with the words *"O Monogenes Yios kai logos to Theou."* Pay attention to the words:

> Only begotten Son and Word of God, although immortal You humbled Yourself for our salvation, taking flesh from the holy Theotokos and ever virgin Mary and, without change, becoming man. Christ, our God, You were crucified but conquered death by death. You are one of the Holy Trinity, glorified with the Father and the Holy Spirit -save us.

Perfect and Sinless Man

The humanity, which the Son of God took upon Himself, was perfect in the sense described above–complete, full and total. But it was "perfect" in another sense, too. Precisely because Jesus' humanity was in complete and intimate communion with His divinity, His humanity was what humanity was created to be spiritually and morally. He was therefore without any trace of sin. Like every human being, He was subject to the physical demands of His body: He became hungry, He thirsted, He experienced tiredness and cold and heat, etc. He was also subject to weariness of soul, and felt emotions of disappointment (with His disciples, for example) and could feel happiness, and know what it meant to rejoice. He could, like us, also be tempted (see the story of the temptations of Jesus in Matthew 4:1-11). But because His human nature was in full and total communion and relationship with the divine nature, He never succumbed to the temptations; as you say "He never did" sin.

That is what the Bible clearly teaches: "He came to take away sins, and in him there is no sin" (1 John 3:5); "he committed no sin; no guile was found upon his lips" (1 Peter 2:22); "it was fitting that we should have such a high priest, holy blameless, unstained, separated from sinners, exalted above the heavens" (Hebrews 7:26)..."who in every respect has been tempted as we are, yet without sinning" (Hebrews 4:15).

Jesus Could Not Have Sinned

So, the question about the possibility of Jesus sinning is a hypothetical one, having nothing to do with reality. The question, however, helps us understand more about ourselves, and how we can reduce the sins in our own lives.

Sin *means* in the last analysis, separation from God. Inasmuch as we human beings are separated from God, we are sinners. Jesus gives us the model for our own lives: His humanity was in full unity with His divine nature, within His person. The human will in Him did not fight its own nature that was created "in the image and likeness of God." Rather, the human in Jesus Christ, because it was full and complete, did not want or desire to do anything else than to be God-like. As a result, Jesus could never sin.

As for us, we are called to realize as much as possible in ourselves this harmony with God in our lives, to realize and complete the fullness of our humanity, which is precisely, the image and likeness of God. Christ's sinlessness is something which we reverence in a worshipful way. But it is equally important to note that each person has the call to move from our "less than full humanity," by reflecting in our life what Christ was through His Incarnation the deep and intimate relationship of the divine and the human in one person. The closer we come to know God in our lives the less we will sin.

That is why, as Orthodox, we cannot separate our beliefs from our deeds; our prayers from our inner dispositions; our sacramental life from our moral life; our membership in the Church, which is the body of Christ, from our love for God and for our fellow human beings.

Jesus Christ did not and could not sin precisely because the human in Him was in full communion with the divine in Him. You and I sin, precisely because our humanity is not in full communion with God. We increase the quality of our humanity as we come closer to God through life in the Church. The closer we come to God, the further away we move from sin. It is not likely that any human being can ever, in this life, be so completely in communion with God, that he or she would become sinless. Yet, this is the direction the Christian's life is called to take.

22. WHO DIED ON THE CROSS?

Q. God did not need saving but man did, with the raising of Christ from the dead on Pascha. Who died on the Cross? Was it God or man, and who was raised from the dead?

– A.C.D., Clinton, MA.

A. This question was discussed frequently during the early period of the Church when the doctrine of the person of Christ was being debated. The answer was given by the Church on the basis of the teaching of the Fourth Ecumenical Council, held in Chalcedon in 451. Christ is both fully human and fully divine in one person. From the moment of His Incarnation, that is, from the moment that the second person of the Holy Trinity, the Son, took on human nature and became a single person, the Divine/Human person Jesus Christ acted as one being-one person (The Greek word expresses this belief much better than any other language–*theanthropos* [meaning God-man]). All His activities and actions belong to the one theanthropic (divine-human) person, Jesus Christ.

In regard to your specific question regarding who it was that died on the Cross, one of our theologians, in summarizing this teaching put it this way: "Only the precious blood of the God/Man (Greek, "Theanthropos"), the unblemished lamb of God, who willingly offered himself upon the Cross in accordance to the preordained and unchanged will of God, was able to remove and cleanse the sin of the world. As the Mediator between God and man, the Lord was able, on the one hand, as the Son of God to relate to the God who was being propitiated, and on the other, as man, He could speak to human beings as one of them Himself. Concurrently, however, as a human being and in the name of the whole of humanity, and as its most exemplary representative, He offered a redemptive sacrifice, which because of the hypostatic union of the two natures in him as the Great High Priest, was of priceless value for the salvation of the world." (Panagiotes Trembelas, *Dogmatike*, vol. 2, p. 159.)

Christ's victory over the enemies of humanity, Death, Sin and Evil, was a victory of the "Theanthropos." We can see how the worship of the Orthodox Church expresses this truth, with the hymn which is intoned before the Cross on Great Friday afternoon in our Churches, during the Service of the Descent from the Cross (Greek, "*Apokathelosis*")

Today He is suspended on a Tree who
    suspended the earth over the waters (three times).
A crown of thorns was placed
    on the head of the King of Angels.
He who wore a false purple robe
    covered the heavens with clouds.
He was smitten, who
    in the Jordan redeemed Adam.
The Groom of the Church was fastened with nails,
    and the Son of the Church was pierced with a spear.
Thy sufferings we adore, O Christ (three times).

In this well-known hymn the person crucified is clearly the one person Jesus Christ, Who is both God (..."who suspended the earth over the waters;" ..."the King of angels;" ...who "covered the heavens with clouds;" ....who "delivered Adam") and a human being. (The one who "is suspended on a Tree;" ...on whose human head was placed "a crown of thorns;" ...who was "smitten" and "fastened with nails." The "Groom of the Church," is the Son of God become a human being.

Who died and was resurrected? It was the Incarnate Son of God, the "Theanthropos," the one person who was concurrently and is forever more into the future and eternity, the Son of God and the Son of Man: Jesus Christ.

23. JESUS CHRIST: Orthodox and Roman Catholic Views

Q. What is the Orthodox view of Jesus Christ, the Church and man? What is the Roman Catholic view of the above? What is "Soteriology?" How do the Orthodox and the Roman Catholics differ on it? Please explain. Thank you!   – *A.C.D., Clinton, MA.*

A. Depending on how you count, there are from five to nine questions in the above! I propose to answer them by talking in four different columns on the topics regarding Jesus Christ, the Church, Humanity and Soteriology (These are located in various sections below in this book). In each the Orthodox view will be explained and information regarding Roman Catholic views on the same subject will be included.

"Who Do Men Say That I Am?"
    In the Gospel of Matthew, it tells how one day Jesus asked His disciples, "Who do men say that the Son of Man is?" Since that was one of the names Jesus used for Himself, Jesus wanted to know how He was perceived by the people. The Apostles answered that the

people thought that He was either St. John the Baptist, or the Prophet Elijah or the Prophet Jeremiah, returned from the dead. Then, Jesus asked them, "But who do you say that I am?" (Matthew 16:15). The Apostle Peter responded for the disciples, saying, "You are the Christ, the Son of the living God!" (Matthew 16:16). Jesus seemed to be very pleased with the response and indicated that this was the foundational truth about Himself.

"Whom do men say that the Son of man is?" is still a pivotal question. Today, there are many who respond in ways which essentially deny Peter's response, or which present Jesus just as a good man, an example for those who honor Him. This has not been the way of the Church in its history.

The Problem of Understanding Who Jesus Christ Is

From the beginning then, the question about who Christ is has been asked. It is asked because Jesus is recorded in the Scriptures as describing Himself and His work as unique and from God in a special exceptional way. His whole life was extraordinary, and the purpose of salvation, which He came to the world to accomplish, meant that in some totally special way, Jesus Christ was different from the rest of humanity. How to understand that was a question asked from the beginning of the Church's history.

The New Testament gives us many different pictures of Jesus Christ, but no systematic response to the question. Very early in the Church's history, people began to think about the question and to try to give some answers. Precisely because Jesus Christ was unique, it was hard to do so, and most of the answers were off target.

Some Early False Answers

The teaching about the person of Jesus Christ is called "Christology." Early in the history of the Church several different "Christologies" were put forth by different people. What they were seeking to explain was how the divine and the human related in the person of Jesus Christ. The name "Jesus" points to the evident human aspect of His person. The name "Christ" which means "the anointed one," the Greek form of the Hebrew name for the Messiah, points to the divine side of Jesus. In the early Church no one doubted that somehow He was divine, and somehow He was human, but the difficult question was *how* He was divine and human at the same time in the same person.

The whole range of possible answers was given. Some said that Jesus Christ was really only God, and that His human side was only an appearance. Some said that for the divine and the human to co-exist in one person, the divine had to take the place of some part of His human nature. For example, they said the divine took the place of His human soul or the human mind. Others approached the problem from the point of view of the divine and said that Jesus was fully human, but He really was not divine, but only divine-like, and so less than God. None of these responses was satisfactory. If Jesus Christ was the Savior of humanity, He had to be fully God and fully human to accomplish the work of salvation. How was this to be understood?

The Answer: The Fourth Ecumenical Council

The reason all the previous answers were wrong, was that each in its own way minimized the evidence for one or the other side of the issue. But by honestly recognizing, on the basis of the Scriptures, that Jesus Christ was both fully divine and fully human, our minds see a problem. According to human logic this cannot be. The Church responded that it is not right to place God under the conditions of the world, which He created. The understanding of the Church saw the answer to the question "Who is Jesus Christ" as a necessary paradox to the human mind, a mystery of faith that could not be reduced to human logical categories. It gave this answer in the Fourth Ecumenical Council.

The central point for the Church Fathers was that in a particular point in time, the second person of the Holy Trinity-the Son-took on human nature in order to redeem humanity from its sinful condition and to empower us to realize the fullness of our humanity. But, as St. Gregory the Theologian put it, "what is not assumed is not redeemed," so God took on a full and complete human nature (without any sin, of course). In 451, the 4th Ecumenical Council in Chalcedon defined for all time the relation between the human and the divine in Jesus Christ.

"We confess one and the same our Lord Jesus Christ, the same perfect in Godhead, the same perfect in manhood, truly God and truly man, the sum of a rational soul and body, acknowledged in two natures, without confusion, without change, without division, without separation, the difference of the two natures being by no means taken away because of the union but rather the distinctive character of each nature being preserved and combining in one person, (*prosopon* in Greek), or entity (*hypostasis*, in Greek). or, in brief, two natures in one person."

Orthodox and Roman Catholic

This is the Orthodox teaching in answer to the question "Who is Jesus Christ?" It remains the bedrock of all of the worship of the Church and our theological reflection on a myriad of issues and questions. In the Roman Catholic Church, the doctrine of Chalcedon remains the official teaching. But modern Roman Catholic theologians have not limited themselves to it, sometimes building upon it on the basis of modern world views, other times being highly critical of it. There is a thread of teaching by some Roman Catholic theologians which seems to have rejected all of the above and descended into thinking of Jesus Christ as just another human being. This is, however, very far from the official teaching of the Roman Catholic Church.

24. CHRIST'S DESCENT INTO HADES

Q. Where in the Bible do we read about Jesus going to Hades?

– Presbytera M.L., Brooksville, FL.

A. It is the consistent teaching of the Orthodox Church from the Bible and the early Church Fathers that following His Crucifixion and before His Resurrection, Jesus "descended into Hades" where those who were dead heard the Gospel preached by Christ. In the Orthodox Church, many Old Testament prophets and holy persons are considered saints of the Church precisely because they responded with faith to the message of salvation conveyed to them in the period between His death and the Resurrection by Christ Himself.

The Biblical Background

The basis for this belief in the New Testament is the belief that Christ came into the world for the salvation of all persons who ever existed, those who died before His coming, those who were alive when He came, and those who were to come. He came as the Savior of all of humanity, and of the whole creation.

In the Gospel of Matthew we learn of a remarkable event which took place during the crucifixion of Christ: "And Jesus cried again with a loud voice and yielded up his spirit. And behold, the curtain of the temple was torn in two, from top to bottom; and the earth shook, and the rocks were split; the tombs also were opened, and many bodies of the saints who had fallen asleep were raised, and coming out of the tombs after his Resurrection they went into the holy city and appeared to many" (Matthew 27:51-53).

Note, that the passage speaks of "the saints" or "holy ones," a term which at that time also referred to the "righteous ancients" of the Old Testament. Note also, that their resurrection followed Christ's Resurrection. Something happened between the crucifixion of Christ and His Resurrection to cause this.

Some hold that the words which Jesus said to the "good (repentant) thief" on the Cross point to the beginning of the work which He accomplished after His death and before His Resurrection in Hades: And he said to him, "Truly, I say to you, today you will be with me in Paradise" (Luke 23:43), something which occurred three hours later when Jesus died.

In his Pentecost sermon, Peter quotes from an Old Testament a prophesy regarding David: ". . . my flesh will dwell in hope. For thou wilt not abandon my soul to Hades, nor let thy Holy One see corruption. . . . " (Acts 2:27). St. Peter then, applies this prophesy to Jesus: "(David) foresaw and spoke of the Resurrection of the Christ, that he was not abandoned to Hades, nor did his flesh see corruption. This Jesus God raised up, and of that we all are witnesses" (Acts 2:31-32).

These passages serve to set the framework of a pattern of death-descent to Hades-Resurrection in the saving work of Jesus Christ. There is, however, one passage which teaches clearly and directly about Jesus' descent into Hades to proclaim the message of salvation to all who were there. It is found in the first letter of Peter, chapter three, verses 18-20. It says:

> For Christ also died for sins once for all, the righteous for the unrighteous, that he might bring us to God, being put to death in the flesh but made alive in the spirit; **in which he went and preached to the spirits in prison, who formerly did not obey, when God's patience waited in the days of Noah**, during the building of the ark, in which a few, that is, eight persons, were saved through water.

As we see from this passage, the subjects who received the preaching are exemplified by those who did not believe Noah, and perished in the Flood. They were "in prison," that is, in Hades. Jesus "went and preached" to the spirits in the prison of Hades. Those who responded to the preaching entered into the Kingdom of God; those who did not, remained in Hades. Like us, at the Second Coming, they will be resurrected, judged and will enter into eternal reward or punishment.

The Teaching of the Church Fathers

In the Orthodox Church, Holy Tradition is the source of our understanding regarding the Revelation of God to us. The Scriptures are a central and major part of Holy Tradition. Other major parts of Holy Tradition are the writings of the Church Fathers. The Scriptures help us understand the Church Fathers and the Church Fathers help us understand the Scriptures. Together, they provide us with a safe and secure understanding of the Christian faith.

When we look at very early teachings of Church Fathers we observe that they taught the Descent into Hades by Christ.

St. Ignatios: The earliest mention we have of the Descent into Hades is by St. Ignatios who lived from 35 to 107 A.D. We have two versions of his letter to the Trallians. The short version includes the following brief phrase, "He was truly crucified, and truly died in the sight of beings in heaven, and on earth, and under the earth (9)." Scholars believe that the long version was an expansion of this made about two hundred years later by an unknown writer. This longer passage says,

> He really, and not merely in appearance, was crucified, and died, in the sight of beings in heaven, and on earth, and under the earth. By those in heaven I mean such as are possessed of incorporeal natures; by those on earth, the Jews and Romans, and such persons as were present at that time when the Lord was crucified; and by those under the earth, the multitude that arose along with the Lord. For says the Scripture, 'Many bodies of the saints that slept arose' (Matthew 27:52), their graves being opened. He descended, indeed, into Hades alone, but He arose accompanied by a multitude; and rent asunder the fence of separation which had existed from the beginning of the world, and cast down its partition-wall" (chapter 9).

St. Justin Martyr: This Christian writer was a defender of the Christian Faith against some of its first enemies. He lived from 100 to 165 A.D. In his *Dialogue With Trypho*, he quotes a passage supposedly from Jeremiah, saying "The Lord God remembered His dead people of Israel who lay in the graves and He descended to preach to them His own salvation." Justin holds that this is authentic Christian teaching.

St. Irenaeus: One of the great early writers of the Church was the Bishop of Lyon, St. Irenaeus, who lived from 130-200 A.D. He provides us with a full statement about Christ's Descent into Hades in his book *Against Heresies*. He says,

> "The Lord descended into the regions beneath the earth, preaching His advent there also, and declaring the remission of sins received by those who believe in Him. Now all those believed in Him who had hope towards Him, that is, those who proclaimed His advent and submitted to His dispensations, the righteous men, the prophets, and the patriarchs to whom He remitted sins in the same way as He did to us" (IV, xxvii, 2).

We see that very early in the Church, Holy Tradition had interpreted and understood certain passages from the Bible, so as to affirm the belief that following His Crucifixion, Jesus Christ descended into Hades and preached the Gospel of Salvation to all those who had previously died.

A Summary of the Biblical/Patristic Teaching

The Church's teachings were summed up in a work titled *The Exposition of the Orthodox Faith* by St. John of Damaskos, who lived from 675-749 A.D. This work still serves as a guide to the teaching of Scripture and the Greek Church Fathers of the first eight centuries of the undivided Church. In the 29th chapter of this work, St. John of

Damaskos writes:

> The soul (of Jesus Christ) when it was deified descended into Hades, in order that, just as the Sun of Righteousness rose for those upon the earth, so likewise He might bring light to those who sit under the earth in darkness and shadow of death: in order that just as He brought the message of peace to those upon the earth, and of release to the prisoners, and of sight to the blind, and became to those who believed the Author of everlasting salvation and to those who did not believe a reproach of their unbelief, so He might become the same to those in Hades: "That every knee should bow to Him of things in heaven, and things in earth and things under the earth" (Philippians 2:10). And thus after He had freed those who had been bound for ages, straight-way He rose again from the dead, showing us the way of resurrection.

There can be no doubt that the Descent of Jesus Christ into Hades is an authentic teaching of the Orthodox Church.

25. CHRIST IS RISEN!

Q. I am 72 years old. For over 60 years I have sung the "Christos Aneste" (the "Christ is risen" hymn) and I enjoyed it! The melody is a happy tune, and a reminder of the Easter season. This year as I sang it, I realized that I do not understand the words or their meaning. Please explain the hymn.   *– P.M., Hudson, FL.*

A. To respond properly to this request, we will need two columns. Today's response begins the explanation. Next week, will be the second part of the explanation. We'll conclude with an enlarged paraphrase of the Paschal Hymn, *Christos Aneste*, or as it is translated into English, the hymn *Christ is Risen*.

A Justified Request

Yours is a common and understandable request. This hymn, in particular, is embedded in many rich, emotion-laden experiences associated with religious life, church services, family observances, strong and beautiful musical resonances, and happy ethnic and cultural traditions. Associated with the singing of the hymn "Christos Aneste" are the smells of incense -and the cooking of the Easter Lamb; the Lamentations of Great Friday -and peanut butter sandwiches for fasting; the Bright Light of Pascha -and the bright faces around the Family Easter Table; the lifting up of the palms on the Sunday before Pascha -and the lifting up of the Easter wine glass; the receiving of red-dyed Easter Eggs in Church -and the receiving of guests in our homes. The hymn *Christos Aneste* is part of a web of wonderful and precious religious, ethnic and cultural traditions.

There is, however, a danger in all of this -the danger which you describe. We can miss the core meaning of what is being proclaimed at Pascha and think of it as only a part (for some, a very small part) of "celebrating Easter."

Paying attention to the words of the hymn *"Christos Aneste"* can help us recover the real meaning of Pascha. It is this meaning that is not only at the heart of the celebration of Easter, but at the center of the Christian Faith.

"Christos Aneste" Translated

Among the many translations into English of the *Christos Aneste* there is one that I feel conveys well the meaning of the Greek. It is the newly revised Patmos Press edition published by Fr. George Papadeas: **"Christ is risen from the dead, trampling Death by death, and bestowing life to those in the tombs."** Let's look at this hymn more carefully, using this translation to enter into its meaning.

Christos Aneste **Explained**

1. The first word in the hymn is **Christ**. Who are we referring to in this hymn? "Christ," you answer. But who is Christ? The Greek word *christos* means, "the anointed one." For the Jewish people it was another way of referring to the expected Messiah. Thus, in the book of Acts we are told about "the Christ appointed for you, Jesus" (Acts 3:19), and the Old Testament is quoted as referring to Jesus Christ, as the Lord's "anointed" (Acts 4:26). About the Apostles, it is said, "And every day in the temple and at home they did not cease teaching and preaching Jesus as the Christ" (Acts 5:42). Of St. Paul it is written, "But Saul increased all the more in strength, and confounded the Jews who lived in Damascus by proving that Jesus was the Christ" (Acts 9:22).

The Church subsequently understood the fullness of that word when it described Him in the Creed as the Son of God, the Second Person of the Holy Trinity, who at a particular point in time, took on human nature, and became a single person who was at the same time a full human being and fully divine: Jesus Christ. He came into the world to redeem humanity from sin.

2. Then, we sing that Christ **. . . is risen from the dead**: This is one of the most important and fundamental teachings about Jesus Christ. It is true that He did many things for our salvation, all of them important. As Peter taught, "(B)y Jesus Christ (he is Lord of all), the word . . . was proclaimed throughout all Judea . . . (and) . . . God anointed Jesus of Nazareth with the Holy Spirit and with power; . . . he went about doing good and healing all that were oppressed by the devil, for God was with him" (Acts 10:36-37).

But in this, one of the earliest sermons of Church, Peter adds as this important truth about Jesus Christ with these words: "And we are witnesses to all that he did . . . They put him to death by hanging him on a tree; but God raised him on the third day . . . . And he commanded us to preach to the people, and to testify that he is the one ordained by God to be judge of the living and the dead. To him all the prophets bear witness that every one who believes in him receives forgiveness of sins through his name" (Acts 10:39-43).

So it was, that the essential element of the first message preached by the Apostles, was "The Lord has risen indeed, and has appeared to Simon!" (Luke 24:34). When we say, "Christ is risen!" and respond "Indeed he is risen!" we are quoting the Bible! But what does that mean for you and me? The answer is in the next phrase of the hymn.

3. We sing then that when He was resurrected from the dead on the third day, Christ was **trampling Death by death**: I believe this translation is particularly good, because it translates the Greek word *thanaton* (death) with a capital "D". This indicates to us that there is a special meaning to the use of the word "Death" in the original Greek phrase *thanato, Thanaton patesas*.

The Bible teaches us that death is a consequence of the sin of Adam: "Therefore as sin came into the world through one man and death through sin, . . . so death spread to all men because all men sinned" (Romans 5:12). "Death" consequently, is also a way of describing our state of sinful separation from God. So, St. Paul says in his letter to the Christians of Rome, "To set the mind on the flesh is death, but to set the mind on the Spirit is life and peace. For the mind that is set on the flesh is hostile to God; it does not submit to God's law, indeed it cannot; and those who are in the flesh cannot please God" (Romans 8:6-8). "Flesh" as it is used here does not refer to the physical body; it is a synonym for sin.

That means that "Death" is the state of living in separation from God, that is, in a state of sin. That is why "the wages of sin is death, but the free gift of God is eternal life in Christ Jesus our Lord" (Romans 6:23). Those in spiritual death are described by St. Paul as "estranged and hostile in mind, doing evil deeds" (Colossians 1:21). And St. John verifies that "He who does not love abides in death" (1 John 3:14), here referring both to love for God and love for neighbor.

The word *"thanato"* ("death" beginning with a lower case "d" in the English translation) refers not only to the death of Jesus Christ on the Cross, but to the whole of His saving work. "And being found in human form he humbled himself and became obedient unto death, even death on a cross" (Philippians 2: 8). Through His Death and Resurrection Christ redeems the world from sin. Contemplate these words of St. Paul! "But in fact Christ has been raised from the dead, the first fruits of those who have fallen asleep. For as by a man (Adam) came death, by a man (Jesus) has come also the resurrection of the dead. For as in Adam all die, so also in Christ shall all be made alive" (1 Corinthians 15:20-22).

26. TRULY, CHRIST IS RISEN!

Q. I am 72 years old. For over 60 years I have sung the "Christos Aneste" (the "Christ is risen" hymn) and I enjoyed it! The melody is a happy tune, and a reminder of the Easter season. This year as I sang it, I realized that I do not understand the words or their meaning. Please explain the hymn.   – P.M., Hudson, FL

A. Last week, we began the response to this question. We pointed out in section 1, that Christ is the Second Person of the Holy Trinity, the Son, who took on human nature, to come into the historical world for our salvation.

In section 2 we said that the proclamation that Jesus Christ is risen from the dead, affirms that the event of the Resurrection of Christ is at the core of the Christian faith.

In section 3 we observed that through His death on the Cross and His Resurrection, Jesus addressed "Death," the condition of humanity separated from the living God. "Death" is the life of sinfulness and broken relationship with God.

"Trampling on Death"
4. The next section deals with the word "trampling," a translation of the Greek word, "*patesas.*"

Trampling is a very interesting word, open to much instruction for us. The Greek word is *"patesas."* It comes from the verb forms *"patein"* and *"patasso."* It can simply mean, "to walk." More intensely, it is used to imply deliberately stepping on something to subdue it. For example, Jesus said in Luke 10:19 "Behold, I have given you authority to tread (*"patein"*) upon serpents and scorpions, and over all the power of the enemy; and nothing shall hurt you." It can mean to squeeze under pressure as in a wine press (Revelation 14:19, 19:15). Translated as "trample" it means to conquer, as we read in Revelation 11:2: "they will trample over the holy city for forty-two months."

"Patasso" in ancient and Septuagint (Old Testament) Greek means to "beat," "knock," "strike," "smite," "afflict," and even to "slaughter." So "trampling" in this case means to conquer Death, or to be victorious over Death and all it represents. It means that through His Resurrection, Jesus conquered the fear of physical death, and overcame spiritual death, sin, evil and all that is demonic.

So, St. Paul rejoices in the Resurrection of Christ: "'Death is swallowed up in victory.' 'O death, where is thy victory? O death, where is thy sting?' The sting of death is sin, and the power of sin is the law. But thanks be to God, who gives us the victory through our Lord Jesus Christ!" (1 Corinthians 15:54-57). Similarly, elsewhere St. Paul says, "The last enemy to be destroyed is death. For God has put all things in subjection under his (Jesus Christ's) feet" (1 Corinthians 15:26-27). Further, in Hebrews we are told that Christ became one like us so that "through death he might destroy him who has the power of death, that is, the devil and deliver all those who through fear of death were subject to lifelong bondage" (Hebrews 2:14-15).

Bestowing life to those in the tombs

5. That leads us to the phrase **. . . and bestowing life to those in the tombs**. Who are "those in the tombs" that the hymn is talking about? The answer is "All those who are spiritually dead!" That

means all human beings who do not share in the victory over Death and in the Resurrection of Jesus Christ.

The New Testament teaches us that we begin sharing in the Death and Resurrection of Jesus Christ through the sacrament of Holy Baptism.

> Do you not know that all of us who have been baptized into Christ Jesus were baptized into his death? We were buried therefore with him by baptism into death, so that as Christ was raised from the dead by the glory of the Father, we too might walk in newness of life. For if we have been united with him in a death like his, we shall certainly be united with him in a resurrection like his" (Rom. 6:3-5).

When we went down into the baptismal waters, we were "buried together with Christ," our old person dying with Him. When we came out of the baptismal water we were raised together with Christ's Resurrection into a new life, and became a new creation. Sacramentally, the gift of the seal of the Holy Spirit in Holy Chrismation and the communion with the Body and Blood of Christ in the Eucharist, maintain our bond of relationship with Christ and contribute to the ongoing "newness of life."

The opposite of "Death" is newness of **"Life"** in Christ. Once baptized, we must make this newness of life real, something we consciously identify with, in our minds, our hearts, our speech, in our way of life and with our deeds. Our Baptism, so to speak, lifted us up out of the kingdom of Death, sin and evil, presided over by the Devil, and placed us in the kingdom of Life, presided over by Christ. Continuing the passage above, St. Paul dramatically describes the new condition in which we find ourselves as baptized Christians:

> We know that our old self was crucified with him so that the sinful body might be destroyed, and we might no longer be

enslaved to sin. For he who has died is freed from sin. But if we have died with Christ, we believe that we shall also live with him. So you also must consider yourselves dead to sin and alive to God in Christ Jesus" (Romans 6:6-8, 11).

In an important sense, this new life is a **bestowing**, that is, a gift of God, which we could never achieve on our own. The victory of Christ over death, sin, evil, demonic forces and the Devil is His gift to us out of God's love for humanity. We did not have a right to it; we did not force it from God; we did nothing to earn it. What Christ did, was a loving gift from God. "For God so loved the world that he *gave* his only Son, that whoever believes in him should not perish but have eternal life. For God sent the Son into the world, not to condemn the world, but that the world might be saved through him" (John 3:16-17).

New Life

7. **Life** is a key word here. We must appropriate for ourselves what Christ did for all of humanity. We must make real the new "life" given to us who were previously residing "in the tombs." Baptism is the entry point into the life of the Kingdom of God. Alone, it doesn't accomplish much unless we respond to it. Through personal commitment to Christ, through the sacramental life, through obedience to His will, through prayerful communion with Him, through faithfulness, through a life of love lived in His service, through a life-long process of continuous growth in the image and likeness of God, we live the new life which has been bestowed upon us.

So, we are told ". . . you, who once were estranged and hostile in mind, doing evil deeds, he has now reconciled in his body of flesh by his death, in order to present you holy and blameless and irreproachable before him, **provided that you continue in the faith, stable and steadfast**" (Colossians 1:21-23).

Christ is Risen! An Expanded Interpretation

Christ, who is the Son of God, took on human nature through His birth from the Theotokos and lived among humanity, teaching, healing, guiding, and finally taking on all the forces of death and evil and sin through His crucifixion. On the third day, however, He overcame the power of death and sin and evil through His Resurrection from the dead. He conquered the power of death over us so that it no longer had necessary control over us. This is the bedrock of the Christian faith about salvation. We share in the Death and Resurrection of Jesus Christ individually and personally through our baptism. Once baptized we are given the gift of the Holy Spirit and share in the Body and Blood of Christ in the Eucharist. We then must cultivate our relationship with God with the aid of the Holy Spirit. Christ's Resurrection is the beginning of our new life, raising us out of the tomb of a life lived without God, which is not true life at all. The new life is nurtured in the Church with the sacraments, learning the meaning of the Christian life, overcoming the residue of sin and evil in us, serving the Lord obediently, living sacrificially in love for God and for others in their need, and growing toward God-likeness.

27. "AND HE SHALL COME AGAIN . . ."

Q. Please explain to me ". . . and He shall come again with glory to judge the living and the dead; whose Kingdom shall have no end" When He comes -the Second Coming–will He reign on the earth for a thousand years? And will we walk this earth again in our resurrected bodies? Or will at the Second Coming will we all be resurrected according to our works, and have spiritual bodies, and the life everlasting will be in heaven or otherwise?   – *W.G., Trenton, NJ.*

A. Questions like this recur frequently, not only during the life of this column, but throughout the centuries. There is a strange inquisitiveness about the events of the "end times" among some people. In August of 1986 this column addressed the question *"Is the Second Coming of Christ Near?"* What follows is a slightly revised version of my answer then, and I think it serves to begin answering your questions. Next week, we'll look more carefully at this issue.

The Expectation of the Second Coming

Because Jesus has promised His coming again to judge the world, Christians expect that He will return one day. Jesus said, "...when I go and prepare a place for you, I will come again and will take you to myself, that where I am you may be also." (John 14:3). The parable of the Second Coming, describing the judgment of Christ, separating the good from the evil (the sheep from the goats) in the 25th chapter of Matthew also teaches the Second Coming of Christ: "When the Son of man comes in his glory, and all the angels with him, then he will sit on his glorious throne..." (Matthew 25:31). There are many other biblical passages which speak of it. Thus, the Church has always expected Christ to return in a Second Coming.

In the Creed, we say, "And He shall come again in glory to judge the living and the dead; Whose Kingdom shall have no end...I await the resurrection of the dead."

The Second Coming - Calculating It

It is interesting that in different places in the Bible there are passages which indicate a kind of "order of events" which will take place before Christ's Second Coming. Yet these are very difficult, if not impossible to put together into a coherent pattern.

For example, in 1 Thessalonians, St. Paul says, "The day of the Lord will come like a thief in the night" (1 Thessalonians 5:2) during a time of peace and security. But in 2 Thessalonians we read, "the day will not come, unless the rebellion comes first, and the man of lawlessness is revealed . . ." (2 Thessalonians 2:3). If we add the difficult-to-understand passages of the Book of Revelation to this mix, we can do one of two things. On the one hand it is possible to spend a lifetime trying to make sense out of the passages so as to harmonize them and make predictions about the Second Coming, according to our subjective understanding. Thus, many Protestants fight among themselves under the banners of Pre-Millenarianism, Millenarianism, various sorts of Dispensationalism, Theologies of the Anti-Christ, etc. Some have predicted the Second Coming, sold their homes, put on white robes, climbed some mountain, and awaited the Second Coming. All have been disappointed.

The Second Coming - Being Ready For It
Another way of dealing with those passages which describe the end times and the return of Christ is to understand them as pointing to the return of Christ itself and the fact that we should be ready for it. This has been the way of the Orthodox Church. Often the parable of the "Ten Wise and Ten Foolish Virgins" is interpreted by the Church to mean that the Second Coming could take place any time; but, in any case, unexpectedly. The main message is that we are to be alert and ready for the Second Coming of Christ, for the Lord can return at any time. For example, in Holy Week we sing the hymn of the Parable of the Bridegroom:

> *Behold the Bridegroom comes in the middle of the night, and blessed is the servant whom He shall find watching; and again unworthy is he whom He shall find heedless...*

In short, the Church's use of those passages is to tell us that we should be ready spiritually and morally every day, in repentance, obedience, loyalty and devotion to Christ.

We Should Not Try To Determine the Date of Christ's Return
The whole concern about the date when Christ will return is not the business of Christians. That is the teaching of the New Testament.

Jesus Himself says: "But of that day and hour no one knows, not even the angels of heaven, nor the Son, but the Father only . . . Watch therefore, for you do not know on what day your Lord is coming . . . Therefore you must be ready; for the Son of man is coming at an hour you do not expect." (Matthew 24:36, 42, 44). So also St. Paul: "As to the times and seasons, brethren, you have no need to have anything written to you. For you yourselves know well that the day of the Lord will come like a thief in the night" (1 Thessalonians 5: 1). On the basis of this, St. Paul counsels: "Now concerning the coming of our Lord Jesus Christ and our assembling to meet him, we beg you brethren, not to be quickly shaken in mind or excited, either by spirit or by word, or by letter purporting to be from us, to the effect that the day of the Lord has come. Let no one deceive you..." (2 Thess. 2:1-3a).

Be Ready! Eternity Starts Now!

Our job is not to be concerned whether His coming is to be sooner or later. We are not to anticipate the date, whether it be soon or delayed. We are not to get excited and worked up about the date. Rather, ours is another responsibility. Our job is to be always ready. Jesus is Coming Soon: FOR YOU.

The Bible is clear that what we do in this life is what will determine our eternal destiny. If we are close to God in this life we will be close to him in the next. If we are far from God in this life, we will be far from Him in the next. Heaven and Hell are a continuation of our lives on earth.

That is why we are to be ready at all times. But if He doesn't come in our life time, then, you and I will go into eternity at our deaths, already prepared for the judgment. Our eternal destiny will be set. St. Paul teaches that to those who are faithful and who suffer for the Gospel, God will "grant rest," and that in them Christ "will be glorified." But they "who do not know God," and "who do not obey the Gospel of our Lord Jesus...shall suffer the punishment of eternal destruction and exclusion from the presence of the Lord and from the glory of his might." This will take place "when the Lord Jesus is revealed from heaven with his mighty angels in flaming fire" (1 Thessalonians 1:5-12).

Life After Death

Since we are taught in the parable of the Rich Man and Poor Lazarus, that those who die already begin to experience their eternal reward or punishment (Luke 16:19-31), the Orthodox Church teaches that when we die, we begin immediately experiencing a foretaste of our eternal destiny. This is known in theological terms as the "Partial Judgment," in contrast to the "General Judgment," which will take place at Christ's Second Coming.

This means that for each of us, personally, the consequences of the Second Coming will begin taking place at our death! In effect, relatively soon (For who knows when he or she will die?) we will each face our own personal equivalent foretaste of the Lord's Second Coming.

When Is Christ Going to Return?

Is Christ Coming Soon? He may come soon. He may not. Our task is not to calculate the date of His Second Coming, but to be always ready. Whether He comes in our lifetime or not, when we die we will face our personal equivalent of Christ's Second Coming. Is Christ coming soon? Maybe! Maybe not! But for sure, He will return! So what should you do now? Jesus says, "Therefore you must be ready; for the Son of man is coming at an hour you do not expect." (Matthew 24:36, 42, 44).

28. END-TIME EVENTS

Q. Please explain to me ". . . and He shall come again with glory to judge the living and the dead; whose Kingdom shall have no end." When He comes -the Second Coming- will He reign on the earth for a thousand years? And will we walk this earth again in our resurrected bodies? Or will at the Second Coming will we all be resurrected according to our works, and have spiritual bodies, and the life everlasting will be in heaven or otherwise. — *W.G., Trenton, NJ.*

A. last week we read the reprinting of an older column which highlighted the following points:

A Summary of the Teaching
1) The Church has always remained in a stance of expectation that Christ will return–The Second Coming.
2) While affirming the Second Coming, it is difficult to have a clear picture about the events that will take place: in the Bible and the Church Fathers are different pictures.
3) The Church teaches that we are to anticipate the Second Coming of our Lord by being always ready for Christ's return, faithfully, spiritually and through our daily way of life, knowing that when He returns, it will be unexpected.
4) Therefore, the Church teaches that we are not to be concerned about dates and details of Christ's Second Coming. Calculating the date and the order of events, spending time and energy on these sorts of speculation violates both the letter and the Spirit of biblical and patristic teaching.
5) Jesus Christ, through His Incarnation, Teaching, Healing, Death and Resurrection did all that was necessary to redeem the world. But we must respond to His saving work. This is the beginning of eternal life for us. It will continue forever, either in communion with God, or if we are not faithful believers, in separation from God. Heaven begins in this life; Hell begins in this life.
6) What is important is our readiness. We are to be ready to meet the Lord whether He comes before we die or whether we die before He returns to the earth in His Second Coming.
7) If we die before He returns, we will experience what Orthodox

theologians call "the Partial Judgment," which consists of a fore-taste of heaven or hell. In the meantime, we await Christ's Second Coming.

8) If Jesus Christ returns before we die, we will see amazing events taking place, but we are not clear about the order and nature of those events. Christ will return for the "General Judgment" in which all persons who ever lived will receive their just reward or their just punishment in eternity.

That is the meaning of the Creed's affirmation "He shall come again with glory to judge the living and the dead; whose Kingdom shall have no end."

Millennialism

You ask, "When He comes –the Second Coming–will He reign on the earth for a thousand years? And will we walk this earth again in our resurrected bodies?" As already indicated, the honest answer to that question is "No one knows." There are scattered passages in the Bible which speak of the coming of the Anti-Christ, of a thousand year reign on earth before the final consummation of things, and similar statements. The main source for these is the book of Revelation, the only "apocalyptic" book of the New Testament.

Some hold that by examining Old Testament apocalyptic writings and coordinating them with statements in the New Testament, it is possible to create an accurate picture of what will happen. And they spend enormous amounts of ink and energy to do this.

This is largely a futile endeavor. The main reason for this is that these various passages were not written to be primarily *predictive*, but to *exhort* believers to remain faithful to the Lord in times of persecution, apostasy and corruption. Because, in one way or another, these phenomena exist in every age, it becomes interesting to apply these writings to specific historical situations. An example is the teaching about the Anti-Christ.

The Anti-Christ

The biblical writings ascribed to John make repeated mention of the Anti-Christ. In one sense, anyone, anything, any teaching that rejects Christ or is opposed to Him is "the Anti-Christ." On the other hand, in 2 Thessalonians and in Revelation we have varying descriptions of the coming of the Anti-Christ as a ruler or power-figure opposed to Christ who deceives many, drawing them away from Christ, before or after the Second Coming. One Orthodox theologian holds that the reign of the Anti-Christ will come as a foretaste of the consequences of disbelief in Christ and as a test of the faithfulness of believers, in all likelihood demanding witness and martyrdom.

The Thousand Year Reign

Much is made of the passage in Revelation 20 which speaks of a "thousand year reign" of Christ on earth before the final consummation of things. The passage is far from a straight-forward prediction. It is written in the past, present and future tenses, filled with allegorical images: "bottomless pit," "great chain," "dragon," "ancient serpent," "thrones," "the beast," "mark on the forehead," etc.

In his book *The Revelation of the Apostle John* (in Greek), Prof. Panagiotes J. Bratsiotes, formerly of the University of Athens, Greece, traces the understanding of this chapter through the Church's history. In the early period of the persecution of Christianity, Revelation was understood as an encouraging vision of Christ's ultimate victory over the enemies of the Church. The persecutions were short in the face of a long-term victory of Christ.

But when extremist heretical groups such as the Montanists began speculating about the end-times and weaving theories that became more important than the Gospel itself, the Church moved to an understanding of the "thousand years" as meaning "a long time" and applying it to the Church as the age of the spread of Christ's redemption to all the world.

Bishop Andrew of Caesarea (6th century) wrote a commentary using the common patristic triple method of interpretation (historical, ethical and mystical) of this difficult book. He contributed greatly to the development of a cautious approach to the Book of Revelation within the Church as both mysterious and as dangerous because of the ease with which it can be misinterpreted and lead to false teachings.

Oecoumenios (6th century), also wrote a commentary on the book Revelation. Between this commentary and that of Andrew of Caesaria, the view came to be established in the Church that the "thousand years" refer to the time of the Incarnation of Christ to the time of the coming of the Anti-Christ, that is, the period between the coming of Christ and the beginning of the end-times. Thus, from this perspective, we are now in the "thousand year" reign of Christ.

What We Need to Know About the End-Times

In short, some day Christ will return. He will judge the living and the dead. His Kingdom will have no end. When Christ returns, our task, whether we are alive on the earth or not, is to do all we can to remain in communion with God and to grow in grace toward God-likeness. The rest is useless speculation. That's all we really have to know.

29. THE HOLY SPIRIT

Q. Jesus told His disciples that the Holy Spirit would be in the world until He returned. What then was the role of the Holy Spirit before Jesus entered and left the earth, and especially what will be the role of this, the third person of the Trinity after Jesus returns.

– J.G.T. Somerville, MA.

A. I am sure that you understand, that to adequately answer these questions would go far beyond the scope of this column. The best way to answer these questions for the column is to be as direct as possible. Otherwise, we will be forced to spend many columns trying to respond to them fully.

The Holy Trinity

The Holy Spirit is the third person of the Holy Trinity. According to the teaching of Jesus, the Holy Spirit is the "Spirit of truth, who proceeds from the Father" (John 15:26). The theological teaching of the Orthodox Church is that the three persons are exactly the same in their divinity, except that the person of the Father is the source (*arche*). The Son is forever born of the Father and the Holy Spirit forever proceeds from the Father.

Among the persons of the Holy Trinity there is such oneness that whatever one of the persons does, the other persons are also present and cooperating. The Bible, however, frequently presents one of the persons of the Holy Trinity as "leading the action," so to speak. Thus, we think of the Father as the Creator. But we also read in the Bible that at the creation "the Spirit of God moved upon the face of the waters" (Genesis 1:2). So, St. Gregory of Nyssa says that the Holy Spirit "is dependent on the Father as the cause from which his being derives and the source from which he proceeds . . ."(*On the Difference Between "Ousia" And "Hypostasis"*. This work is sometimes attributed to St. Basil).

The Holy Spirit Before Christ

Before Christ came, the Holy Spirit is often presented as sustaining the created universe and being present throughout the created world. As one of the Psalms asks, "Whither shall I go from thy Spirit?" (Psalm 139:2). Most importantly, the Holy Spirit acted to guide the leaders of Israel and to inspire the prophets. Thus, in Judges 11:29 we read how the Spirit of the Lord came upon Jephthah." The Prophet Ezekiel begins his prophecy with the words "The Spirit entered into me . . . and I heard him speaking to me. And he said to me, 'Son of man, I send you to the people of Israel . . .'" (Ezekiel 2:2).

The Psalmist expresses personal experience of the Holy Spirit as the source of life and holiness when he says, "Take not Thy Spirit from me" (Psalm 51:11). Prophecy that refers to the coming of the Messiah and the Kingdom of God sees it as a special gift of the Holy Spirit: "I will pour out my Spirit upon all flesh" (Joel 2:28).

That prophecy continued on from the Old Testament period into the New. St. Gregory of Nyssa expresses the tradition of the Church when he says in his Life of Moses that "The law and the prophets trumpeted out the divine mystery of the incarnation . . . The Spirit expressing itself through various instruments made the sound successively more impressive and more forceful. For prophets and apostles were all instruments giving utterance to one spiritual sound."

The Holy Spirit and the Work of Christ

Jesus announced the beginning of His public ministry by saying that "the Spirit of the Lord is upon me," quoting from the Old Testament book of the Prophet Isaiah (Luke 4:18).

He began by going to St. John the Baptist who recognized him for who He was, proclaiming that Jesus will baptize with the Holy Spirit, while he just baptized with water (Mark 1:8).

Jesus was accompanied in His saving work by the Holy Spirit, for at His own baptism by John the Baptist, the Spirit came upon Him in the form of a dove (Matthew 3:16). It was the Spirit that led Jesus into the wilderness where He fasted forty days, after which He was tempted and overcame the temptation.

Christ's teaching, healing, and saving work on the Cross and through the empty tomb took place with the Spirit and the gifts that come to us from that saving work are through the Holy Spirit. Thus, St. Gregory of Nyssa says in the work mentioned above "Every good thing which comes to us from the divine power is, we say, the working of the grace which works all in all. As the apostle says, 'All these things are the work of the one same Spirit distributing them separately to each man as he wills' (I Corinthians 12:11)." St. Gregory ties it all together with these words, "Thus the Spirit, who is the source of the entire supply of good things which flows forth upon creation, is linked to the Son in that the two are known in a single act of apprehension."

An example of this close tie between the work of Christ and the Holy Spirit is seen in Acts 2:2 where the giving of commandments by Christ to His disciples is described as taking place "*through* the Holy Spirit."

The Holy Spirit In The Church

At His Ascension, Jesus promised His disciples that they would "receive power when the Holy Spirit has come upon (them)" (Acts 1: 8). That happened several days later at Pentecost. "And they were all filled with the Holy Spirit and began to speak in other tongues, as the Spirit gave them utterance" (Acts 2:4).

Since then, the Holy Spirit has been sustaining the Church and its members in their growth in God-likeness. Jesus promised that "The Holy Spirit will teach you . . ." (Luke 12:12). He said, "When the Spirit of truth comes, he will guide you in all truth" (John 16:13). On the other hand, the Bible teaches us how we are to relate to the Holy Spirit. "Walk by the Spirit, and do not gratify the flesh" (Galatians 5:16); "maintain the unity of the Spirit in the bond of peace" (Ephesians 4:3); "do not grieve the Holy Spirit of God" (Ephesians 4:30); "do not quench the Spirit" (1 Thessalonians 5:19). Above all, as Jesus taught, we worship in the Spirit. "But the hour is coming, and now is, when the true worshipers will worship the Father in spirit and truth, for such the Father seeks to worship him. God is Spirit, and those who worship him must worship in spirit and truth" (John 4:23-24).

The Holy Spirit After The Second Coming

It is hard to determine the activity of the Holy Spirit after the Second Coming of Christ. We know that Jesus will "sit at the right hand of the Father" in all eternity, according to the Creed. What that means exactly we cannot know, however. The book of Hebrews in the New Testament tells us also that Christ does His work through the "eternal Spirit," so the Holy Spirit will of necessity be participating in the activities of the Father and the Son. Whatever we might say about life eternal in God's Kingdom after the Second Coming, will without question include the Holy Spirit. As St. Gregory of Nyssa says, "It is not possible to conceive of the Son but only in inseparable conjunction with the Holy Spirit; for no notion of the Son is possible unless one is first enlightened by the Spirit."

This much we can be sure of: the Holy Spirit will continue to unite us with Christ and with God the Father throughout eternity.

30. THE ROLE OF THE HOLY SPIRIT

Q. What was the role of the Holy Spirit before Pentecost, and what will be its role after the return of Jesus, after the Parousia?

– J.G.T., Somerville, MA.

A. When St. Cyril of Jerusalem (315-386) undertook to write about the Holy Spirit in his *Catecheses,* he said, "Truly I need spiritual grace if I am to discourse on the Holy Spirit. I do not mean, to enable me to speak as the subject deserves, for that is not possible, but simply to run through what is said in Holy Scripture without imperiling my soul. For what is written in the gospels, of Christ saying unequivocally, 'Whoever speaks a word against the Holy Spirit, will not be forgiven, either in this world, or in the world to come' (Matthew 12:32), truly makes one very much afraid" *(Catechetical Lecture 16).*

Needless to say, I feel the responsibility and fear even more, as I seek to respond to your question, so today, I will try to let one or two of the Fathers of the Church speak for me regarding the work of the Holy Spirit. I take "before Pentecost" to mean before the Christian dispensation, since we are all familiar with the work of the Holy Spirit in the Annunciation, the Birth of Christ, the Work of Christ, and the mission of the Apostles.

When we speak of the Holy Spirit, we speak of the third person of the Holy Trinity, we affirm that the Holy Spirit is fully God and forever proceeding from the first person of the Holy Trinity, the Father, and who is sent into the world for its salvation by the Son. The Nicene Creed says that the Holy Spirit is "the Lord, the Giver of life, who proceeds from the Father, who together with the Father and the Son is worshiped and glorified, who spoke through the prophets."

Yet, we also affirm that there are not three gods, but one God, Who in His very being is a community of divine, interpenetrating persons: Father, Son and Holy Spirit. We stand before a mystery that simply transcends the categories of thought available to us as created human beings.

Nevertheless, there are some specific things that we can and do say as Orthodox about the work of the Holy Spirit. St. Athanasios (296-373), in his third letter to Serapion, says:

> The Holy Spirit is supreme power, a divine and ineffable reality. For he is alive and rational, and sanctifies everything that has been brought into being by God through Christ. He enlightens the souls of righteous men. He was in the prophets, and under the new covenant he was in the apostles.

In the same letter, St. Athanasios adds:

> (The Holy Spirit) it is who through the prophets predicted the things of Christ, he again who worked mightily in the apostles. To this very day it is he who in the sacrament seals the souls of those who are baptized. . . . Every grace is given by the Father, through the Son, together with the Holy Spirit.

Before Christ

In the Creation: The first thing to note about the work of the Holy Spirit before Christ is that the Holy Spirit was present and participated with the Father and the Son in the creation of the world. St. Athanasios, again is our guide:

> For it is written concerning him in the one hundred and third Psalm: 'Thou shall take away their spirit, and they shall die and return to their dust. Thou shall put forth thy Spirit, and they shall be created, and thou shall renew the face of the earth' (Psalm 103 [Septuagint]:29-30).

As it is thus written, it is clear that the Spirit is not a creature, but takes part in the act of creation. The Father creates all things through the Word in the Spirit; for where the Word is, there is the Spirit also, and it is out of the Spirit from the Word that the things which are created through the Word have their power to exist. Thus it is written in the thirty-second psalm: 'By the Word of the Lord the heavens were established, and by the Spirit of his mouth is all their might' (Psalm 33:6).

In Providence: The whole created world is sustained and maintained in existence by the presence and power of the Holy Spirit. St. Athanasios says that:

It follows from this that the Spirit too cannot be a creature; for he is not in separate places assigned to him, but fills all things and yet is outside all things. Thus it is written: 'The Spirit of the Lord has filled the world' (Wisdom 1:7). And David sings, 'Whither shall I go from thy Spirit?' (Psalm 139:7), inasmuch as he is not in any place, but is outside all things and in the Son, as the Son is in the Father.

In the Holy Scriptures: The Holy Spirit also inspired, guided and illumined the Holy Prophets and other writers of the Scriptures. As St. Athanasios says:

The Spirit is so clearly indivisible from the Son that what we are saying leaves no room for doubt. When the Word came upon the prophet, it was in the Spirit that the prophet used to speak the things he received from the Word. Thus it is written in the Acts, when Peter says: `Brethren, the Scripture had to be fulfilled which the Holy Spirit spoke beforehand' (Acts 1:16). In Zechariah it is written, when the

Word came upon him: 'But receive my words and my statutes, which I charge in my Spirit to the prophets' (Zechariah 1:6). And when, a little farther on, he rebuked the people, he said: 'They made their heart disobedient, lest they should hear my laws and the words which the Lord Almighty has sent by his Spirit in the hands of the prophets of old' (Zechariah 7:12).

In All that is Good: It is the belief of the Church that God inspires every good thing wherever it is to be found. St. Cyril of Jerusalem speaks of the Holy Spirit, which we should "contemplate (as) the great guardian and dispenser of the several graces, who, throughout the world, is giving to this one chastity, and to that one lifelong virginity, making another a generous giver, and detaching another from care for worldly goods, while on yet another he bestows the gift of driving out evil spirits. And just as daylight, by one act of the sun's radiation, enlightens the whole earth, so too the Holy Spirit gives light to all who have eyes to see."

In the Eschaton
The New Testament book of Revelation indicates that in the End Times (the Eschaton) the Holy Spirit will be present as we must necessarily expect. We read: "'I Jesus have sent my angel to you with this testimony for the churches'. . . . The Spirit and the Bride say, 'Come.' And let him who hears say, 'Come.'" (Revelation 22:16-17).

Since the Holy Spirit unites us with Christ and the Father in this life, we must assume that the Holy Spirit will continue to do so in the eternal Kingdom of God.

31. THE HOLY SPIRIT IN PRAYER

Q. When in prayer, how do you know that the Grace of the Holy Spirit is upon you?   – *C. M., Baltimore, MD.*

A. Your question is not an easy one to answer. The issue, of course, is what is meant by "to know." Certainly, if we pray genuinely and honestly, with commitment and without reservations, it means that we will be in communion and union with God. He certainly will manifest himself to us in the whole of our lives. The first impact on us will probably be on our feelings. But that is not the only way we know that the Holy Spirit is with us. There are many ways. What follows in this column is a recording of some biblical passages, which illustrate this response to your question.

The Emotions - Joy and Peace: The first sense which we have of the grace of the Holy Spirit in our lives is a sense of peace and joy. St. Paul spoke of "joy inspired by the Holy Spirit" in the Thessalonian Christians (1 Thessalonians 1:6). To the same people he exhorted, "Rejoice always, pray constantly, give thanks in all circumstances; for this is the will of God in Christ Jesus for you. Do not quench the Spirit" (1 Thessalonians 5:16-19). In the New Testament book of the Acts of the Apostles, we learn that "the disciples were filled with joy and with the Holy Spirit" (Acts 13:52). Saint Paul also instructs us that life in the Kingdom of God, which begins with our baptism, includes such experiences: "the kingdom of God is not food and drink but righteousness and peace and joy in the Holy Spirit" (Romans 14:17). We are even told that Jesus experienced such feelings: "In that same hour he rejoiced in the Holy Spirit" (Luke 10:21).

There is another feeling which the Scriptures speak about; it is the feeling of being in God's caring love. Thus, one of the Psalms says, "But truly God has listened; he has given heed to the voice of my prayer. Blessed be God, because he has not rejected my prayer or removed his steadfast love from me!" (Psalm 66:19-20). But it is not enough just to experience these feelings. The presence of the Holy Spirit will also impact on our thinking.

The Holy Spirit Keeps Us in the Truth: So, St. Paul speaks to Timothy, his disciple, indicating that the Christian truth is protected by the Holy Spirit. "Follow the pattern of the sound words which you have heard from me, in the faith and love which are in Christ Jesus; guard the truth that has been entrusted to you by the Holy Spirit who dwells within us" (2 Timothy 1:13-14). And elsewhere, St. Paul gives witness of the influence of the Holy Spirit in his telling of the truth, when he said "I am speaking the truth in Christ, I am not lying; my conscience bears me witness in the Holy Spirit" (Romans 9:1).

The Holy Spirit Encourages Us to Pray: The more we are "in the Holy Spirit," the more we want to pray and thank God. As St. Paul says, in the second letter which he wrote to the Christians in Corinth: "so that as grace extends to more and more people it may increase thanksgiving, to the glory of God" (2 Corinthians 4:15).

Increased Need For, and Desire to Worship: Right after the first Christians received the gift of the Holy Spirit at Pentecost, the Acts of the Apostles tells us, they showed a tremendous increase in the desire to worship together: "And they devoted themselves to the apostles' teaching and fellowship, to the breaking of bread and the prayers" (Acts 2:42).

Crisis Assistance: We can be confident that the Holy Spirit is with us, when in times of trial and crisis, we are guided in what we should say and do, for didn't our Lord promise it? "And when they bring you before the synagogues and the rulers and the authorities, do not be anxious how or what you are to answer or what you are to say, for the Holy Spirit will teach you in that very hour what you ought to say" (Luke 12:11-12).

With this we see that the presence of the Holy Spirit is also with us in our external circumstances, not just in our inner life. For example, how we behave in our lives toward ourselves and toward others is a sign that the Holy Spirit is with us. Here are some examples.

The Holy Spirit and Our Bodies: When we respect our bodies and keep ourselves from bodily sin, because we are able to overcome any temptations which seek to lead us to those kinds of sins, we know the Holy Spirit is with us. St. Paul put it so powerfully when he said, "Do you not know that your body is a temple of the Holy Spirit within you, which you have from God? You are not your own; you were bought with a price. So glorify God in your body" (1 Corinthians 6:19-20).

Other Behavior: We know that the Holy Spirit resides in us when our behavior in general is directed with a measure of ease toward pleasing God and serving God's purposes. For example, *when we speak:* "Therefore I want you to understand that no one speaking by the Spirit of God ever says 'Jesus be cursed!' and no one can say 'Jesus is Lord' except by the Holy Spirit" (1 Corinthians 12:3). Christians who are rich in the presence of the Holy Spirit do not swear or blaspheme the name of God. Nor do we gossip, or lie, or deceive. As St. Peter says, "He that would love life and see good days, let him keep his tongue from evil and his lips from speaking guile; let him turn away from evil and do right; let him seek peace and pursue it. For the eyes of the Lord are upon the righteous, and his ears are open to their prayer" (1 Peter: 3:10-12). Also, prayer in the Holy Spirit must influence our conduct. Thus, St. Paul says, "I desire then that in every place men should pray, lifting holy hands without anger or quarreling" (1 Timothy 2: 8).

In general, we know the Holy Spirit is present in our lives when we follow God's ways. Thus, the book of Acts speaks of "the Holy Spirit whom God has given to those who obey him" (Acts 5:32).

Special Gifts: To each of us, God gives special gifts to fulfill His will. To all is the gift given to build up the Church, which each of us, clergy and lay, do in our own unique way. St. Paul thus says, "So with yourselves; since you are eager for manifestations of the Spirit, strive to excel in building up the church" (1 Corinthians 14:12). And in general, the Lord sends His varied gifts to all that are "in the Spirit". In the New Testament book of Hebrews we read, therefore, that "God...bore witness by signs and wonders and various miracles and by gifts of the Holy Spirit distributed according to his own will" (Hebrews 2: 4). All these are signs of the presence and power of the Holy Spirit, not only in our prayers, but also in our whole Christian life.

Be Aglow in the Spirit

I wish to end this column with a beautiful passage from Saint Paul about the presence of the Holy Spirit in our lives, which encompasses nearly everything which has been said above.

"Never flag in zeal, be aglow with the Spirit, serve the Lord. Rejoice in your hope, be patient in tribulation, be constant in prayer. Contribute to the needs of the saints, practice hospitality. Bless those who persecute you; bless and do not curse them. Rejoice with those who rejoice, weep with those who weep. Live in harmony with one another; do not be haughty, but associate with the lowly; never be conceited. Repay no one evil for evil, but take thought for what is noble in the sight of all. If possible, so far as it depends upon you, live peaceably with all"

(Romans 12:11-18).

32. ACQUIRING THE HOLY SPIRIT

Q. As Orthodox Christians, our goal is to acquire the Holy Spirit. What does this mean and how do we know we have reached this goal?

– *G. V., New York, N.Y.*

A. Very briefly, the answer to your question is as follows: acquiring the Holy Spirit is the unending process of growth in communion with God, fulfilling our purpose as Christians-which is, to become God-like, as much as is possible for us as human beings. We may grow in the Holy Spirit but we never "reach" the goal, we are always in the process of appropriating into our lives the gifts and presence of the Holy Spirit. This is a vast subject. In this column I can only touch upon a few aspects of it.

Christ, the Holy Spirit, and Salvation

After His resurrection, and at His Ascension, Jesus instructed His disciples to return to Jerusalem, and to wait until He sent His Holy Spirit to them (Acts 1:4-8). At Pentecost, fifty days after His resurrection, Jesus sent the Holy Spirit upon his disciples and the Church of God was born (Acts 2:1-4). One of the tasks of the Church is to renew this pentecostal experience of the giving and receiving of the Holy Spirit for every person who enters the life of faith in Christ. What Christ did through his Incarnation, teaching, healing, death, resurrection and ascension for the salvation of the whole world in every age, is made available personally to each of us through the Holy Spirit.

The Person and Work of the Holy Spirit

The Holy Spirit is the third person of the Holy Trinity, that is, God. The special and unique work of the Holy Spirit is to complete and fulfill the work of salvation in us, both as the Church and as individual persons. In the Orthodox Church we have a very high awareness of the Holy Spirit. Here are two hymns from the Pentecost services of our Church which tell us much about the biblical and patristic teaching regarding the Holy Spirit.

> The Holy Spirit has ever been, is, and ever shall be; for he is wholly without beginning and without end. Yet he is in covenant with the Father and the Son, counted as Life and Life-giver, Light and Light-giver, good by nature and a Fountain of goodness, through whom the Father is known and the Son glorified. And by all it is understood that one power, one rank, one worship are of the Holy Trinity.

> Light, Life and a living supersensuous Fountain is the Holy Spirit, good, upright, supersensuous Spirit of understanding, presiding, and purifying offenses, God and deifying, Fire projecting from Fire, speaking, active, Distributor of gifts, through whom all the Prophets, the Apostles of God, and the Martyrs are crowned; a wondrous Report, a wondrous sight, a Fire divided for the distribution of Gifts.

> *Ainoi of Orthros of Pentecost*

The Gift of the Seal of the Holy Spirit

Every Orthodox Christian has received the gift of the Holy Spirit right after Baptism, through the sacrament of Holy Chrismation; you were anointed with the "seal of the Gift of the Holy Spirit." As a result, God "has put his seal upon us and given us His Spirit in our hearts as a guarantee" (2 Corinthians 1:22) of our salvation and of our membership in Christ's body, the Church. All of us have received gifts of the Holy Spirit, in many cases different gifts among us that complement each other: "There are varieties of gifts, but the same Spirit....To each is given the manifestation of the Spirit for the common good....All these are inspired by one and the same Spirit, who apportions to each one individually as he wills." (1 Cor. 12:4, 7, 11).

More generally speaking, the Holy Spirit produces in us all the Christian virtues by illuminating, directing, guiding, strengthening and co-working with us in the process of growing in God-likeness. Thus, St. Paul teaches us: "the fruit of the Spirit is love, joy, peace, patience, kindness, goodness, faithfulness, gentleness, self-control...(Galatians 5:22).

Both A Gift and Something to be Obtained

But the obtaining of these fruits is not an automatic thing. It is both a gift and something we must desire and act so as to acquire. As a gift from God, the Holy Spirit provides us assurance and confidence that we have been forgiven and freed from the dominion of evil, sin, death and the Devil. Further, the gift of the Holy Spirit assures us that we belong to Christ and that we are members of His body, the Church.

But that is only a beginning. We are called upon to grow as Christians, both as members of Christ's body, the Church, and as individuals. See what St. Paul says about this:

You are no longer strangers and sojourners, but you are fellow citizens with the saints and members of the household of God, built upon the foundation of the apostles and the prophets, Christ Jesus himself being the cornerstone, in whom the whole structure is joined together and grows into a holy temple in the Lord; in whom you also are built into it for a dwelling place of God in the Spirit" (Ephesians 2:19-22).

As a result, we are to grow in the Christian life, as the Bible clearly teaches us (Ephesians 4:15, 1 Peter 2:2, 2 Peter 3:18).

Acquiring the Holy Spirit

So, we have the Holy Spirit; but since we need the Holy Spirit to grow in God-likeness, we must also be in the process of acquiring the Holy Spirit. This we are taught by the New Testament with absolute clarity.

In (Christ) you...were sealed with the promised Holy Spirit, which is the guarantee of our inheritance until we acquire possession of it, to the praise of his glory (Ephesians 1:14).

How do we acquire the Holy Spirit? We are taught by the Bible to "earnestly desire the spiritual gifts" (1 Corinthians 14:1). We must want with our hearts to receive the gifts of the Spirit and to grow in Christ, both individually and as members of Christ's Church. St. Paul says, "since you are eager for manifestations of the Spirit, strive to excel in building up the Church" (1 Corinthians 14:12). Ours is a constant process of "renewal in the Holy Spirit" (Titus 3:5),

-by constant repentance for our sins;
-by participating in worship and in the sacramental life;
-by frequently receiving in Holy Communion;
-by listening attentively to the preaching of God's word, reading the Bible and other good books of the Church;
-by living our lives in obedience to the will of God; and,
-by sharing in all things and communicating the love of God.

Also, one of the most important ways of acquiring the Holy Spirit is prayer.

A Prayer for the Holy Spirit

We can begin our conscious effort to acquire the Holy Spirit as we grow in our spiritual life by praying for the Holy Spirit to come into our lives. Here is one of the prayers of our Church that helps us do this. Pray it daily.

O heavenly King, the Comforter, Spirit of Truth, who is present in all places and who fills all things; treasury of blessings, and Giver of life; come and dwell in us, cleanse us from every stain, and save our souls, O Good One. Amen.

The Creation

33. GOD AND CREATION: A TEMPORAL GAP?

Q. The visible world was created in time. It has a beginning. God is without beginning. He is *Anarchos*. Don't you think this teaching of the Church creates a temporal gap, and puts God in an awkward position of being alone without creation for a long time? How do you explain then, that God after being alone for billion and trillion of years without a creation, finally decided to create first the angels and then the visible world? Why? He needed somebody to worship Him? After the angels and the inanimate world and the animals he created man in His image. Why? To worship Him?   – *K.H., Niagara Falls, NY.*

A. I'll respond to your observations one by one. It is true according to Orthodox Christian doctrine that God is without beginning and that the Creation was brought by God into being in time. The book of Genesis speaks of the Creation this way: "In the beginning God created the heavens and the earth" (Genesis 1:1).

A Temporal Gap?

There is no "temporal gap" precisely because time itself came into existence with the Creation. Time did not exist before the Creation. Time measures the relationship between at least two different bodies, for example, a year is how long it takes for the earth to revolve once around the sun. If there is only one being (God, that is) there can be no time. This is so because there was nothing else that could be in relationship with God. So there were no "billion and trillion years." Thus, there is no "awkward position" for God to be in loneliness.

Further, God is –in Himself– a community of Divine Persons: Father, Son and Holy Spirit. In this sense, God has been forever in a relationship of persons. Therefore, God has never been "alone." Consequently, God neither needed nor needs anything outside of Himself. God is complete in Himself.

Does God Need Worship?

Then, why did God create angels, the inanimate cosmos, the animal world and human beings? Because he needed worship? The answer to this question is "no," precisely because God has no need of anything outside His own existence, including praise and worship from us. Yet, God's existence is characterized by love. His love could have been realized exclusively by the inner relationships of the Holy Trinity, that is, the love of each of the three persons for each of the other three persons.

But God in His goodness, compassion, love and kindness reached out of Himself in what theologians call "ecstatic love" to create those realities which are other than Himself. In a sense, God "went outside of Himself" to create. The Greek words that make up the English word "ecstatic" explain it somewhat: *ek* means "out" and *stasis* means "a stopping or a stepping place." This means that God didn't have to create the world and all that is in it. He chose to create it.

God's Choice to Create

Why, then, did God choose to create? God created so that something other than Himself could share in existence. But full existence for the created world precisely means being in communion with the Creator. Hence, "the heavens declare the glory of God and the firmament proclaims his handiwork" (Psalm 19:1), the animals seek "their food from God" (Psalm 104:21). Regarding humanity, St. Gregory of Nyssa put it this way, "God made man for the purpose of sharing in his own goodness" (*Catechetical Oration*, 5).

The Creation Communes With God

The concluding words of the Psalm read at every Orthodox vesper service is, I think, a good way to end this response.

May the glory of the Lord endure for ever,
may the Lord rejoice in his works,
who looks on the earth and it trembles,
who touches the mountains and they smoke!
I will sing to the Lord as long as I live;
I will sing praise to my God while I have being.
May my meditation be pleasing to him,
for I rejoice in the Lord.
Let sinners be consumed from the earth,
and let the wicked be no more!
Bless the Lord, O my soul!
Praise the Lord! (Psalm 104:31-35.)

Angels and Devils

34. ANGEL NAMES

Q. On November 8 the Orthodox Church celebrates the Synaxis of the Archangel Michael and the Other Bodiless Powers: The angels names listed are, Michael, Gabriel, Raphael, Uriel, Selaphiel, Jegudiel, and Barachiel. Of the names listed, Michael and Gabriel I find in both the Old and the New Testaments. Raphael and Uriel I find in the Apocryphal books of Tobit and Esdras. Also mentioned in a book on *All the Angels in the Bible*, are Jermiel and Metatron.All the remaining names of angels listed I haven't been able to find in the Bible. Can they be found in the Scriptures? Have I just overlooked them? If so, where are they to be found? *– M.N. Barton, OH.*

A. This question has caused me some puzzlement. I have checked the Greek *Menaion* (Monthly Service Book) for November 8 and read every word of the service. I did not find the names of the angels in question. Actually, only the names Michael and Gabriel are mentioned. Also, there is no mention of any angel names other than the Archangels Michael and Gabriel in the Greek *Megas Synaxaristes tes Orthodoxou Ekklesias* (Great Book of Saints of the Orthodox Church) for the November 8 entry (2nd Ed., Victor Matthaios, ed., Athens, 1964).

However, I did find on the Greek Orthodox Archdiocese web site "ACCESS" the following entry for the November 8 Feast of the Archangels.

THE SYNAXIS OF ARCHANGELS MICHAEL AND GABRIEL AND ALL THE OTHER HEAVENLY BODILESS POWERS. In the fourth century, Pope Sylvester and Patriarch Alexander established today when the nine orders of the angels are celebrated nine months after the world was created. This is thought to have happened in March. Angels, the first created beings, are not to be worshipped according to a canon of the fourth century Council of Laodicea. The following is the hierarchy of the nine orders. There is perfect unity as well as obedience between the orders. (1) Six-winged Seraphim (2) Many-eyed Cherubim (3) Godly thrones (4) Dominions (5) Virtues (6) Powers (7) Principalities (8) Archangels (9) Angels.

There are seven leaders of the heavenly powers: (1) Michael is the leader of the angelic army. His name means "Who is like God." Michael said the now familiar words to the remaining half of the angels in heaven when Lucifer and his followers had been cast out: "Let us give heed! Let us stand aright! Let us stand with fear!" Michael defends the Garden of Eden, told Abraham not to sacrifice Isaac, told Lot to flee Sodom, protected Jacob from Esau, took the soul of Moses from the devil, and he changed the course of a river in Asia Minor to protect a holy spring in a church. Michael is seen on the left side of the icon screen. (2) Gabriel which means "The power of God," is seen on the right side of the icon screen. He announces the mysteries of God. (3) Raphael means "God the Healer".(4) Uriel means "Light of God". He guards the underworld. (5) Salathiel means "One who prays to God". (6) Jequdiel means "One who glorifies God". (7) Barachiel means "The blessing of God". (8) Jeremiel means "God's exaltation". He awakens the thoughts of man that inspire him towards God. Every nation and every Christian each have their own guardian angels. They record every thought, word, and deed of man that will be revealed on Judgment Day.

This is apparently the source for the question. It is supplied by "The Orthodox Calendar Company" of Allison Park, Pennsylvania and appears to have been adapted from the book *The Prologue From Ochrid: Lives of the Saints and Homilies For Every Day of the Year, Part Four: October-November-December,* by Bishop Nikolai Velimirovic (Birmingham: Lazarica Press, 1986), I am sorry to say that I have not been able to find the three names Selaphiel, Jegudiel, and Barachiel in any of my reference sources. So, I cannot give you any more information about your question.

Dimensions of Angelology

From your own study, the book *All the Angels in the Bible* does not show these three names as being from the Bible. (By the way, the Orthodox Christian Church considers Esdras and Tobit to be part of the Old Testament, sometimes referred to as "Deuterocanonical" but never "Apocryphal.")

We might find some solution to this question if we take into consideration that great numbers of names of angels have been listed in many religious traditions outside Christianity, including Islam and many earlier religious traditions such as Zoroastrianism. It is also true of the medieval Jewish mystical tradition of the Kabbala, beginning around 1150. They developed theosophist theories and spoke of ten *"sefirot"*, which were variously understood as powers internal to God, or as ranked intermediaries between the infinite reality and limited created reality, or -like angels- instruments of divine activity.

All of these were closely related to the Gnostic heresies which sought to undercut the true Christian faith in earlier generations and which had been strenuously fought by the Church Fathers. That is why the Prologue correctly says that "the first created beings, are not to be worshipped according to a canon of the fourth century Council of Laodicea." Scholars hold that often names of angels were created by these groups by borrowing from other religions or making "angelic," various kinds of natural forces and attributes. In the genuinely false writings that presented themselves as scripture, but were not recognized or accepted by the Church -known by the names Apocrypha and Pseudepigrapha- there were increasing numbers of angel names.

Regarding these, *The Interpreter's Dictionary of the Bible,* (1st ed., vol. 1, p. 133) writes the following from the perspective of the history of religions (edited):

> *Specific angels.* (In the late Prophets, the Dead Sea Scrolls, the Talmud, the Apocrypha and the Pseudepigrapha) Angels tend to be designated by specific names—e.g., the archangels, Michael, Gabriel, Raphael, and Uriel: 'the angel who is over the lights [Hebrew word].' In Enoch 6:7; 8:3-4; 69:2, a catalogue is given of the names of the fallen angels. Most of these are, to be sure, unintelligible in the Ethiopic and Greek texts; but with the aid of a parallel list in a medieval Hebrew version, they may be recognized as personifications: of celestial phenomena—e.g., Baradiel, from (Hebrew word for) 'hail'; Ruhiel, 'wind'; Ziqiel, 'wind'; Kokbiel, 'star.' Similarly, in Enoch 82:13, the angels of the four seasons bear specific names—viz., Melkiel, Helemmelek, Melejal, and Narel—though the basis on which these are chosen remains obscure. Sometimes, too, the names are determined by the special functions of the angels who bear them—e.g., Raphael, the angel of healing, from (Hebrew word for) 'heal'; Raguel, 'who takes vengeance on the world of the luminaries' (Enoch 20:4), from (Hebrew word for) 'disquiet.' In the Talmud, names of angels are often evolved out of fanciful exegesis of a scriptural text-e.g., Lailah, the angel of conception (Nid. 16b), from Job 3:3.

The Dangers of Angel Speculation

I don't know the sources of the names "Selaphiel, Jegudiel, and Barachiel" as found in the *Prologue*, but not the Bible. They may well be patristic, but I could not find them in the 37 volumes of the Nicene and Post-Nicene Fathers. My guess is that they have been adapted from the literature discussed above. If any of our readers has specific information about them, please write to me. In the meantime, it seems to me that the Church wants us to focus on our life in Christ not on speculative angelology. It distracts us from the life of the Church and our life in Christ. St. Paul says, "Let no one disqualify you, insisting on self-abasement and worship of angels, taking his stand on visions, puffed up without reason by his sensuous mind, and not holding fast to the Head (Christ), from whom the whole body, nourished and knit together through its joints and ligaments, grows with a growth that is from God" (Colossians 2:18-19).

35. ORTHODOX TEACHINGS ABOUT ANGELS

Q. On November 8 the Orthodox Church celebrates the Synaxis of the Archangel Michael and the Other Bodiless Powers: The angels names listed are, Michael, Gabriel, Raphael, Uriel, Selaphiel, Jegudiel, and Barachiel. Some of these are in the Bible and some are not. Tell me about those who are not.   – *M.N. Barton, OH.*

A. In the first part of the response to this question, the question of angelic names was discussed. In this second part, the column presents a slightly edited chapter on angels from the 8th century Church Father, St. John of Damascus.

Orthodox Doctrine Regarding Angels

"God is Himself the Maker and Creator of the angels: for He brought them out of nothing into being and created them after His own image, an incorporeal race, a sort of spirit or immaterial fire: in

the words of the divine David, "He maketh His angels spirits, and His ministers a flame of fire"(103 [104]:4): and He has described their lightness and the ardour, and heat, and keenness and sharpness with which they hunger for God and serve Him.

"An angel, then, is an intelligent essence, in perpetual motion, with free-will, incorporeal, ministering to God, having obtained by grace an immortal nature: and the Creator alone knows the form and limitation of its essence. But all that we can understand is, that it is incorporeal and immaterial. For all that is compared with God Who alone is incomparable, we find to be dense and material. For in reality only the Deity is immaterial and incorporeal.

"The angel's nature then . . . is changeable in will, or variable. For all that is created is changeable, and only that which is un-created is unchangeable. Also all that is rational is endowed with free-will. . . and as it is created, it is changeable, having power either to abide or progress in goodness, or to turn towards evil. Angelic nature is not susceptible of repentance because it is incorporeal. For it is owing to the weakness of his body that man comes to have repentance.

"It is immortal, not by nature but by grace. For all that has had beginning comes also to its natural end. But God alone is eternal, or rather, He is above the Eternal: for He, the Creator of times, is not under the dominion of time, but above time.

"They are secondary intelligent lights derived from that first light which is without beginning, for they have the power of illumination; they have no need of tongue or hearing, but without uttering words they communicate to each other their own thoughts and counsels. Through the Word therefore, all the angels were created, and through the sanctification by the Holy Spirit were they brought to perfection, sharing each in proportion to his worth and rank in brightness and grace.

"They are circumscribed: for when they are in the Heaven they are not on the earth: and when they are sent by God down to the earth they do not remain in the Heavens. They are not hemmed in by walls

and doors, and bars and seals, for they are quite unlimited.

"It is not as they really are that they reveal themselves to worthy persons to whom God wishes them to appear, but in a changed form which the beholders are capable of seeing.

"*Further, apart from their essence they receive the sanctification from the Spirit:* through the divine grace they prophesy: they have no need of marriage for they are immortal. Seeing that they are minds they are in mental places, and are not circumscribed after the fashion of a body. For they have not a bodily form by nature, nor are they tended in three dimensions. But to whatever post they may be assigned, there they are present after the manner of a mind and energise, and cannot be present and energise in various places at the same time.

"*Whether they are equals in essence or differ from one another we know not.* God, their Creator, Who knows all things, alone knows. But they differ from each other in brightness and position . . .
and they impart brightness to one another, because they excel one another in rank and nature. And clearly the higher share their brightness and knowledge with the lower.

"*They are mighty and prompt to fulfill the will of God*, and their nature is endowed with such swiftness that wherever the Divine glance bids them there they are immediately found. They are the guardians of the divisions of the earth: they are set over nations and regions, allotted to them by their Creator: they govern all our affairs and bring us assistance. And the reason surely is because they are set over us by the divine will and command and are ever in the vicinity of God.

"*With difficulty they are moved to evil*, yet they are not by nature absolutely immovable from goodness: but now they have become altogether immovable, not by nature but by grace and by their nearness to the Only Good.

"*They behold God according to their capacity*, and this is their food. They are above us for they are incorporeal, and are free of all bodily passion, yet are not passionless: for the Deity alone is passion-less.

"They take different forms at the bidding of their Master, God, and thus reveal themselves to men and unveil the divine mysteries to them. They have Heaven for their dwelling-place, and have one duty, to sing God's praise and carry out His divine will.

"Moreover, as that most holy, and sacred, and gifted theologian, Dionysius the Areopagite (500 A.D.) (*The Heavenly Hierarchy,* ch. 6), says, All theology, that is to say, the Holy Scripture, has nine different names for the heavenly essences. These essences St. Dionysios, that divine master in sacred things, divides into three groups, each containing three. The first group, he says, consists of those who are in God's presence and are said to be directly and immediately one with Him, that is, the Seraphim with their six wings, the many-eyed Cherubim and those that sit in the holiest thrones. The second group is that of the Dominions, and the Powers, and the Authorities; and the third, and last, is that of the Rulers and Archangels and Angels.

"Some Church Fathers, like Gregory the Theologian (329-389), say that these were before the creation of other things. He thinks that the angelic and heavenly powers were first and that thought was their function. Others, again, hold that they were created after the first heaven was made. But all are agreed that it was before the creation of humanity. For myself, I am in harmony with the Theologian. For it was fitting that the mental essence should be the first created, and then that which can be perceived, and finally humanity itself, in whose being both parts are united.

"But those who say that the angels are creators of any kind of essence whatever are the mouth of their father, the devil. For since they are created things they are not creators. But He Who creates and provides for and maintains all things is God, Who alone is uncreated and is praised and glorified in the Father, the Son, and the Holy Spirit. (St. John of Damascus, *Exposition of the Orthodox Faith,* Book II, Chapter III.)

36. SATAN, THE DEVIL AND DEMONS

Q. When you consider the number of demons loose in the world, there must have been a LOT of angels who sided with Lucifer when he rebelled against God. What do you suppose would make them do that? Couldn't they see the risk they were taking? Finally, were all of today's demons former inhabitants of Heaven, or do you think Satan has the power to create new ones?   – *J. K. Phoenix, AZ.*

A. This question directs our attention to the other side of the question on angels discussed in the last two columns. In this column, a brief answer will be offered to your questions, and a passage about the Devil and demons from St. John of Damascus will be added.

Getting Terms Straight: Satan, the Devil and Demons
According to the New Testament, Satan (described by other names, such as "the Devil," "the Evil One," "the Accuser," "the Tempter," "the Divider," [Greek, "*o diabolos*"]), is aided in his work against God and against God's people, by demons (sometimes also called devils, evil spirits, principalities, authorities, powers of evil).

For practical purposes, there is no real distinction in the New Testament between the use of the word Satan and the Devil ("*diabolos*"). However, there is a distinction between Satan (the Devil) and his angels, otherwise referred to as demons. Thus, Jesus speaks of "the eternal fire prepared for the devil and his angels" (Matthew 25:41).

In broad outline, the Church's teaching is that at the beginning of creation Satan was created as a good angel. But he rebelled against God, was expelled from the presence of God, taking with him "innumerable" angels who subsequently do his bidding. Thus, there is no way to know the exact number of demons serving Satan, just as there is no way of knowing the number of angels serving God, according to New Testament teaching.

Freedom of Choice and the Habitual Condition of Good or Evil

The angelic and demonic exercise of choice regarding good and evil has led to a habitual commitment to one or the other in particular beings.

According to Orthodox teaching, following the fall of Satan, the remaining angels became firm in their goodness and relationship with God, so that they no longer were practically capable of falling. The same is true of Satan and his demons. They are beyond repenting; theirs is the sin against the Holy Spirit, which is precisely full and total opposition to God's saving grace (Mark 3:28-29).

You question whether Satan and his devils couldn't see the consequences of their evil choice in rebelling against God. As you state it, you imply that if they did see the consequences of their evil choice, they would not have acted as they did. Again, I must speculate. Let us look at ourselves. We human beings do the same thing. We often reflect on the consequences of our acts, and even forsee that undesirable results can be predicted in doing morally and spiritually wrong things. Yet, we do them anyway. Why? Because we also see consequences which we find desirable. For example, before starting the use of illicit mind-destroying drugs, many people opt for the "excitement," the promise of the pleasure of a "high" experience. They know the possible consequence of addiction, but discount it. For Satan, it was pride, according to the Church Fathers. This must have taken over and minimized concern with negative consequences of rebellion against God. Is it any different with us?

Can Satan Create New Demons?

What about your question regarding the possibility of Satan creating new demons? This is speculative. I have not read anything about this issue elsewhere. So I must reflect on it myself. Since Satan is not God, it would seem to me that he is not capable of creating new demonic spiritual beings out of nothing. Since in the spiritual world there is no sexual reproduction (Luke 35:36), and we know nothing of "spiritual reproduction," it would seem that Satan could not bring new demons to birth. Apparently, Satan will have to be content with his "innumerable" legions of demons! I am not comfortable with this speculation about angels and devils. It seems to feed on an inordinate curiosity with little or no practical application.

However, there is at least one practical aspect to your question, if we look at it in our own human perspective. This is what I mean. If we human beings are capable of becoming "children of God" (John 1:12), we are also capable of becoming "children of the evil one" (St. Ignatius, *To the Trallians*, Chapter xi). If angels are those who do God's will; and demons do Satan's will, then those of us who commit ourselves to doing evil (Satan's will), function similarly to Satan's demons.

Thus, there is a potential for an almost limitless increase of "Satan's demons," if by that phrase, we mean human beings who willfully do evil. So the New Testament teaches us: "By this it may be seen who are the children of God, and who are the children of the devil: whoever does not do right is not of God, nor he who does not love his brother" (1 John 3:10). We can still exercise our freedom of choice. St. Paul put it this way to us: "now you are light in the Lord; walk as children of light (for the fruit of light is found in all that is good and right and true), and try to learn what is pleasing to the Lord. Take no part in the unfruitful works of darkness" (Ephesians 5:8-11).

St. John of Damascus on "The Devil and Demons"

The 8th century Church Father who summarized the central teachings of the Orthodox Church for his time, St. John of Damascus, wrote both about angels and demonic powers. Here is part of what he wrote, expressing Orthodox teaching.

> He who from among these angelic powers was set over the earthly realm, and into whose hands God committed the guardianship of the earth, was not made wicked in nature

but was good, and made for good ends, and received from his Creator no trace whatever of evil in himself. But he did not sustain the brightness and the honor which the Creator had bestowed on him, and of his free choice was changed from what was in harmony to what was at variance with his nature, and became roused against God Who created him, and determined to rise in rebellion against Him: and he was the first to depart from good and become evil. For evil is nothing else than absence of goodness, just as darkness also is absence of light. For goodness is the light of the mind, and, similarly, evil is the darkness of the mind. Light, therefore, being the work of the Creator and being made good (for God saw all that He made, and behold they were exceeding good) produced darkness at His free-will. But along with him an innumerable host of angels subject to him were torn away and followed him and shared in his fall. Wherefore, being of the same nature as the angels, they became wicked, turning away at their own free choice from good to evil.

Hence they have no power or strength against any one except what God in His dispensation hath conceded to them, as for instance, against Job and those swine that are mentioned in the Gospels. But when God has made the concession they do prevail, and are changed and transformed into any form whatever in which they wish to appear.

Of the future both the angels of God and the demons are alike ignorant: yet they make predictions. God reveals the future to the angels and commands them to prophesy, and so what they say comes to pass. But the demons also make predictions, sometimes because they see what is happening at a distance, and sometimes merely making guesses: hence much that they say is false and they should not be believed, even although they do often, in the way we have said, tell what is true. Besides they know the Scriptures.

All wickedness, then, and all impure passions are the work of their mind. But while the liberty to attack man has been granted to them, they have not the strength to over master any one: for we have it in our power to receive or not to receive the attack. Wherefore there has been prepared for the devil and his demons, and those who follow him, fire unquenchable and everlasting punishment.

Note, further, that what in the case of man is death is a fall in the case of angels. For after the fall there is no possibility of repentance for them, just as after death there is for men no repentance." (*Exposition of the Orthodox Faith,* Book II, Chapter iv).

Human Beings

37. WHY WERE HUMAN BEINGS CREATED?

Q. I have asked many persons this question, but I have as yet not received a satisfactory answer. Maybe there is no answer. The question is, "Why was humanity created by God?" I know the "how" and the "circumstances," but not the "why."   – *D.A.C., Augusta, GA.*

A. One way of answering your question would be to say simply, we have no direct revelation on the subject in the Bible, and so we can't answer your question, since "No one has ever seen God; the only Son, who is in the bosom of the Father, he has made him known" (John 1:18), and to my knowledge, Jesus has not revealed the answer to this question.

But this is an excellent example of the place of Holy Tradition in the life of the Church, which is guided by the Holy Spirit in the understanding of the great truths about God, and described in the New Testament as "the church of the living God, the pillar and bulwark of the truth" (1 Timothy 3:15). Some of these questions have been addressed by the Spirit-filled Fathers of the Church, for "as it is written . . . no one comprehends the thoughts of God except the Spirit of God" (1 Corinthians 2:9, 11).

The Background

The Bible does tell us about the creation of the world, that is, of everything existing, visible and invisible, which is not God. God created everything "in the beginning" (Genesis 1:1). This teaching, in spite of many misunderstandings, does not preclude the scientific study of the material world and the inferences that can be made about it from observed data. There are numerous scientific theories that speak about the creation of the world. In nearly all of them, there is an assumption of some elementary energy forms which eventually formed the world as we know it. Science, of course, can neither prove the existence of God nor the non-existence of God. We come to our knowledge of God through the experience of faith. So in Hebrews 11:3 we read this profoundly religio-scientific affirmation: "By faith we understand that the world was created by the word of God, so that what is seen was made out of things which do not appear." In current scientific understanding, these things "which do not appear" are the protons, neutrons and electrons out of which everything material is made.

In addition, God is the creator of the non-material, spiritual angelic world, which has an existence different from the material world.

But the Church's theology pushes this truth even further. The Church teaches that even before such basic energy sources of matter, and before there were any other spiritual beings, there was nothing. Out of that nothingness, God brought into being the forces from which come atoms, elements, chemical compounds and everything made from them, mineral, plant and animal, as well as the spiritual realities of non-material creation about which we know almost nothing. St. Irenaeus (130-200 A.D.) expressed this teaching in his book *Against Heresies* in this way:

> While men, indeed, cannot make anything out of nothing, but only out of matter already existing, yet God is in this point pre-eminently superior to men, that He Himself called into being the substance of His creation, when previously it had no existence" (Bk. 2, ch. 10).

This creation was an act of the Holy Trinity: God the Father created the world through the Son and in the Holy Spirit.

Why, Indeed?

Your question was also asked by the God-inspired Fathers of the Church. Why, indeed, did God bring into existence the creation and with it humanity?

The potential answers to this question are that God created the world out of capriciousness, out of need for Himself, or because it was not willed by Him, but occurred as an unwilled outflow of His divinity. In the first case, it would mean that God acts without reason and in an arbitrary, erratic and fickle way. Nothing we know of God through divine revelation as it appears to us in the Bible, or which is consistent with our understanding in Holy Tradition about God allows us to believe that the creation came into existence as some kind of cosmic divine joke. We must eliminate that potential answer to this question.

Perhaps God might have willed the existence of the creation because there was some need that He had in Himself for the creation to exist. Was there something in the "divine psychology" that pressed God to decide to bring into being something which did not exist, to satisfy some requirement of His being? Some people answer "yes" to that question, saying "God created the world so that He could have something and someone to love." But that is wrong, because, as a Trinity of Divine Persons relating in eternal love, God did not need the creation to love for His own sake. There is nothing, then, "necessary" which forced God to will the creation into existence.

The third response takes the creation out of the willed decision of God, and sees it as an "outflowing" from God's divine nature, an emanation from God, and descending in being from the divine to the material. This would mean that the creation was a part of God Himself, a form of pantheism. This teaching is the exact opposite from the belief that God brought into being everything other than Himself. So, it too must be eliminated as an answer.

The Answer of the Church Fathers

The Church Fathers understood this dilemma, and sought to find an answer to the question "why" God created the world, and in particular, why He created humanity.

The answer given by the Fathers is that God freely chose out of the fullness of His goodness to share the goodness of existence with beings other than Himself. Being in communion with God, all creation would thus enjoy a relationship with the Ultimate Reality, Who is God.

St. Irenaeus, once again shows us the way:

> Nor was God influenced by any one, but of His own free will created all things, since He is the only God, the only Lord, the only Creator, the only Father, alone containing all things, and Himself commanding all thing into existence (*Against Heresies,* Bk. 2, ch. 1).

God acted freely, in an unforced way, motivated by His loving desire to share the goodness of existence with a new, created reality. Origen (185-254), the first Christian theologian, said "When God in the beginning created those beings which He desired to create, that is, rational natures, He had no other reason for creating them than on account of Himself, that is, His own goodness" (*On First Principles*, Bk. 2, ch. 9). St. Irenaeus put it this way: "In the beginning, therefore, did God form Adam, not as if He stood in need of man, but that He might have some one upon whom to confer His benefits" (*Against Heresies* Bk. 4, ch. 14).

St. John of Damascus (675-749) summed up the Church's teaching in his *Exposition of the Orthodox Faith* this way:

> God, Who is good and more than good, did not find satisfaction in self-contemplation, but in His exceeding goodness wished certain things to come into existence which would enjoy His benefits and share in His goodness" (Bk. 2, ch. 2).

"Why?" Because God is good and wills to share His goodness with the creation in general, and with human beings in particular.

38. HUMANITY: DIFFERING VIEWS

Q. What is the Orthodox view of...man? How do the Orthodox and Roman Catholics differ on it?   – A.C.D. Clinton, MA.

A. Today's question deals with the Orthodox teaching about what it means to be a human being.

The Human Mystery

To understand our humanity is an impossible task. Just as seeking to understand God and Jesus Christ and the Holy Spirit is shrouded in unfathomable mystery, so is human existence a mystery of the most profound sort. Many seek to explain human existence. Some by means of philosophy, some by means of more or less exact sciences, some only to express the human condition by the arts. There is a sense in which the Church includes all of these and more, as it tells its story of the human situation and the nature of human existence. Here we can only outline the Orthodox teaching regarding what being human means.

"In the Image and Likeness"

The beginning of the Church's understanding of human existence is found in the first book of the Bible, Genesis, where we read: "Then God said, 'Let us make man in our image, after our likeness; and let them have dominion...over all the earth. So God created man in his own image, in the image of God he created him; male and female he created them'" (Genesis 1:26-27).

The Fathers of the Church point out that the words "image" and "likeness" as they appear in Greek (Septuagint) translation of the

Old Testament imply two different things. The "image" points to all of the characteristics that differentiate human beings from the animals. These are our reasoning ability, our free choice, our perception of right and wrong, our creativity, etc. On the other hand, the "likeness" points to the potential we have to realize those abilities to their fullest. The Orthodox Church, thus, teaches that, as created, human beings are not perfect, but capable of being perfected and realizing a potential unique to human beings, that is, to be God-like.

Special: "A Microcosm"

There is another Genesis passage which informs the Orthodox teaching about human existence. We read "...then the Lord God formed man of dust from the ground, and breathed into his nostrils the breath of life, and man became a living being" (Genesis 2:7). This indicates two things. On the one hand, we have been created like all else in this world. On the other, we have been created differently from all other creatures that were created only by the word of God. In humanity, there is the divine "breath of life." This means that only human beings share in both the spiritual world and the material world. The Church Fathers sometimes call humanity a *"microcosm"* (a little universe), joining within the human being the totality of all things, material and spiritual.

For Good or For Evil

Consequently, humanity can lead all of creation toward its fulfillment. Or, it can do the opposite, by leading it to its destruction. By means of faithful communion with God, accomplishing His purposes in life and realizing the potential of God's likeness in our existence, we fulfill our own nature and purpose, and we realize as well the purposes of God for His whole creation. This is symbolized in the Genesis story of the naming of the animals. "So out of the ground the Lord God formed every beast of the field and every bird of the air, and brought them to the man to see what he would call them; and whatever the man called every living creature, that was its name" (Genesis 2:19). The "dominion" which humanity was given over creation was not for exploitation, but for responsible use, and to lead the creation to its fulfillment through human communion with God and His purposes.

The Condition of Sin

But freedom to choose means humanity can choose to rebel against God, to reject communion with Him and obedience to His will. That is the meaning of the story of the Garden of Eden. In fact, humanity in many ways rejects God, becomes the source of rebellion against God and the image and likeness of God in us. Our condition of sinfulness distorts our humanity, robs us of the potential to become God-like, causes us to, in fact, be "less than truly human." The story of Noah and the great flood highlights that truth about our existence. "The Lord saw that the wickedness of man was great in the earth and that every imagination of the thoughts of his heart was only evil continually" (Genesis 6:5). And elsewhere in the same book, it is affirmed that "the imagination of man's heart is evil from his youth" (Genesis 8:21) as a description of tendencies within each of us.

Ways of Limiting Evil: Law and Wisdom

The evil of human ways results from human separation from God and His will. In the Old Testament, two main means were provided by God to limit and restrain evil in human existence. The first consisted of the commandments and the laws of God given to guide human behavior. Thus, we have the Ten Commandments. For instance, "You shall do no murder" (Exodus 20:13). For the Fathers of the Church this is a law that is built into human existence, a natural commandment to be found in every society. Further, the laws have sanctions, that is, punishments. Thus, we read "Whoever sheds the blood of man, by man shall his blood be shed; for God made man in his own image" (Genesis 9:6).

The second way of leading humankind away from sin is the teaching of "wisdom." The Bible teaches that in spite of human sinfulness which has darkened our minds, enfeebled our wills, distorted our perception of right and wrong, weakened our resolve, human beings are not totally depraved and incapable of doing some good. We are still capable of struggling against evil and for good. Humanity still remains a "little less than God," (Psalm 8:4-5) compared to the rest of creation.

Knowledge of the will of God is important and leads to a measure of happiness for humanity: "For the commandment is a lamp and the teaching a light, and the reproofs of discipline are the way of life" (Proverbs 6:23). And "Happy is the man who finds wisdom, and the man who gets understanding, for the gain from it is better than gain from silver and its profit better than gold" (Proverbs 3:13-14). So there could be righteous persons, even in such a situation. "A righteous man turns away from evil" (Proverbs 12:26). The Church Fathers identify such persons as Old Testament Saints, such as Moses and Isaiah the Prophet. Some even identify such righteous persons among the non-Jews. But these are exceptions. Thus the empirical description of human existence is the "less than fully human existence" of immersion in sin.

A Different View

For the Orthodox Church, this is the human predicament. In the traditional Roman Catholic teaching, the human condition is seen, rather, as basically "natural." For Roman Catholicism sin has caused us to lose "Supernatural Grace." This is why the Roman Catholic Church has a very strong dependence upon natural law in its teaching, and gives it much more importance than do the Orthodox. In this view, without divine Grace, we are simply what we were originally created. Also, strongly present in Roman Catholic teaching is the idea of guilt, closely connected with sin, in contrast to the primary Orthodox understanding of sin as our broken relationship with God.

While post-Vatican II teaching has modified this teaching, it still remains a different view of human existence.

39. BODY AND SOUL

Q. I am a clinical psychologist and a professor at the University of Sao Paulo, Brazil. I am very interested to read about the way the Greek Church thinks about the relationship between body and soul. This subject is very important in clinical psychology, especially when patients are suffering from physical diseases. Would you give me information about this subject? — *T. V., Sao Paulo, Brazil.*

A. The application of the Church's views to clinical psychology is something for specialists in the field to do. Here we can only describe and illustrate the Church's teachings.

Different Perspectives

There are different attitudes that exist on the question of the relationship of body and soul. *Materialists* hold that there is no soul because everything that really exists is matter and nothing else. Then, there are the *Intellectualists* or *Spiritualists* for whom spirit and soul are the ultimate reality. They see matter as a sort of degenerated form of true reality (Plato and Neoplatonism).

Most thinkers acknowledge the existence of both matter and spirit (soul), but rank them differently. So some give priority to matter and the body, and see the soul as arising out of it as an "epiphenomenon." Many in the field of psychology hold to this view: the physical dimension produces and conditions the soul dimension. Others acknowledge that we have a physical side, but how we think and the state of our soul is what determines our physical condition. So, the religious group known as *Christian Science* holds that all illness, including physical illness, is the result of wrong thinking.

The Orthodox Christian Approach

The Church's view starts with the Creation Story (Genesis 1 and 2) that: God created the human body first, then gave it "the breath of life," but also, God created humanity "in His image and likeness". Since both body and soul are God's creations, both are good and necessary. On the level of ordinary existence a human being is a composite of both body and soul. Both are essential to human existence.

But, there is more. In the teaching of many of the Church Fathers, a truly complete human being -what a human being "ought to be" is further defined as composed of body, soul *and the Holy Spirit,* where all elements work together to reflect our creation in God's image and likeness.

However, when we look at our selves, individually and in community, we confirm that we are not what God created us to be. Our human condition, because of sin, shows that our relationship with God is broken; our physical existence is drawn to sinful passions, and our soul seeks for what corrupts us, and not what fulfills our humanity.

That is why to be fully human, we need to share in the saving and redemptive work of Jesus Christ, to participate in the sacramental life, to live a life of repentance that re-orients the inner world of our souls and bodies, so that body and soul are in harmony with life in the Holy Spirit.

The wisdom of the Church gives priority to the spiritual aspect of our life, knowing however, that it is often overtaken and subdued by physical cravings. But the physical side of the human being is essential so it can never be abandoned or minimized. We are "psychosomatic wholes" (soul-bodies) who can only have a wholesome relationship of soul and body, when we are also in communion with the living God.

The soul should lead the body, and the body ought to be the instrument of the soul. And both should be enlightened, guided, directed and illuminated by the Holy Spirit.

Body / Soul in the Church's Life

Almost every aspect of the life of the Church expresses this perspective. Here are two examples.

Doctrine: The Church teaches that Jesus Christ is both fully God and fully human in one Person. He is "Theanthropos," the only fully "divine-human person." This means that the humanity of Jesus Christ consists of both His body and His soul in their fullness. In fact, because of His Ascension to Heaven, He will always be *Theanthropos*.

Another doctrine that emphasizes the close relationship between body and soul is the resurrection of the body at the Last Judgment. We, too, will forever be not just "eternal souls" but we will be souls together with our "spiritualized bodies" into eternity. Human beings are body and soul together forever.

Sacramental Life: Every aspect of our Church's worship and sacramental life includes both bodily and spiritual dimensions. Think how candles, architecture, cloth, metal, wood, glass, flowers, smells (incense), colors, sounds (bells), hymns, and art are physical instruments for the soul in the worship of the Church. Think of icons, which are "windows on heaven" and "spiritual books" for the faithful. Think of water which washes us of sin and into which we are buried with Christ and out of which we are resurrected with Christ to a "new creation" ("*Kaine Ktisis*") Think of bread and wine which become the Body and Blood of Christ. Think of consecrated oil with which we are anointed "with the gift of the seal of the Holy Spirit" and with which we receive the unction of healing. For the Orthodox Church, the material and the spiritual are inextricable.

Church Fathers on Body and Soul

St. Irenaeus (+ 202 A.D.), said in his book *Against Heresies,* "The whole person, soul and body, receives the Spirit of the Father. This is the perfect human being."

St. Gregory of Nyssa (+394) said: "just as the spirit takes its proper perfection from its likeness to the beauty of the universal

Model, so the body, ruled by the spirit, finds its proper embellishment in the beauty of the spirit" (*The Creation of Man,* 12).

St. Cyril of Jerusalem (+386) said, "It is not the body that sins, but the soul. The body is only an instrument; it is like the outward clothing of the soul. It becomes impure if it is used for fornication, but it becomes the temple of the Holy Spirit if it is united to his sanctity" (*Catecheses,* 4)

St. John Chrysostom (+407) said, "When the body is ill, the soul is badly affected. In the great majority of cases, in fact, our spiritual capacities behave according to our physical condition; illness lays us low and makes us different, almost unrecognizable from when we are well. . . . It is the same with the body. It can do a great deal of harm to the soul." The body should be "a ready instrument of the soul." (*On Hebrews,* 29).

The message? The human person is body and soul together, mutually influencing dimensions of a single being, achieving its potential through growth in relationship to God.

40. ANCESTORAL SIN

Q. How can "Original" or "Ancestral" sin be transmitted to or inherited by one born of baptized Christian parents, since by their own individual Baptisms they were each "washed clean" from original sin and thus became a "new creation in Christ?" *–K. L., Chicago, IL.*

A. There are several implied questions here. Let's begin by looking at the two background ideas in this question: "Ancestral" or "Original Sin;" and, the effects of Baptism. A similar question was dealt with early in the Church's history.

The Human Condition
In Christian teaching, one of the most important doctrines deals with the human condition. By this we mean who we are and what our

circumstance is in relationship with God, with ourselves, with others and with the rest of creation. What does being human mean?

The story that defines the human condition is the story of Adam and Eve. It describes and gives form in a dramatic way to the Christian teaching about humankind, called in Theology, "Christian Anthropology."

In brief "Adam" (which means "human being" in Hebrew) was created by God in His own "image and likeness" (Genesis 3). Humanity is thus seen as sharing in divine-like characteristics that distinguish human beings from the rest of the creation, both spiritual and animal. Both spiritually (soul, spirit, mind, heart) and physically (body), humanity was created good with the potential to achieve the fullness of life. The story of the "forbidden fruit" was a test of obedience of the first created human beings. Obediently communing with God's will would have produced true and full life. Disobedience would produce spiritual and, ultimately, physical death.

Our Human Condition - Ancestral Sin

Adam and Eve's disobedience and expulsion from Paradise strikingly describes the consequences of the breaking of humanity's relationship with God. The self-willed choice to disobey is a description of our present inner world. It consists of our real loss of the potential to realize God-likeness. Together with this is the real distortion and darkening of our intelligence, our creativity, our sense of God, our ability to properly discern good and evil -and even more so, our inability to consistently do what is good and to avoid what is evil. Though all these characteristics of our creation in God's image remain, they are crippled in their expression and function.

The name we give to this distorted and darkened condition is *Ancestral Sin* (in Greek, *"Propatorikon Amartema"*). In this condition of separation from God, we retain, for example, intelligence -but we cannot exercise it fully. Also, we have the ability to choose -but our whole being, body and spirit, is not fully focused on the good and we frequently choose wrongly. Consequently, our bodies and our spirits are not fully synchronized with God and we are incomplete.

As a result, we are in a condition of broken relationship with ourselves, with our environment, and with God. The cause of this fallen and distorted condition is our broken relationship with God. Consequently, what we see in our empirical existence is not our true nature, that is, being fully "the image and likeness of God." It is in fact, less than natural, a distortion of our nature. The Church Fathers call this not "nature" (*"physis"*), but "deficient nature" (*"para physin."*).

Baptism

So, in his *Spiritual Works*, Diadochos, Bishop of Photike (5th century) says, "Ever since the sin of Adam, not only has the soul been contaminated, the body also tends gradually towards corruption."

How were we to be freed from this condition? We could not do it ourselves: neither laws, nor education, nor science, nor arts, nor philosophy, nor religions could change our condition. Only God's love for us, in sending Jesus Christ for our salvation could change that. St. Paul described the situation this way in his letter to the Romans:

> Therefore as sin came into the world through one man (Adam) and death through sin, and so death spread to all men because all men sinned. . . . death reigned from Adam to Moses, even over those whose sins were not like the transgression of Adam. . . . If, because of one man's trespass, death reigned through that one man, much more will those who receive the abundance of grace and the free gift of righteousness reign in life through the one man Jesus Christ. . . . For as by one man's disobedience many were made sinners, so by one man's obedience many will be made righteous. So that, as sin reigned in death, grace also might reign through righteousness to eternal life through Jesus Christ our Lord" (Romans 5:12,14,17,19,21).

In that same Letter, St. Paul tells us that we share in the death and resurrection of Jesus Christ through our Baptism. And Simeon the New Theologian (949-1022), summarized that message succinctly: "if God has himself been made a human being and has deigned to be called the brother of the human race, we ought to be born again, in water by the grace of the Holy Spirit *(Theological and Ethical Treatises)*, Through our Baptism, another early writer, Theodore of Mopsuestia (350-428) says "the curse which was on us on account of sin has been broken by Him who 'became a curse for us' (Galatians 3:13). . . . For as, in that we are of earth, we all die in Adam, so, in that we are reborn from above of water and spirit (Baptism), we are all brought to life in Christ (see John 3:3,5; 1 Corinthians 15:22). *(On the Incarnation)*.

The Question

So the question appears logical. If baptized Christians are freed from the condition of Ancestral Sin, shouldn't their children also be freed from it? Something similar was addressed by the Council of Neocaesaria (a city in Pontos of Asia Minor) in 315 A.D. In its 6th canon, we read, "Concerning a woman with child, it is determined that she ought to be baptized whensoever she will; for in this the woman communicates nothing to the child, since the bringing forward to profession is evidently the individual privilege of every single person." The commentary in the *Pedalion* says that "inasmuch as the embryo in the womb is part of the pregnant woman . . . some took it that a woman ought not to be baptized when pregnant, but only after she gave birth. . . . In opposition to those who say this, the present canon decrees that a pregnant woman who is a catechumen may be baptized whenever she wishes, since she does not impart the illumination and baptism to the embryo in her womb, but on the contrary, she alone is baptized."

Consequently, the Church teaches us that the consequences of saving Baptism are not automatically passed on to the children of

Christians. They must receive Baptism either by personal choice or through the agency of a Sponsor.

41. OUR FREE CHOICE AND GOD

Q. I have a question concerning the dilemma of the omniscience of God and humankind's free will. If I were hungry and there were three blueberry muffins on a table (and I liked blueberries), would God know which muffin I would choose, whether I would eat one, two or three of them, or abstain from eating any of them? Would I really have a choice in the matter, and at the same time, would God know what I would do, ahead of time?   *–J.G.T. Somerville, MA.*

A. Let's first clarify your question. "Omniscience" is a theological term from the Latin that means "All-knowing." In Greek, the word is "*Pantognosia*." It means that God knows everything: past-present-future. Your example of the blueberry muffins raises a theological dilemma. If God knows everything that we will do, are we then free to do it? As you say, is there "real choice in the matter"? In short can we reconcile God's "Omniscience" with human freedom (self-determination)?

God's *Pantognosia*

Both the Bible and the Holy Tradition of the Church teach us of the omniscience of God. For example, in the Old Testament book of Job we read "He looks to the ends of the earth, and sees everything under the heavens" (Job 28:24). In the Psalms we are told "he knows the secrets of the heart" (Psalm 44:21) and in Proverbs we read "The eyes of the Lord are in every place, keeping watch on the evil and the good" (Proverbs 15:3). In the New Testament we read "Before (God) no creature is hidden, but all are open and laid bare to the eyes of him with whom we have to do" (Hebrews 4:13).

One of the earliest Church writers, Clement of Alexandria (150-215 A.D.) expressed the Church's clear teaching about God's knowledge: "God knows all things-not only those which exist, but those also which shall be-and how each thing shall be. And foreseeing the particular movements, 'He surveys all things, and hears all things,' seeing the soul naked within." (Stromata, 6,17).

So, it is clear that the Church consistently teaches that God knows all things, past, present and future.

Human Freedom / Self-Determination

The Bible presupposes that human beings, by their very creation, are free, in the sense that they are able to determine their choices, having true self-determination. Thus, God speaks to the Hebrew people, "I call heaven and earth to witness against you this day, that I have set before you life and death, blessing and curse; therefore choose life" (Deuteronomy 30:19). And Jesus also shows we have a choice when He says to us "If any man would come after me, let him deny himself and take up his cross daily and follow me" (Luke 9:23).

The Church teaches the same. Another very early Church writer, Origen (185-254) put it briefly this way: "the Creator granted to the minds that He made the power of free and voluntary movement, so that the good which was in them might become their own through being preserved by their own free-will" (*On First Principles,* 9, 2) St. Gregory of Nyssa, in talking about sin and evil in our lives, teaches that we are responsible for it, not God.

> Evil comes in some way or another from within. It is the product of free choice, whenever the soul withdraws in any way from the good . . . Since the distinctive character of free-will is freely to choose what pleases it, God is not the cause of your present evil state. He provided you with a free and independent nature; it is your folly that has chosen the worse instead of the better (*Catechetical Oration* 5).

Freedom in Choosing Blueberry Muffins

Now these two things may seem to be contradictory. If we are free, it would seem that knowing in advance what we will do (choosing none, one, two or three muffins) couldn't take place.

But let us suppose that truly, God does know everything about us. God is like a person at the top of a mountain who is watching a car speed downward around the winding mountain road. The driver can only see twenty or thirty feet in front of the car. But the person at the top of the mountain can see that the road has been washed out fifty feet ahead, around the next turn of the mountain road. He "knows" that the car will fly off the road and crash. He "knows," but his knowledge does not cause the crash. The driver was free not to drive down the road, or to drive down the road more cautiously, or to obtain a report of road conditions before he began his descent.

In a more complicated way, God would know how many, if any, muffins the hungry person would choose. But knowing that would not determine the choice. The muffin-eater would determine what he did, not God.

Life Is More Than Muffins

The real issue connected with this question is our freedom to choose for good and against evil. God's fore-knowledge does not determine the moral choices we will make. He teaches us to choose good and not evil. If we seek His help, we will more likely choose the good. If we separate ourselves from God, it will be more likely that we will choose evil. But, with our choices we can either place ourselves closer to God, or further away from God. It is up to us. St. John of Damascus (675-749) resolves the dilemma for us like this:

> We ought to understand that while God knows all things beforehand, yet He does not predetermine all things. For He knows beforehand those things that are in our power, but He does not predetermine them . . . (I)t is not His will

that there should be wickedness nor does he choose to compel virtue . . . (We) have it in our power either to abide in virtue and follow God, Who calls us into ways of virtue, or to stray from the paths of virtue.

42. THE CHRISTIAN LIFE AND SIN

Q. Is the Christian life in sin? Sin, as defined by the Orthodox Church and by many other Churches is not clearly understood by many Christians as "separation from God." How can the fullness of life be achieved under these circumstances? How is our relationship with God affected by this?   *–J.T.H. Hudson, FL.*

A. "Is the Christian life in sin?" sounds like a strange question. Yet, it is not. It is a way of asking what you as a Christian are to think and do about the reality of not living up to the fullest expectations of your Christian identity.

All of us have experienced moments when we reflect on our attitudes and actions, and find them falling short of what they ought to be. Often we know we are guilty of doing wrong things. Sometimes we feel that burden deeply, and over a long period of time.

The word that has been used by the Church from the earliest of times to describe this "falling short of what ought to be" in the Christian life, is "sin." We have to understand what sin is, before we can answer the question "Is the Christian life in sin?"

The Modern Rejection of Sin

We live in a time and an age that almost completely avoids the idea of sin. The media, psychology, and recently, genetics, imply that sin is an old fashioned idea that doesn't apply to the "enlightened" contemporary person. There are three reasons for this development. First, sin implies that there is something wrong about our attitudes and behavior. Many people try to escape being considered "bad," "morally wrong," or identified as "sinners," by denying that "sin" exists. As it is said so often today, "I'm O.K., your O.K."

Secondly, since the development of modern psychology, the idea that we are responsible for our actions and "guilty" when we do what is wrong has been under attack. For the last one hundred and fifty years we have been taught by some psychological disciplines that the experience of guilt for sin should be neutralized through self-oriented psychological "adjustments."

Finally, as this question indicates, "sin" does have something to do with people's relationship with God. If God is not part of your world-view, that is, the way you understand reality, then sin doesn't have much meaning for such unbelieving persons.

The Meaning of Sin

What do we mean when we use the word "sin"?

There are two ideas that have a place in the teaching of the Church about sinning on the practical level. The one is "rule-based" and the other is "goal-based". The "rule-based" aspect of sin sees it as the violation of a pre-existing rule or commandment. An example is one of the Ten Commandments that says, "You shall not bear false witness against your neighbor" (Exodus 20:16). If you tell lies about your neighbor, you break the rule and commit the sin of lying.

The other practical way of understanding sinning is when you don't live up to the best that is expected of you as a Christian. An example of this is when Jesus instructed His followers in the Sermon on the Mount, to "be perfect, as your heavenly Father is perfect." (Matthew 5:48). We are to be "God-like" in our thoughts and behavior because we are created to be the "image and likeness of God" (Genesis 1:26). When we don't live up to that goal of the Christian life, we "sin."

In the Church's mind both of these aspects of sinning are real and both should be avoided. But the "goal" based understanding of sin is more inclusive. It not only includes our actions, but also the quality of our inner dispositions. Further, our understanding of sin makes us give attention to the fundamental orientation of our lives.

"Sin" and "sins"

The Greek word for sin is *amartia*. In ancient Greek, it means "missing the mark." From the Orthodox Christian perspective, the "goal" of all of our lives is growing toward God, or as it is frequently described by the Church Fathers, *growing toward Theosis*.

One of the most important dimensions of *Theosis* (that is, growing toward God-likeness) is communion with God. Since God is a Divine Trinity of Persons, Father, Son and Holy Spirit, who are in communion with each other, for human beings to be "like God," means that they, too, must be in communion with God. Whenever our communion with God is broken, we are "missing the mark." We are deflected from our path whose goal is to be God-like.

There are at least two levels on which this takes place. The first deals with the whole orientation of our life. If you reject God, if most of your life ignores your relationship with God, you are a Sinner, with a capital "S." Your focus may be on money, pride, cars, sex, or whatever. Even people who have been baptized and are members of parishes may be so alienated from any relationship from God, that they are in this category.

Little "s" sins, are the second level we are talking about. If you are a committed and faithful Christian who tries to live the Christian life, it means that you are moving in the right direction in your relationship with God. But you will often still "miss the mark," precisely because you are growing toward God-likeness and haven't reached it yet. When you don't live up to your Christian calling, you "sin" (with a little "s"), but it is not at all the same as denying and rejecting God in the capital "S" sense.

As Christians we are in a constant struggle against **temptations** to think and do things which draw us away from our proper relationship with God. The Orthodox tradition calls these inner attitudes which tempt us to sin, *the passions*. They are attitudes and behaviors like pride, greed, sexual immorality, envy and jealousy. Christians, by definition, battle **against** the passions and **for** God-like ways of living, which are often called *the virtues*. This struggle is ongoing and never-ending. The Church's experience shows that "standing still" is almost impossible. If you are not growing in God-likeness, you are in all probability, sliding backwards! This means that there is always a danger in the Christian life. If we don't deal with the little "s" sins, they will eventually lead us to an almost total break in our relationship with God -big "S" Sin! So, sins and Sin are dangerously inter-connected!

For both of these kinds of sin, there is one remedy: repentance. But the repentance for Capital "S" Sin is a total reorientation of life and values to a new way of life. The repentance for small "s" sin is a daily change in tack, like a sailor does in adjusting the course of his sailing ship toward his final destination.

Is the Christian Life in Sin?

So now the answer to your question is clear. From the sense of the basic orientation of life toward God, if you are identifying your life with Jesus Christ, seeking to live out the consequences of your baptism in faith, hope and love, responding to the saving work of Christ, praying, worshipping, seeking to grow toward "perfection" as a member of the body of Christ and His household, the Church, you are not "in Sin."

To the contrary you are a member of Christ's holy body, the Church. You are walking the life of salvation (Ephesians 5:2,8,15, Galatians 5:16,25). As St. Paul put it, "Now you are the body of Christ and individually members of it" (1 Corinthians 12:27).

However, in the second sense of the word "sin" (with a little "s"), Christians continue to sin whenever our inner attitudes and motives, our words and our actions, do not "fit" our calling as Christians to be living and growing in God-like ways. When we don't think and act like the "image and likeness of God" that we were created to be, we sin.

That's why in the life of the Church there is always repentance, confession of sins, receiving of forgiveness, and repeated "new starts." That's why our Lord taught us to pray daily, "forgive us our trespasses."

The Church

43. WHAT IS THE CHURCH?

Q. What is the Orthodox view of... the Church...How do the Orthodox and the Roman Catholics differ on it? *—A.C.D., Clinton, MA.*

A. This is a fundamental question for both the Orthodox and Roman Catholic Churches. All Orthodox Christians need to have a clear idea regarding the Church. Here are some basic understandings about it.

What is the Church?

Many volumes have been written to answer this question, and all admit that it is not possible to give a complete response. For, as is the case with all of the central teachings of the Church, there is an unknowable element since the Church is alive and growing toward its ultimate fulfillment at the end of time. The mystery of the Church will never be fully understood by us in this life.

Nevertheless, we can try to answer your question. What follows is my own attempt to summarize the self-understanding that the Orthodox Church has about its own existence. Obviously others could say it differently.

One Way of Saying What the Church Is

The Church is the body of people united with Christ as sharers in His death and resurrection through baptism, and life in the Holy Spirit through the sacraments, the truth of God and the life in Christ.

The Church as a body is one, holy, catholic (universal), and apostolic, and it exists so as to continue the work of salvation for all the world, and to build up each of the faithful so as to grow in God's image toward God-likeness (*theosis*), until the time that the final consummation of all things takes place in God's plan. As such, it is the body of Christ, an organic whole composed of believers in the process of growth and distinguished into clergy and laity, who in their own way seek to fulfill the work of salvation in the Church and for the whole world. The Church is at once local (the diocese and the parish) and universal (the One, Holy Catholic and Apostolic Church) and it has organic continuity through the centuries to the time of Christ, the Apostles, and the giving of the Holy Spirit at the birth of the Church at Pentecost.

The Church is the place of God's self-disclosure, His self-revelation that proclaims the truth about God as Trinity, about humanity, about the world's status in relationship to its Creator, about redemption and salvation.

The task of the Church is to continue the three-fold work of Christ's salvation: the teaching (prophetic) role, the governing (kingly) role, and the redeeming (high priestly) role of Christ for the sake of the salvation of humankind. No individual person can be fully a Christian outside the Church, yet in spite of this, in greater or lesser measure, every living person shares in some of the grace of the Church, whatever they believe and whatever they do. But the dividing line of membership in the Church is baptism and participation in the sacramental life of the Church, and the basic true moral and spiritual orientation of life, which enables it.

That is a minimum. However, Church members are called to grow and develop in God-likeness, a course of spiritual development which requires unity in the body of Christ. This is realized, if only partially in this world, in love, personal discipline to overcome sin in one's life, and to develop in constant communion with God -a life which realizes the image and likeness of God in us. What is true of the individual is true of the whole body of the Church. In its empirical existence, it too, seeks to manifest the life of the Kingdom of God in its total way of life. The most visible manifestation of this existence is in the sacramental life, and especially the Eucharist, and in the experience of love for God and our fellows both within and outside the Church.

All this has begun already with Christ's Death and Resurrection and the granting of the Holy Spirit, but will not be fulfilled until the consummation of the age when Christ will come to judge the living and the dead and will realize His Kingdom in all fullness.

It is our conviction that all these factors and conditions come together and have been maintained through the centuries in their fullness in only one ecclesial body-the Orthodox Church.

The Orthodox and the Roman Catholic Understanding of the Church

One of the aspects of the Church, which the Orthodox Church has retained in its teaching and practice, is the sense of the Church as a body.

St. Paul spoke of the Church in this way when he said, "For just as the body is one and has many members, and all the members of the body, though many, are one body, so it is with Christ. For by one Spirit we were all baptized into one body—Jews or Greeks, slaves or free—and all were made to drink of one Spirit" (1 Corinthians 12:12-13). Though there are clergy, i.e. bishops, presbyters and deacons, whose task it is to oversee the work of the Church, they cannot -and do not-function without the laity, nor without each other, just as the various organs of the body cannot function without each other. At the head of the Church is Christ: "Christ is the head of the church, his body, and is himself its Savior" (Ephesians 5:23).

This all means that the Orthodox understand the Church as a great council, a synod, a corporate reality, which in all aspects of its existence, reflects this truth.

Here is to be found the major difference between the Orthodox and the Roman Catholics regarding their understandings of the Church. The Roman Catholic Church, in spite of the changes of Vatican II, still sees the Church as a monarchy, with the Bishop of Rome as its supreme controlling authority. Therefore, the main difference between the Orthodox understanding of the Church and the Roman Catholic understanding of the Church is the Papacy.

44. THE UNITY OF THE FAITH

Q. During the Divine Liturgy we pray "for the unity of the faith." Please explain the meaning of this phrase. What does the Church mean by "unity"? What specifically is meant by "the faith"?

– C.K., Norwood, MA.

A. I believe it is possible to answer your questions on at least two levels. Let's first look where the phrase "unity of the faith" is found in our liturgical tradition.

"Unity of the Faith"

You have encountered the phrase in the Divine Liturgy. The phrase is found in the Divine Liturgies of St. John Chrysostom, St. Basil and the Liturgy of the Pre-Sanctified Gifts. It is included in a set of petitions just prior to the repetition of the Lord's Prayer. The Priest or Deacon says "Having prayed for the unity of the faith and the communion of the Holy Spirit, let us commend ourselves and one another, and our whole life to Christ our God."

We do not find this precise wording, interestingly, in similar sets of petitions in the Vesper or the Orthros services. In the Divine Liturgies of St. John Chrysostom and St. Basil it follows this petition, to which it seems to refer: And grant that with one voice and one heart we may glorify and praise Your most exalted and magestic name of the Father, and of the Son, and of the Holy Spirit, now and always and forever and ever. Amen."

The phrase "for the unity of the faith," is also part of a prayer at the end of the Service of the Hours and the Service of Compline (Apodeipnon). This prayer begins with the words "You who at all times and at every hour. . . "(Greek, *"O en panti kairo kai pasi ora..."*).
In the Service of the Hours and the Compline, this is the context in which the phrase is found:

Do you, O Lord, also receive our supplication at this present hour, and direct our lives according to your commandments. Sanctify our souls; purify our bodies; set aright our minds; cleanse our thoughts; and deliver us from all calamity, wrath and distress. Compass us round about with your holy angels, that guided and guarded by their hosts, we may attain to the *unity of the faith* and to the comprehension of your ineffable glory.

If you read these two passages carefully, you will note that the phrase "unity in the faith" is something we are praying will be given to us in the future. In the first case we are asking God to grant it to us; in the second we are asking that "we may attain to the unity of the faith." By adding the phrase "and to the comprehension of your ineffable glory" an end-times character is given to the phrase. Theologians call this an "eschatological hope or expectation" for when the Kingdom comes in fullness.

The Source - Ephesians 4

Where does this phrase come from? It is used once in the New Testament in St. Paul's letter to the Ephesians in chapter 4, verse 13. I think that it is worth seeing the phrase in its biblical context, because it is part of one of the most magnificent passages in the New Testament that speaks about the character of the Christian life. We are thus also able to understand it more fully.

Chapter four of the letter to the Ephesians begins with an appeal by St. Paul to the Christians in Ephesus, *"to lead a life worthy of the calling to which you have been called, with all lowliness and meekness, with patience, forbearing one another in love, eager to maintain the unity of the Spirit in the bond of peace"* (Ephesians 4:1-3). Here, "unity of the Spirit" is presented as something which the Christians have and experience, but which needs to be maintained in a spirit of mutual harmony and peace.

The next few verses emphasize the sense of unity and oneness that St. Paul describes as a characteristic of the Church. This already existing unity binds Christians, their Lord, their endeavors and existence as a Church into one comprehensive reality. Verses 4 through 6 say: *"There is one body and one Spirit, just as you were called to the one hope that belongs to your call, one Lord, one faith, one baptism, one God and Father of us all, who is above all and through all and in all."* Here "one faith" is seen as integral element in the oneness of the Church body that is constituted of the Holy Spirit, of the one hope in Jesus Christ, the one liturgical life as seen in baptism, of the one heavenly Father who pervades all of the Christian Church's existence.

Verse 7 then speaks of the individual members of the one body, the Church, who are all different and who all receive diverse and special gifts from God as is fitting for each: *"But grace was given to each of us according to the measure of Christ's gift."* Verses 11 and 12 describe some of these gifts: *"And his gifts were that some should be apostles, some prophets, some evangelists, some pastors and teachers."*

For what purpose were these gifts given to individuals in the one Church? St. Paul is clear. The gifts were given, he says, in verse 12, *"to equip the saints for the work of ministry, for building up the body of Christ."*

It is in verse 13 that we find the phrase under discussion. The gifts given are to enable the members of the Church to serve in various ways to build up the members of the Church. This passage underlines the goal toward which this "building up of the Church" is leading us. We are to keep using our gifts to build up the body of Christ, "until we all attain to the unity of the faith and of the knowledge of the Son of God, to mature manhood, to the measure of the stature of the fullness of Christ."

Note that this is fully future oriented. On the one hand there is already "one Lord, one faith, one baptism, one God and Father of us all." So there is already one level of unity in the visible Church. But, all of this exists so as to make possible a process of growth and development in each of us and all of us together that leads to the unity of the faith and knowledge of Christ that will truly fulfill our humanity. The "unity of the faith" is at once a reality in the teaching and beliefs of the Church; while at the same time it is not yet fully realized.

The prayer for "the unity of the faith," coupled with the prayer for the "knowledge of the Son of God" provokes our growth into "mature" human living that is measured and compared with the ultimate goal of the God-Manhood of Jesus Christ. So here, too, there is a future orientation to the appeal for "unity of faith."

Unity of Faith in the Here and Now

As we have seen, while the fullness of the unity of faith is asked for and anticipated as the future realization of our life in Christ's Church, there is also a sense in which the basic beliefs and teachings of the faith are present now. As the passage continues, the expectation and hope arising from the giving of these gifts is *"so that we may no longer be children, tossed to and fro and carried about with every wind of doctrine, by the cunning of men, by their craftiness in deceitful wiles. Rather, speaking the truth in love, we are to grow up in every way into him who is the head, into Christ."* (Ephesians 4:1-14).

Consequently, there is a Christian truth, a Christian faith, that can be known now in some accurate measure within the unity and oneness of the Church's faith teaching. In the famous "love passage" of St. Paul in his first letter to the Christians of Corinth, he noted that:

> our knowledge is imperfect and our prophecy is imperfect; but when the perfect comes, the imperfect will pass away ... For now we see in a mirror dimly, but then face to face. Now I know in part; then I shall understand fully, even as I have been fully understood (1 Corinthians 13:10,12).

So there is a present truth and knowledge of the faith which is adequate for our salvation. But its purpose is to open up a future of growth that will bring us eventually to a fuller and more intimate knowledge and communion with the things of God.

Likewise, there is a unity in the faith in God that exists now in the empirical and historic Church. It is the Orthodox Christian Faith, enshrined in the tradition of the Church. It is a given. But at the same time, it is also a potential that is not yet fulfilled. This is the "unity of the faith" for which we pray.

45. ONE CHURCH

Q. In the Creed we profess our belief "in one, holy, catholic and apostolic Church." What is meant by **one** Church?   –C. K., Norwood, MA.

A. This question is a continuation of last week's column on the topic "The Unity of the Faith." In that column, readers will remember, the source of that phrase was identified both biblically and liturgically. We noted how the phrase is used both to describe the existing unity of the faith and its future fulfillment. It is a gift from God, but also something we strive to achieve with God's grace. It is found, preserved, taught and lived in the Church. It is precisely the claim of the Orthodox Christian Church that it contains, expresses, promulgates and lives, in its institutional existence as Church, that very Faith, given by Christ and the Holy Spirit to the Church.

In today's column, the focus changes somewhat to the doctrinal unity of the Church's teaching and the practice based on it.

"One, Holy, Catholic and Apostolic"

The context of the emphasis on the unity, purity and truth of the Christian teaching, as preserved, taught and lived in the Orthodox Church is the teaching that the Church is "One, Holy, Catholic and Apostolic." This phrase, found in the Creed, expresses the New Testament's teaching that there is a Church which Jesus Christ founded and which the Holy Spirit preserves and inspires. The "oneness" or unity of the Church is given by Christ and preserved by the Holy Spirit for the glory of God the Father. Christ never speaks of establishing many churches with differing or contradictory teachings and practices. The Bible speaks of "one Church."

Christ the Son of God - Foundation of the Church

There is a passage from the Gospel of Matthew which is often discussed as to whether or not it supports the idea that the Pope of Rome has primacy over the rest of the church. This passage, however, has a more basic meaning. You remember how it describes that Jesus asks his Disciples, "But who do you say that I am?" Peter's answer on behalf of all of the Disciples, is an unambiguous faith affirmation: "You are the Christ, the Son of the living God." Jesus then blessed Peter for his expression of this truth and points to the fact that this is not mere human knowledge, but knowledge given by God the Father—in short, it is divine revelation: ". . . flesh and blood has not revealed this to you, but my Father who is in heaven." Peter (whose name in Greek is identical with the Greek word which means "rock," that is, *petra*) then hears that the doctrinal affirmation, which affirms that Jesus Christ is the Son of God the Father is the "rock" upon which Jesus says, "I will build my church." We should note that "His church" is singular, not plural. The assumption of the Gospel of Matthew, as it points to Jesus' establishment of His Church is that there is "one Church," and that this *one Church will live into eternity: "the powers of death shall not prevail against it"* (Matthew 16:15-18).

To this, we can add a second passage from the Gospel of Matthew: You might remember this passage also referred to frequently in a different context:

> If your brother sins against you, go and tell him his fault, between you and him alone. If he listens to you, you have gained your brother. But if he does not listen, take one or two others along with you, that every word may be confirmed by the evidence of two or three witnesses. If he refuses to listen

to them, tell it to the church; and if he refuses to listen even to the church, let him be to you as a Gentile and a tax collector" (Matthew 18:15-17).

There are two things to learn from this passage that bear on our question. First, it is "THE Church" that is being spoken about.

While it is true that often the New Testament speaks about the various local Churches in different cities or regions (example, "the church of Jerusalem"), this geographic identification is practical, while reference to "**the Church**" is doctrinal. Secondly, there is a distinction between what ordinary Christians do (the counseling some fellow Christians) and what "**the Church**" does. Implied in this statement is the authority of the Church in regard to spiritual matters. There is a status which "the Church" has especially in the area of determining doctrine that individual Christians do not have.

"The One Church"

Here are some examples of biblical passages in which the various authors refer not to "local churches" but to "the Church:"

-Colossians 1:18 "He (Jesus Christ) is the head of the body, the church;"

-Colossians 1:24 "Now I rejoice in my sufferings . . for your sake, and . . . for the sake of his (Jesus Christ's) body, that is, the church;"

-1 Corinthians 5:12-13 "what have I to do with judging outsiders? Is it not those inside the church whom you are to judge? God judges those outside;"

-1 Corinthians 10:32 "Give no offense to Jews or to Greeks or to the church of God;"

-1 Corinthians 12:28 ". . . God has appointed in the church first apostles, second prophets, third teachers, then workers of miracles. . .;"

-1 Corinthians 14:4 "He who speaks in a tongue edifies himself,

but he who prophesies edifies the church.;"
-1 Corinthians 14:12 ". . . strive to excel in building up the church;"
-1 Corinthians 15:10 "I (St. Paul) "persecuted the church of God;"
-Ephesians 3:21 "To him (God the Father) be glory in the church
   and in Christ Jesus to all generations,for ever and ever. Amen.";
-Ephesians 5:23 "...Christ is the head of the church, his body,
   and is himself its Savior;"
-Ephesians 5:25 "Christ loved the church and gave himself up
   for her."

The Church: Bulwark of the Truth

This one Church, established by Christ and inspired by the Holy Spirit is the vehicle for knowing and experiencing the truth of God. Thus, the Bible records Saint Paul as writing to his disciple Timothy the following very important message:

> I hope to come to you soon, but I am writing these instructions to you so that, if I am delayed, you may know how one ought to behave in the household of God, which is the church of the living God, the pillar and bulwark of the truth. Great indeed, we confess, is the mystery of our religion" (1 Tim. 3:14-16).

The "truth" about which this passage speaks is about Christ Himself; that is, it is doctrinal, dealing with some of the most fundamental beliefs of the Church.

It is in this sense that the Orthodox Church understands itself to be identical with that very same Church of almost two thousand years ago. "Orthodox" means "true believing," so the claim of the Orthodox Church is that it maintains, teaches, and seeks to live in accordance with that true belief. St. Cyril, Bishop of Jerusalem (4th century) in his *Catechesis* put it this way:

The Church . . . teaches fully . . . and without any omission every doctrine which ought to be brought to men's knowledge, concerning things visible and invisible, in heaven and on earth. . . it brings a universal remedy and cure to every kind of sin whether perpetrated by soul or body, and possesses within it every form of virtue that is named, whether it expresses itself in deeds or words or in spiritual graces of every description.

St. Cyprian (300 A.D.) said in his letter to his son Anfagnus, "The testimony of divine Scripture shows that the Church cannot be outside, that it cannot be split or divided against itself, but that it possesses the unity of a single indivisible house."

46. ORTHODOXY AND HETERODOXY

Q. In the Creed we profess our belief "in one, holy, catholic and apostolic Church." What is meant by "**one** Church." –*C. K., Norwood, MA.*

A. The answer to this question, the third in a series, points to an important theological teaching about the nature of the Church. The Church is the "Body of Christ." St. Paul said "Now you are the body of Christ and individually members of it" (1 Corinthians 12:27). All Orthodox Christians are part of the Body of Christ.

Consequently, being active members of the Church means that together we form the body of Christ. St. Paul parallels our physical bodies with the Church understood as the "Body of Christ," when he says, "For just as the body is one and has many members, and all the members of the body, though many, are one body, so it is with Christ. For by one Spirit we were all baptized into one body — Jews or Greeks, slaves or free — and all were made to drink of one Spirit" (1 Cor. 12:12-13).

But a body has many different parts to it: head, hands, feet, internal organs. Likewise the Church has different parts to it. Christ is the "head of the Church." In the earliest history of the Church Christ's Apostles exercised this leadership in the Church as Christ's representatives; preaching, deciding, and guiding the infant Church. Subsequently, the Apostles ordained Bishops, Presbyters and Deacons to continue the work of the Church, along with the laity.

Bishops and the Unity of the Church

It is the Bishops of the Church who mark out the unity of the Church within its boundaries, by clarifying the faith of the Church, its discipline and its order. This is exercised on a local level within a Diocese, Archdiocese or other kind of church province. But it is most fully manifest when Bishops gather together canonically in a Synod. The highest way that the faith of the one Church is expressed is in an Ecumenical Council. At a Council of the Church, only Bishops decide the Church's teaching, though they may be advised by Deacons and Presbyters and Lay persons.

Heterodoxy

Often in the history of the Church, there have been divisions based on differences in doctrinal beliefs, and often divisions have been created on the basis of sacramental separation and other breaks in Church unity, based on the lack of communion with or among the canonically ordained Bishops of the Church. There are two types of division. The first is "heresy," which is division on account of differences in faith; the second is "schism," which is administrative division where the schismatic group is not in communion with the canonical bishop.

Unfortunately, such divisions have existed from the beginning of the life of the Church. For example, in the first pastoral letter to Timothy in the New Testament, we read:

> Now the Spirit expressly says that in later times some will depart from the faith by giving heed to deceitful spirits and doctrines of demons, through the pretensions of liars whose consciences are seared. . . . If you put these instructions before

the brethren, you will be a good (servant) of Christ Jesus, nourished on the words of the faith and of the good doctrine which you have followed" (1 Timothy 4:1-2,6).

One of the major responsibilities of the clergy (Bishops, Priests and Deacons) is to protect the integrity of the Christian Faith within the Body of Christ, the Church. Thus, to the clergy of Antioch, St. Paul said,

> I did not shrink from declaring to you the whole counsel of God. Take heed to yourselves and to all the flock, in which the Holy Spirit has made you overseers, to care for the church of God which he obtained with the blood of his own Son. I know that after my departure fierce wolves will come in among you, not sparing the flock; and from among your own selves will arise men speaking perverse things, to draw away the disciples after them" (Acts 20:27-30).

You can see in this passage that there is a sense of the unity of the Faith as it is preserved in the Church. It is the contention of the Orthodox Church that it has maintained this original Faith given to the Holy Apostles and preserved in the Church through the centuries. Jesus said to His Apostles, very clearly, "To you has been given the mystery of the kingdom of God" (Mark 4:11).

That is why we not only affirm in the Creed that the Church is "one"; it is also "Apostolic." Communion in that fundamentally unchanged Apostolic Faith is a sign of membership in the Body of Christ, the Church. Teachings that deviate from that Apostolic Faith, are heresies and false doctrine. There are many expressions of this "rule of Faith," of the Church. One example is the Creed that Orthodox Christians recite every Sunday in the Divine Liturgy. Another is an early affirmation of belief dealing with the person of Christ, found in the New Testament letter of St. Paul to the Colossians:

He (Jesus Christ) is the head of the body, the church; he is the beginning, the first-born from the dead, that in everything he might be pre-eminent. For in him all the fullness of God was pleased to dwell, and through him to reconcile to himself all things, whether on earth or in heaven, making peace by the blood of his cross. And you, who once were estranged and hostile in mind, doing evil deeds, he has now reconciled in his body of flesh by his death, in order to present you holy and blameless and irreproachable before him (God the Father), provided that you continue in the faith, stable and steadfast, not shifting from the hope of the gospel which you heard, which has been preached to every creature under heaven" (Colossians 1:18-23).

This passage is significant because it emphasizes the early Christian exhortation to Christians to remain committed and faithful to the core beliefs about the person of Christ: that He is both divine and human; that He saved us from the broken condition of sin through His death and His resurrection; that we must respond in faith and in life-style marked by steadfastness and commitment to these beliefs about Jesus Christ in order to be saved.

Orthodoxy = "Unity in Faith"

The great doctrinal controversies throughout history have aimed on the one hand, to clarify the faith of the Church with the goal that "unity of the faith" can be realized now and empirically in the life of the Church on earth. The Orthodox hold that this basic unity in faith is essential for sacramental and jurisdictional unity in the Church here on earth. At the same time, it is the foundation for the unity of faith for which we pray to be fully realized in the future Kingdom.

One way of defining the Orthodox Church's self-understanding, is that it is the Church of Christ in which the true (*"Orthe"*) Christian Faith and worship (*"doxa"*) are lived, taught and experienced.

For example, on the first Sunday of Lent, the Sunday of Orthodoxy, in which we commemorate the decision of the 7th Ecumenical Council to restore the icons, there is a hymn in the Orthros among those known as the "Praises" or *"Ainoi"* whose text is the following:

> A Feast of joy and gladness is revealed to us today. For the teachings of the true faith shine forth in all their glory, and the Church of Christ is bright with splendor, adorned with the holy icons which now have been restored; **and God has granted to the faithful unity of mind.**

The practical message for the Orthodox Christian is expressed by St. Paul as he speaks of the stance that Christians should take now, in anticipation of the future coming of Christ: "Be watchful, stand firm in your faith, be courageous, be strong. Let all that you do be done in love" (1 Corinthians 16:13-14).

47. THE CHURCH, RELIGION AND HATE

Q. The God-fearing editor of the *Readers Digest* wrote a very angry article against the Supreme Court for refusing once again to allow prayers in schools. The article was titled "Let Us Pray." I wrote to him my own answer. I am sure you would be interested in it, I also hope you will enjoy my own ideas about praying and how effective prayers are. *–A. L., Marblehead, MA.*

A. This letter was accompanied by a copy of a typed three-page letter to the Editor of the Readers Digest, not simply opposed to the idea of prayer in public schools, but also expressing the ideas that prayer is ineffectual, and that religions stand for "hate. . .Blood (shedding) . . . and tears . . . ." Here are just a few of the paragraphs in the letter:

"'Let Us Pray!!!' What an appeal in absolute futility when thousands upon thousands of religious fanatics in Europe proceeded to slaughter each other in nine religious wars in a period of only forty years.

'Let Us Pray!!!' did not do much good to the native Americans because God in usual stupidity plus indifference, mixed with cruelty, forgot to immunize the natives against God's given horrible diseases brought here by the European Christians.

'Let Us Pray!!!' for the twenty million children God kills every year, either by his own diseases or by hunger.

'Let Us Pray!!!' for all the blind, the deaf, the blind plus deaf, plus retarded children that God creates every year."

From these paragraphs the reader will understand the position of the letter writer. In his view prayer is totally ineffective, essentially because religion itself points to a God who causes suffering, pain, illness, who does it from hate-filled and cruel dispositions.

Though this letter is not a question, but a statement, what can we, as Orthodox Christians say to such charges?

It is not the first time that this correspondent has expressed similar ideas. Even though I have in the past tried to clarify for him and the readers of the column the mistaken presuppositions in these and similar statements, he has chosen to ignore the responses. I will try to restate them.

Mistaken Presuppositions

Most Christians who read the statement in the preceding section (including, I would suppose, the Editor of the *Readers Digest*), would not recognize the presuppositions in this letter. My understanding of most other religions is the same. Let's look at the presuppositions.

1. The first presupposition is that God is identical with the processes of nature as we know them today.

2. The second presupposition is that God not only creates evil,

disease, tragedies of every sort, but that God delights in them.

3. The third presupposition is that God determines the actions of cruel and evil men and women, so that God is ultimately responsible for their actions.

4. The fourth presupposition is that prayer to God is effective only if it magically produces what is asked for.

If I am correct in understanding these presuppositions, then I must ask if these, in truth, represent Christian perspectives about God. Though I am not an adequate spokesman for Judaism and Islam, I believe I can also speak for these religions as well, in categorically denying that these are Christian, Jewish or Muslim beliefs about God. Let's look at these presuppositions from an Orthodox Christian perspective.

Is God Identical with the Process of Nature?

This presupposition holds that because there are accidents, germs, illness, these are direct actions of God. Since they happen, it is God who causes them to happen.

On a theoretical level, we need to point out that one of the most fundamental affirmations of Orthodox Christianity is that the CREATOR is qualitatively distinct from the CREATION. God is one thing, the created world another. That does not mean that God is unrelated to the created world, but God is not the same as the created world. God created the world good, but not perfect, with the potential of achieving its purpose. This is dependent upon human beings, who were also created good, but not perfect, with the potential of achieving their purpose, as a result of free choice between real alternatives. Nature is not now what God created it to be. Influenced by the corruption of sin, the Bible teaches that "the whole creation has been groaning in travail together until now" (Romans 8:22). If there are germs and illnesses it is a sign of the evil in the world, a reflection of its disharmony and lack of continuity with God. Just the opposite of what the letter writer thinks is the Christian teaching.

Does God Delight in the Evil People do to Each Other?

There is only one sense that we could even vaguely say that this approaches Christian teaching. Christians hold that in an ultimate sense, this is a moral universe. The good is ultimately rewarded and evil is ultimately punished, bringing with it its own sanctions. Nevertheless, many times the good is honored and brings good consequences in this life. Similarly, many times persons who do evil in this life reap the consequences of their deeds and are punished. When justice triumphs, the Bible, especially the Old Testament presents God as being pleased. This, however, does not mean that God is pleased with the suffering itself, experienced by the evil doer. Rather, the evidence of the Bible and the Church's teaching about God points in a very different direction: beyond the concerns of justice, God is concerned with human welfare. God abhors the evils we inflict upon each other, condemns them and counsels us to act accordingly. The clearest statement of this is the simple biblical teaching "God is love" (1 John 4:8).

Does God Make People Do What They Do?

This is probably the biggest and most significant mistake of the letter writer. He holds that God determines the actions of cruel and evil men and women, so that God is ultimately responsible for their actions. The letter writer doesn't want to accept the truth that people are responsible for their own actions. Christian teaching is that God directs us toward the good, but we must make the choices. The definition of sin itself is "breaking our relationship with God." Evil acts are the clearest examples and consequence of this broken relationship with the source of all goodness, who is God.

Christianity teaches us about a good God who also expects us to be good. For example, St. Gregory of Nyssa, in his book *The Life of Moses* (sec. 166) says, "Religion can be divided into two halves, one part being concerned directly with God, the other with the establishment of good conduct (for purity of conduct is also a part of religion). First a man must learn what he needs to know about God. . . . Then the second part is taught and he learns the kind of practices which go to make up the good life." The Bible puts it this way:

> Beloved, let us love one another; for love is of God, and he who loves is born of God and knows God. He who does not love does not know God; for God is love. In this the love of God was made manifest among us, that God sent his only Son into the world, so that we might live through him. In this is love, not that we loved God but that he loved us and sent his Son to be the expiation for our sins. Beloved, if God so loved us, we also ought to love one another. No man has ever seen God; if we love one another, God abides in us and his love is perfected in us (1 John 4:7-12).

The reader's mistake is to identify what some people actually do (whether they are Christians or not) with what God wants them to do. If God forced them to "do good" then the "good" they did would not be really good because it would not be done freely.

Is Prayer Magic?

The difference between magic and religion is that magic assumes that incantations will automatically produce the desired results. Prayer is not magic. Prayer is conversation with God. Christians know that they can pray to God and that God can give different kinds of answers. Sometimes God says "No!" Sometimes He says "Yes!" Sometimes God responds in ways that are different than what we expect. And often that means new insights and growth for us.

A Concluding Word

The God that our letter writer has in mind is not the God of the Christians (or the Jews or the Muslims). It is a philosophical God that no one believes in, to my knowledge. The writer needs to accept the God of love and salvation and find in Him peace for his soul.

Saints

48. QUESTIONS ABOUT THE SAINTS

Q. As Orthodox Christians, are we encouraged to pray to the Saints? Also, are there certain Saints to whom we pray for specific requests?
— *F.C.C., Brookline, MA.*

A. The context for understanding how and why we pray to the saints in the Orthodox Church is the Church itself. The Church is made up of all the believers who accept as their own the faith of the Church about God, Christ, the Holy Spirit, salvation, the sacramental life, etc.; who acknowledge the spiritual role of saints in the Church, and the teaching of the Church about the saints.

Holiness and Sainthood

For us Orthodox, it is good to remember that the original word in Greek used to speak about saintly persons is the same word exactly which is used to describe God's "holiness" and whatever is sacred, for that matter. The Greek word is *aghios*. So, in our minds we must keep ever highlighted the extremely close connection between the holiness of God and the saintliness of human beings.

There are early references in the New Testament to holy people, or saints. Significantly, the word is always in the plural and refers to all of the members of the Church. For example, in many of his letters St. Paul addresses the members of the local Church to which he is writing as "the saints" of that particular place. Thus, writing to the Christians in the city of Ephesus in Asia Minor, St. Paul begins his letter to them with these words: "Paul, an Apostle of Christ Jesus, by the will of God to the saints who are at Ephesus and faithful in Christ Jesus..." (Ephesians 1:1).

A First Level Meaning: All Christians

This clearly does not mean that all of the Christians at Ephesus were morally and spiritually perfect, because in this letter and in nearly all of his other letters, St. Paul speaks of shortcomings and sins and spiritual failings on their part. In this first meaning of "sainthood," the word "saint" was a description of those who were separated away from the others of their city by a special standing which they had. For, as Christians, they had believed and accepted the saving work of Christ, and through His Church they had entered into a new relationship with God. This was different in substance and quality from the relationship to God of others who were not Christians. In this sense, "Saint," means someone who is "set apart" for God.

The sign of that sainthood was Baptism, by which the "old man (*anthropos*") died "with Christ," and the "new man (*anthropos*") rose out of the water to new life in the resurrection of Christ. This made, in this first understanding, every baptized person a saint!

Another Meaning: "Saint" as "Friends of God"

But clearly, there is another meaning to this word. It also signifies that a person in a special way has realized and put into practice a holy and God-like existence. In other words, a saint is a person who in a special way has made the potential of Baptism into an experienced spiritual and moral reality in his or her life. The Church understands that this happens only when there is intense communion with God and love for God. Thus, a saint, in this sense, is a special "Friend of God."

This is illustrated in the writings of St. Paul. As seen above, he refers to all the baptized Christians in Ephesus as "saints" as compared to those in Ephesus who were not baptized, and therefore, not "saints." But in his letters to the Romans and to the Corinthians, St. Paul says something slightly different.

He speaks of Christians whose sainthood is yet to be realized. For example, he addresses his letter, "to all God's beloved in Rome, who are called to be saints" (Romans 1:7). This sense of living in accordance with our "holiness," on the one hand, as well as the sense of seeking to make our holiness real and developing it, is thus equally part of the New Testament teaching about holiness. So, in his letter to the Ephesian Christians, St. Paul says that special gifts are given to the Christians "for the equipment of the saints, for the work of ministry, for the building up of the body of Christ." This takes place, says St. Paul, so that we may "attain the unity of the faith and of the knowledge of the Son of God, to mature manhood, to the measure of the stature of the fullness of Christ" (Ephesians 4:12-16). Growth into sainthood is the theme here.

Sanctity as Every Christian's Goal

Sanctity then, is a given, but it is also to be sought after and something to be done, as well. Speaking of himself, St. Paul says, "we have behaved...with holiness and godly sincerity" (2 Corinthians 1:12). And in the same letter, he calls on the Corinthian Christians to make holiness a reality in their lives: "Since we have these promises, beloved, let us cleanse ourselves from every defilement of the body and spirit, and make holiness perfect in the fear of God" (2 Corinthians 7:1).

Who Are the Saints?

All Christians are saints in the sense that all are baptized and united to God through the saving work of Jesus Christ, as we have seen. But this holiness is at the same time a call to all of us to grow toward the fulfillment of this new relationship with God. It is important that each of us understand the holiness of our Christian calling and the sanctity of our existence as believers and therefore, as "saints in the making."

Some Christians, throughout the history of the Church, have, in fact, spent their lives so completely in "making holiness perfect" that they have impacted dramatically on the rest of the Church's membership. It is these wonderful people, these examples of what faithfulness to God can do for the life of human beings, whom we refer to in the special sense of "the saints of the Church" whom we honor in icons and hymns. It is these very special persons who stand as an example for the rest of us, an encouragement, a proof that the Christian life can be lived to its fullness in this life. And it is these very special members of the Church of Christ, whom we call upon to pray for us, to intercede on our behalf.

Kinds of Saints

The first persons honored as saints of the Church were Christ's Apostles. Thus, we read that Christ made His revealed teaching known "to his holy apostles and prophets by the Spirit" (Ephesians 3:5). Very early in the history of the Church, the Mother of our Lord, the "Theotokos" was honored by Christians as a most unique and important holy person and saint. As a result of the persecution of the Church, thousands of saints were honored by the Church because of their courageous witness for the faith; the "martyrs" gave their lives, while the "confessors" suffered for the sake of Christ in different ways. Later, when monasticism developed in the Church, many monks and nuns were acknowledged by the Church as luminaries of the spiritual life. In the history of the Church many thinkers, teachers and pastoral leaders, whom we name "Fathers of the Church," were also honored for their saintliness. Many saints were bishops, priests and deacons. So, also, were the healing saints, the "Holy Unmercenaries," the faithful and devoted heads of Orthodox nations, the dedicated virgin saints, married saints, soldier-saints, missionaries, simple folk who responded to persecution in later years such as the "neo-martyrs," and many other saintly figures.

As the New Testament book of Hebrews says, "we are surrounded by so great a cloud of witnesses." They have expressed through their lives the holiness to which all Christians are called. How are we ordinary Christians to respond to them? What is the relationship we should have with the saints? Next week, we will examine this question in a practical way, in specific and concrete ways.

49. THE SAINTS AND US

Q. How should we pray to the various saints?

–D. P., Cleveland, OH.

A. Last week "The Question Box" responded to this question in a general way, speaking about the meaning of "sainthood" as the term applies to all Christians, as well as how it is used to refer to those special "friends of God" who stand out among Christians and who have shown in their lives the results of their full commitment to Christ. We saw, also, that the saints have many different backgrounds.

Today's column will build on this information answering, directly and practically, your request for information about how we should pray to the various saints.

Pray to the Saints in God

The saints should never be prayed to separate from our faith and commitment in God; God the Father, the Son of God Jesus Christ, and the Holy Spirit of God. The saints are not "gods." The saints are saints, precisely because of their love for the Father, their salvation in Christ, and their deep communion with the Holy Spirit.

To use a homey analogy, our prayers to saints are as if we were asking an elder brother or sister to speak on our behalf to our parents; or, as if we were asking a fellow employee to intercede on our behalf with our employer. It is not that we can't speak for ourselves. We can do it, and do it every day. But, we call upon the "friends of God," to aid and support our prayer. As the Bible says, "the prayer of a righteous man has great power in its effects" (James 5:16). It is precisely the saints who were "righteous," and so it is to them that we go when we want "great power" for our requests and petitions.

But ultimately, the saints intercede for us before the throne of God. God is the source of our salvation and the giver of every good gift. Because the saints live in communion with God, we shouldn't pray to them in isolation from our whole Christian faith commitment to God. So, pray to the saints, always asking them to intercede for you before God. That is the basic way we should pray to the saints.

Pray to the Saints With Confident Faith

Our Church teaches us that the saints are ready and eager to hear our requests and to intercede, that is, to pray themselves for us. So we should not hesitate in asking for their assistance and help.

Just as we would not hesitate in asking another Christian to pray for us, in the same way we should feel free to call upon our "fellow Christians"-the saints-to speak to God on our behalf. The reason we can do this is that we Christians who live on earth, and the saints who already have entered in some ways into the eternal Kingdom of God, are co-members of One Church. We are members of that part of the Church which is still battling to fulfill our Christian calling; we are called "the Church Militant." They are members of that part of the Church which has completed the Christian struggle with victory; they are the Church Triumphant. But the two are part of a single whole which is the Church. "Pray for one another," the Bible says (James 5:16).

Pray to the Saints With Knowledge of Their Lives

Knowing the lives of the saints helps us pray to them because we are able to call upon them for the blessings, which the members of the Church have found them to be most effective in their intercessions. A common example is the prayer people offer to St. Phanourios to help them find lost things. More deeply spiritual is the great devotion which the whole Orthodox Church has for the mother of our Lord, the "Theotokos." The Church sees the Theotokos as our human representative in the whole mystery of the Incarnation of

Christ, as the first among the saints, as the beloved "Mother of God," whose intercessions are "most effective."

Another example of saints whom we call on for special intercessions are the *"Aghioi Anargyroi,"* that is, the "Holy Unmercenaries" such as St. Panteleimon, and Sts. Cosmas and Damian, who were Christian physicians and healed their poor patients without charge. Often Orthodox Christians will seek their intercessions for the healing of sickness in themselves and in their families.

The list is almost endless, and it would take several columns just to describe the various "specialties" of the saints. That is one reason for Orthodox Christians to become familiar with the lives of the saints. An example of a popularly written collection of the lives of the saints for the whole year are the volumes written by Fr. George Poulos. You can order them from the any Orthodox bookstore.

Pray to the Saints As Examples

Many of the saints exemplify particular virtues which are examples for all Christians in their efforts to grow in the Christ-like life. We are all familiar with the phrase "the patience of Job," for example. When we read the lives of the martyrs, we are impressed by their steadfastness, commitment to Christ, and unwavering strength in the face of torture and persecution. Reflecting on their lives, and calling upon them in our own temptations is a powerful source of strength for us. Every life of a saint whose biography we read can inspire us in one way or another to a more Christian life. When we ask the saint to intercede for us for the specific character trait, or way of behaving, we make that influence even greater.

Pray to Your Patron Saint

Every one of us, who is a baptized Christian has received a "Christian name." For most of us, that is a "saint's name." It is important that we each become familiar with the life of the saint after whom we have been named. That saint is special to us, precisely because our name is special to us, and because the saint after whom we have been named is our patron saint. We should ask our namesake saint to intercede for us, not only in general ways, but specifically. For example, my patron saint is St. Stylianos, who is known for his love for children and for his intercessions for their protection. Each morning as I complete my prayers, I ask my patron Saint, St. Stylianos, to intercede before God for the health and well-being of my children. I ask the Theotokos to intercede for my wife, and Saint Nektarios (who was a Seminary Dean and Professor) to intercede for my seminarian students, to mention only a few saints.

Pray to Honor the Saints

Many of the hymns of our Church are not primarily requests for intercessory prayers by the saints on our behalf, but prayers of honor for the saints. Here is an example of a hymn regarding the Theotokos which simply honors her for whom she is and for what she has done:

> Today the virgin Theotokos, Mary, the fortified chamber of the heavenly groom, is born by the will of God of a barren woman, being prepared as a chariot for God the Word; for to this she had been foreordained, since she is the divine gate and the Mother of Life in truth. (September 7, Kontakion, Feast of the Preparation for the Nativity of the Theotokos)

But the intercessory aspect is not absent from many of these kinds of hymns, either. Here is another example regarding the Theotokos:

> Rejoice, O virgin Theotokos, full of grace, O haven and intercessor for humankind; for from thee was the Deliverer of the world incarnate; and thou alone are Mother and Virgin, blessed and glorified always. Intercede therefore,

with Christ God, to grant safety to all the universe. (September 1, Troparion, Feast of the Indiction.)

Pray to the Saints Through Their Icons

In each Orthodox home there should be a "family shrine," which should have a vigil lamp and icons. An icon of Christ and the Theotokos are essential. But also, the icons of the patron saints of the members of the family are appropriate. Thus, there should be icons of the patron saints of the spouses who head the family, as well. We honor the saints individually when we reverence their icons. Icons should be in our homes. When we go to Church, we should also reverence their icons, thus honoring them through their icons. A book title, *Praying With Icons*, properly expresses the Church's teaching.

Pray to the Saints on Their Feast Days

Each day is a feast day of one or more saints. The popular saints' days are well-known, such as St. George (April 23), The Archangels (November 8), St. Demetrios (October 26), St. Katherine (November 25), and St. St. Nicholas(December 6) and many, many more. In local parishes Divine Liturgies are conducted on these and other saints' days. Check your church calendar daily. If you are able, you should attend the Divine Liturgy on the feast day of your Patron Saint and receive Holy Communion, asking especially on that day for the intercessions of your Patron saint.

Concluding Thoughts

We have hardly exhausted the topic here. Much more could be written. But I suppose we could draw everything together by observing that living close to the life of the Church, and sharing in the spirit, mind and heart of the "communion of the saints" is probably most pleasing to the saints themselves.

50. THE THEOTOKOS

Q. Protestants believe the blessed Virgin Mary holds no spiritual importance to them. How did this belief come about? If only they knew that denying belief in the Theotokos makes them self-condemned. Isn't that blasphemy?   *–N.T., Rhodes, Greece.*

A. The Protestant form of Christianity came about as a result of perceived abuses in the Roman Catholic Church in the sixteenth century. Among the errors which they perceived, was an excessive devotion to the Mother of Jesus, to the point that people seemed to be worshipping Mary instead of Jesus Christ and God. Instead of reforming the abuses, they essentially removed the Virgin Mary from the Protestant experience of faith.

Developments in Roman Catholic Attitudes

In reaction, the Roman Catholic Church asserted even more strongly the importance of the Virgin Mary for their Church. This expressed itself in increasing devotions to the Virgin Mary, exemplified by the doctrine of the Immaculate Conception, a belief that the Virgin Mary was born without Original (Ancestral) Sin. After theological doubt about this doctrine in the Medieval period, the Roman Catholic Church made it a required teaching in 1854.

As of late, however, less focus has been placed on these teachings, while more emphasis is put on the role of the Virgin Mary in salvation, and in her as a model as is seen in the title of a 1984 book by Andre Feuillet, *Jesus and His Mother: According to the Lucan Infancy Narratives, and According to St. John: The Role of the Virgin Mary in Salvation history and the Place of Woman in the Church.* Another book published in 1990 by a bishop of the Roman Catholic Church, Francis Cardinal Arinze, also points to practical Christian living dimensions of the life of the Virgin Mary for the Church: *Motherhood and Family Life, the Blessed Virgin Mary, Christian in Christ.*

Developments in Protestant Attitudes

Protestants, in the meantime continue to have varying attitudes to the Virgin Mary. Most fundamentalist and evangelical Protestants do not consider her important for the Christian faith; there are still many who reject her in their teachings.

Some, however, have begun rethinking her importance and place in Protestantism. In 1971, Protestant author Heiko Augustinus Oberman, wrote a small book titled *The Virgin Mary in Evangelical Perspective*, with an introduction by a Roman Catholic scholar. One of the greatest Protestant theologians of the past generation was Karl Barth. In 1977 scholar Andrew Louth published a study with the title *Mary and the Mystery of the Incarnation: An Essay on the Mother of God in the Theology of Karl Barth*. A recent study which exemplifies a deeper appreciation of the Virgin Mary among mainline Protestants is Methodist George H. Tavard's 1996 book *The thousand faces of the Virgin Mary*.

Unfortunately, some of the extreme liberal fringe elements of Protestant writings (and those of some former Roman Catholics) have gone in another direction, influenced by psychologism, secularism and extreme feminism. Some, like Marina Warner, psychologize belief in Mary as a denigration of women! Others such as Ruth Vanita, connect the Virgin Mary to homosexuality! And some, like William Bond and Pamela Suffield, depict the Virgin Mary as a goddess! This indeed, is blasphemy!

The Theotokos in the Orthodox Tradition

In the Gospels, the earliest mention of Mary, points to her role in the Incarnation of the Son of God (Mark 3:31-35, 6:3). Matthew 1:18-24 tells us of the Virgin birth. Of all the Evangelists, Luke tells us the most about the Theotokos: the Annunciation (1:26-28), her visit to Elizabeth (1:39-56), Jesus' birth (2:1-7), the Presentation at the Temple (2:22-39) and the finding of 12 year old Jesus teaching in the Temple (2:41-52). All of these events point to the Incarnation of

Christ, showing Mary's unique involvement in the divine plan of salvation.

She herself is presented to us in Luke and Acts, as one authority puts it, "as the servant of the Lord (1:38), who sings the praises of the Lord (1:46-55), and brings him into the world (2:6-7), but who must accept his return to the Father (2:49); show(ing) her as a type (*typos* = model) of the church and underlin(ing) her ecclesiological nature. Later, in Acts 1:13-14, Mary the Mother of Jesus is presented as a disciple at prayer."

In the Gospel of John, we see her at the Marriage in Cana, instructing the servants to obey Jesus (2:1-12). She is present at the Crucifixion of Christ, where Jesus pays special attention to her, giving John responsibility for her care. In both cases, Jesus refers to His mother as "woman" something totally unprecedented. This points to her person and role as the new Eve, contrasting her faithful commitment to God with that of Eve's disobedience, just as St. Paul would identify Jesus as the new Adam, contrasting Jesus' obedience to God with Adam's disobedience (1 Corinthians 15:22, 15:45-49, Romans 5:11-19).

Given this important place in the Gospels for the Virgin Mary, it should not surprise us that the Church conformed to her own prediction in her song of praise: "For behold, henceforth all generations will call me blessed" (Luke 1:48).

From the beginning Mary as *Theotokos* (= "birthgiver of God") was invoked by the Church Fathers to affirm Christ's physical birth, incarnating in human nature the divine reality of the second person of the Holy Trinity, the Son. Such statements are to be found in the letters of Ignatios (35-107 A.D.). Justin Martyr (100-165 A.D.) in his *Dialogue With Trypho* makes explicit the identity of the Theotokos as the New Eve, emphasizing also her virginity. Irenaeus (130-200 A.D.) developed in his book *Against Heresies* the Eve/Mary parallel in the salvation of humanity, but he made a clear distinction between Christ's saving work and Mary's prayerful intercessions for humanity.

When in the fifth century, Nestorios sought to deny the real divinity of Jesus Christ, Cyril of Alexandria (died 444 A.D.) emphasized Mary's title as the "Birthgiver of God." This title was officially affirmed at the Ecumenical Council in Ephesus in 431.

Soon after, others sought to reject or minimize the human nature of Jesus Christ. Again, Christ's full humanity was defended by the Church with the affirmation of the title for the Virgin Mary as "The Mother of God," emphasizing the physical and human reality of the birth of Jesus Christ.

The Church Fathers and writers also emphasized Mary's churchly (ecclesiological) role as the first among the saints, her holiness, and her virtue, including her purity in her perpetual virginity, protected and inspired by the Holy Spirit, which "over-shadowed" her, keeping her from sin.

Many sought to honor her and numerous stories and legends were told in Apocryphal writings, some of which became the basis for Church feasts such as her Birth (September 8), her Entrance into the Temple (November 21) and her death and translation to heaven, the Dormition of the Theotokos (August 15).

Among some of the most careful, beautiful and instructive patristic writings about the Virgin mother of our Lord are the *Homilies on the Theotokos* of St. John of Damascus (675-749 A.D.) which affirm the main lines of the Orthodox understanding of the Theotokos. She is honored as "Theotokos" as "Mother of God," as "All-holy" (*Panagia*), as "Intercessor for Christians," and as "Guide of Christians." (*Hodegetria*) are a few of many of her other titles.

Her role in the Incarnation of Christ is expressed in the large icon depicting her holding the Christ child on the wall behind the Altar Table (the Apse), and in many other kinds of icons.

To this day, the Orthodox Church has maintained the biblical and patristic tradition regarding the Virgin Mary, neither over-emphasizing nor under-emphasizing her place in the Church.

Read About the Theotokos in the Orthodox Tradition

To learn more, you may want to read these books about the Theotokos: Dennis Michelis, *The Virgin Mary* (1994); Holy Apostles Convent, *The Life of the Virgin Mary, the Theotokos* (1989); Constantine Callinicos, *Our Lady the Theotokos*, tr. by George Dimopoulos (n.d.); and Georgia & Helen Hronas, *The Illustrated Life of the Theotokos for Children* (1990).

Salvation

51. SALVATION

Q. What is *"Soteriology?"*   *–A.C.D., Clinton, MA.*

A. Concern about salvation and how we are saved is a source of common discussion in our country among Christians of different backgrounds. In theology, this topic is called the study of "Soteriology."

The Christian Doctrine of Salvation

The word "Soteriology" comes from two Greek words. *Soteria* means "salvation" and *logos* in this case, means "the study of." Thus, "Soteriology" is the part of theological study that deals with the topic of salvation. Christianity is very rich in teachings and images of salvation. Here we can just touch on the topic of "Orthodox Soteriology."

Salvation from What?

It is Orthodox teaching that the sinful human condition results from the broken relationship between humanity and God. This condition of sin, however, has a further step. Not to be in communion with God, means that we have come under the dominion of the demonic, influenced and controlled by "death, sin and the Devil." As St. Paul says, we had become slaves to sin. "Formerly, when you did not know God, you were in bondage to beings that by nature are no gods" (Galatians 4:8).

In the Orthodox understanding, then, humanity, in its distorted "less than fully human" condition, is in bondage to the forces of evil and sin, and lives a spiritual death in spiritual darkness. That is why, in the Gospel of John, the human condition is described as "death" and "darkness." Humanity needed to be saved from that condition of "death," understood as separation from God and godly ways.

The Savior

It is the teaching of Scripture that God initiated the redemption of humankind from its enslavement to death, sin, darkness and the demonic influence over its existence. How was this to take place? Because it was God who was sinned against by His creature, God had to be involved. Because it was humanity that broke the relationship with God through sinful pride, humanity also had to be involved in the work of salvation.

Thus, the second person of the Holy Trinity at a particular point in time took on human nature and came into the world for the salvation of the world. As the New Testament teaches, "For God so loved the world that He gave His only-begotten Son..." (John 3:16). It also teaches that "when the time had fully come, God sent forth his Son, born of woman, born under the law, to redeem those who were under the law, so that we might receive adoption as sons... So through God you are no longer a slave but a son, and if a son then an heir. (Galatians 4:4-7).

The Work of Salvation

How did Jesus Christ save humanity from its enslavement to sin, the demonic, evil, darkness and death? The work of Christ can be understood under three headings. First, Christ was a teacher, instructing humankind so that we understood our condition. We learned of God's saving love for us. Then, He gave us direction as to how we ought to live and behave. He is the Lord and Master of all, King and Ruler of all, but especially of those who are being saved. Lastly, Jesus Christ functioned as a High Priest, who offered Himself upon the Cross to die for the world's sins, to take upon Himself the brunt of the powers of the demonic in our place, and then to conquer the Devil, sin, evil, darkness and death, through His resurrection. St. Paul calls this teaching "of first importance." "For I delivered to you as of first importance what I also received, that Christ died for our sins in accordance with the scriptures, that he was buried, that he was raised on the third day in accordance with the scriptures (1 Corinthians 15:3-4). You'll recognize that very similar language has been included in the Creed said at each Divine Liturgy.

The Results of the Saving Work of Jesus Christ

Christ's death and resurrection restored to humanity the "likeness," that is, the potential to realize our full humanity that was created in the image of God. It meant it was now possible for each person to be freed from the dominion of the Devil, to escape from spiritual darkness and to be released from spiritual death. As the Bible teaches: "But God, who is rich in mercy, out of the great love with which he loved us, even when we were dead through our trespasses, made us alive together with Christ (by grace you have been saved), and raised us up with him...." (Ephesians 2:4-6).

For the Orthodox Church, the death of Christ cannot be separated from His resurrection, for the resurrection is the source of the new life of humanity. "For if while we were enemies we were reconciled to God by the death of his Son, much more, now that we are reconciled, shall we be saved by his life" (Romans 5:10). As a result of the saving work of Christ, humanity has become "a new creation" (Galatians 6:15).

A Liturgical Expression of Orthodox Soteriology

Nowhere is this more fully expressed than at the midnight Easter Service in the Orthodox Church. Just before midnight all the lights in the Church are extinguished. It represents the darkness and dominion of the Devil in the world. Darkness and spiritual death dominate our existence. Then, the Royal Gate opens and the Priest comes forth holding high a lighted Paschal candle, as Christ came forth, resurrected, from the tomb. His resurrection brings light and life into the darkened world of sin. Soon the light fills the Church, as each person's candle receives "light from the unending light." A procession follows, and the Gospel story of the discovery of the empty tomb is read. "Why do you seek the living among the dead?" (Luke 24:5) "He is not here; for he has risen" (Matthew 28:6). Then we sing, over and over again, the hymn, which expresses fully Orthodox "Soteriology." "Christ is risen from the dead, trampling down 'Death' by (his) death, and to those in the tombs, He gives 'Life'." The Divine Liturgy that follows, is the most glorious celebration of the new life in the Kingdom of God.

Making Christ's Work of Salvation Ours

How do we make what Christ did for the whole world, and for every human being, personally our own? How are we able to move from being dominated by death and sin and evil and the demonic, to coming once again into full communion with God, so as to begin restoring in us the image and likeness of God?

We need to accept in faith that this work of salvation is a gift from God, an act of His grace, and to live in communion with God as a result. "For by grace you have been saved through faith; and this is not your own doing, it is the gift of God" (Ephesians 2:8). "Consequently (Jesus Christ) is able for all time to save those who draw near to God" (Hebrews 7:25). The way we share in the death and resurrection of Christ is by believing in Christ through the sacramental life, especially baptism (Romans 6:3-14) and Holy Communion (John 6), and by our struggle to follow His way of life. Christ "became the source of eternal salvation to all who obey him" (Hebrews 5: 9). Thus, being a Christian, means realizing the potential of Christ's work of salvation in our own lives, and as members of Christ's body, the Church. It is a life-long process of growing, with the help of the Holy Spirit, in God-likeness, so that we might more and more "be conformed to the image of (God's) Son" (Romans 8:29).

52. JUSTIFICATION

Q. I have some questions about "Justification." 1) What is the difference between salvation and justification since both are through a dynamic relationship with Christ? 2) What is the difference between deification and justification? 3) How do the sacraments justify? I have read the statement on "Justification" in the Orthodox Study Bible. — *J. C., Charlotte, NC.*

A. The Orthodox view of salvation could be summarized as a process on a time line of: a) *Past* -"I have been saved through the redeeming work of Jesus Christ"; b) *Present* -"I am now in the process of being saved by Jesus Christ through the Holy Spirit in the Church"; and c) *Future* -"I will be saved in fullness in the eternal Kingdom of God." What is the role of "Justification" in this?

Salvation and Justification

In the first part of St. Paul's letter to the Romans, his purpose is to show that Jews, who have the Mosaic Law with its ritual requirements, and Gentiles (pagans) who have the natural inborn moral law, were both incapable of living up to them. Both always fell short. Both, thus, were separated from God because of their sinful condition and acts. All human beings, consequently, are sinners and in need of salvation.

St. Paul says that we can't, therefore, save ourselves. None of us by ourselves can accomplish our salvation on the basis of our own righteousness, our own *dikaiosyne*. None of us is capable of being just (*dikaios*) on our own. Justification *dikaiosis* is not our doing. It is God's doing. It is a gift. It is grace (*charis*).

The only way for *dikaiosis* to be realized in our lives is through the saving and redeeming work of Jesus Christ. He taught, guided, died and was resurrected for the salvation of all of humanity. Only by connecting with that saving work can we be in truth and in fact made just, justified, that is, and become righteous in God's eyes and in reality.

How do we connect with the saving work of Jesus Christ? By faith. God has offered to us the opportunity to respond to what Jesus Christ has done for us. The way we respond is to believe in Him, love Him, obey Him and serve Him. Here is what St. Paul says:

> For no human being will be justified in his sight by works of the law, since through the law comes knowledge of sin. But now the righteousness of God has been manifested apart from law, although the law and the prophets bear witness to it, the righteousness of God through faith in Jesus Christ for all who believe. For there is no distinction; since all have sinned and fall short of the glory of God, they are justified by his grace as a gift, through the redemption which is in Christ Jesus, whom God put forward as an expiation by his blood, to be received by faith. This was to show God's righteousness, because in his divine forbearance he had passed over former sins; it was to prove at the present time that he himself is righteous and that he justifies him who has faith in Jesus" (Romans 3:20-26).

So, we cannot claim salvation on the basis of our own following of the law, ritual or morality. Through faith we receive what God has done through the saving work of Jesus Christ. When we are justified through our faith, we have taken the first step in the process on the road of salvation. In this sense, through what Christ has done, "We have been saved."

But since salvation is a process, the first step must be continued. St. Paul put it this way:

> Since, therefore, we are now justified by his blood, much more *shall* we be saved by him from the wrath of God. For

if while we *were* enemies we *were* reconciled to God by the death of his Son, much more, now that we *are* reconciled, *shall we be saved* by his life" (Romans 5:9-11).

Notice the tenses: formerly we **were** enemies, but "We are **now** justified." Yet, "we **shall** be saved;" "We are reconciled," but in the future "**shall we be saved**."

Justification and Deification

Being made righteous by God as a result of our step into the life of faith begins something real. On every step of the way, we travel the road of salvation enveloped in the divine energies of God, His *charis*, Divine Grace. But we must also conform ourselves freely to His promptings as much as is possible for human beings to live God's way. So while the whole of the Christian life is lived in the sphere of divine grace, we must continue to believe, "commiting ourselves and one another and our whole lives to Christ, our God."

That is why in Romans, St. Paul provokes us, saying, "Do not be conformed to this world but be transformed by the renewal of your mind, that you may prove what is the will of God, what is good and acceptable and perfect" (Romans 12:2).

And that is why St. Peter tells us that we are involved in a process of growth and development:

> become partakers of the divine nature. For this very reason make every effort to supplement your faith with virtue, and virtue with knowledge, and knowledge with self-control, and self-control with steadfastness, and steadfastness with godliness, and godliness with brotherly affection, and brotherly affection with love (2 Peter 1:4-7).

What begins with justification continues with growth toward holy God-like living, which the Church calls "Deification."

How Do the Sacraments Justify?

The Sacraments "justify" precisely because they are the means by which our faith becomes "connected" with the grace that forgives and redeems us. We must also be incorporated into the Body of Christ. Note that in St. Paul's teaching, justification is intimately connected with the sacrament of Baptism:

> So that the law was our custodian until Christ came, that we might be justified by faith. But now that faith has come, we are no longer under a custodian; for in Christ Jesus you are all sons of God, through faith. For as many of you as were baptized into Christ have put on Christ" (Galatians 3:24-27).

In the Sacrament of Chrismation we receive "The gift of the seal of the Holy Spirit" and the Holy Eucharist is "for the forgiveness of sins" and without it "we have no life in us" (John 6:53).

Justification

The most important thing about the teaching regarding "Justification" is the truth that salvation is a gift from God. St. Irenaeus (130-200 A.D.) summed it up:

> Christ redeems us righteously from the apostasy of sin by His own blood. But as regards those of us who have been redeemed, He does this by grace. For we have given nothing to Him previously" (*Against Heresies,* V, ii, 1).

53. "BORN AGAIN"

Q. I am interested in learning where the term "born again" comes from in the Bible. What does the original Greek say, and how is this phrase translated in various versions in English?

–M.P., New Port Richey, FL.

A. This question is valuable because it help us clear up the meaning of this widely used phrase in our country. Often the phrase is used to define Christianity, other times it is condemned because it is used by some to denigrate the religious experience people who have been Christians from childhood.

Rebirth and Regeneration in Baptism

In the teaching of the Church, expressed in the Bible, the phrase "born again" has been applied exclusively to the spiritual rebirth we have received in Baptism and Chrismation with the grace of the Holy Spirit. This is how an early Church Father, St. Justin Martyr (100-165 A.D.) spoke of it, speaking of Baptism.

> We lead (the candidates for Baptism) to a place where there is water, and they are regenerated in the same manner in which we ourselves were regenerated. In the name of the God, the Father and Lord of all, and of our Savior, Jesus Christ, and of the Holy Spirit, they then received the washing with water. For Christ said: 'Unless you be born again, you shall not enter into the kingdom of heaven'" (John 3:3).

The issue has risen when certain Protestant groups developed a new theology regarding being "born again." This view ignored the new birth in Baptism and claimed that even though someone was baptized, that person actually became "born again" when they made a personal confession of faith in Jesus Christ as their Savior. The

Orthodox (as well as Roman Catholics and other "mainline" Protestants such as Lutherans and Reformed groups) hold to the view that this was not being "reborn" for those already baptized. Rather, it was repentance and renewal.

The Bible and References to the New Birth

This question moves us to look more carefully at the Bible passages that are connected with he idea of rebirth, and especially the original Greek and some of the translations.

Perhaps the most important New Testament statement about Christian rebirth comes from St. John's description of the conversation between Jesus and Nikodemos. We read:

> Jesus answered him (Nikodemos), 'Truly, truly, I say to you, unless one is *born anew*, he cannot see the kingdom of God.' Nikodemos said to him, 'How can a man *be born* when he is old? Can he enter a second time into his mother's womb and *be born*?' Jesus answered, 'Truly, truly, I say to you, unless one is born of water and the Spirit, he cannot enter the kingdom of God'" (John 3:3-5).

For the early Church and to this day, the "rebirth" being spoken about here clearly refers to Baptism.

The translation above is the Revised Standard Version. The older, King James Version translates it this way (note the italicized words). "Jesus answered and said unto him (Nikodemos), 'Verily, verily, I say unto thee, Except a man *be born again*, he cannot see the kingdom of God. Nikodemos saith unto him, How can a man be *born* when he is old? can he enter the second time into his mother's womb, and be *born*? Jesus answered, Verily, verily, I say unto thee, Except a man be *born* of water and of the Spirit, he cannot enter into the kingdom of God." The New English Bible translates this passage differently. It refers to being *"born over again."*

Now let's look at what the original Greek text says. What is translated as "born anew" by the Revised Standard Version; and "born again" by the King James and the New King James Versions; and "born over again" by The New English Bible–Version doesn't say that at all in the Greek!

The Greek original says *"Ean me tis **gennethe anothen**, ou dynatai eidein ten basileian tou Theou."* The phrase *"gennethe anothen"* literally means **"born from above."**

The New Revised Standard Version translates the verse correctly: **"Very truly, I tell you, no one can see the kingdom of God without being born from above."**

1 Peter

Two other words that can be translated differently that refer to this same idea are rooted in the Greek verb *"anagennan."* This word is usually translated "regenerate." Usually, it refers to something already living, but which reproduces an organ (frogs "regenerate" lost legs). There are only two verses in the New Testament that use this word. Both are from 1 Peter. The New Revised Standard Version translates the verb form *anagennesas* like this in verse 1:3: "Blessed by the God and Father of our Lord Jesus Christ! By his great mercy he has given us a new birth (*anagennesas emas*) into a living hope through the resurrection of Jesus Christ from the dead . . . ." Since Baptism, according to St. Paul is participation in the Death and Resurrection of Christ (Romans 6:3-11), this general reference to "regeneration" cannot refer to some "rebirth" or "new birth" after Baptism.

The other passage is found in 1 Peter 1:23. Its context is the ongoing living of the Christian life, not as a new beginning after someone has been baptized. The Revised Standard Version puts it this way.

> Through him (Christ) you have confidence in God, who
> raised him from the dead and gave him glory, so that your
> faith and hope are in God.

Having purified your souls by your obedience to the truth for a sincere love of the brethren, love one another earnestly from the heart.

You have been born anew (*anagennemenoi*), not of perishable seed but of imperishable, through the living and abiding word of God; for . . . 'the word of the Lord abides for ever.' That word is the good news which was preached to you.

So put away all malice and all guile and insincerity and envy and all slander.

Like newborn babes (*artigenneta brephe*), long for the pure, spiritual milk, that by it you may grow up to salvation; for you have tasted the kindness of the Lord (1 Peter 1:21-2:3).

St. Peter is talking to newly baptized Christians about their spiritual state, "like newborn babies" and encouraging them to "grow up to salvation." It is growth from spiritual infancy to Christian maturity.

Spiritual Rebirth Refers to Baptism and Repentance

Orthodox Christians properly use the words "born from above," "reborn," "born anew, or even "born again," to refer to their Baptism. But as the passage from St. Peter points out, we also "grow up to salvation." This is a life-long process. Every time we fall, we need to personally repent, regenerate our spiritual lives, and move closer to God. After all, we say repeatedly in our worship, "Let us commit ourselves and one another and our whole life to Christ our God." But never let anyone tell you that you are not "born from above." As an Orthodox Christian, you have been Baptized and Chrismated with the gift of the Holy Spirit!

54. SALVATION TEACHINGS: DIFFERENT VIEWS

Q. I attend a private school run by the Presbyterian Church. I have had conversations with my history and bible teachers about differences between the Presbyterian Church and the Orthodox Church, such the place of the saints in the Christian faith. One topic that isn't clear to me is the differences between the Calvinist/Reformed view and the view of the Orthodox Church regarding salvation. In my school they teach the Calvinist view, which I find difficult to grasp and it seems to contradict itself sometimes. Could you please write a short response that I could present to my class on this subject?

–G. J. K., Tampa, FL.

A. Let us begin by seeing both the Orthodox and the Presbyterian Churches in their historical contexts. Then, we can address the approach of the Orthodox and this particular tradition within Protestantism to the doctrine of salvation. Finally, I want to show how there are different ways to approach this and other doctrines which can be illuminating to all Christians. In this column, we will describe briefly the historical contexts of the two Churches; and describe the distinctive way that the Orthodox Church tells the "Salvation Story."

Looking At The Backgrounds

The Orthodox Church traces its life *historically* to the earliest existence of the Christian experience. It understands itself as founded by Jesus Christ with the sending of the Holy Spirit at Pentecost. Its authoritative recorded sources are rooted in Jesus Christ, the Holy Spirit and the Apostolic Tradition. Its administrative life, through the Apostolic Succession of its Bishops, indicates unbroken continuity from Jesus Christ and the Apostles through the centuries in canonical unity to the present day. Orthodox Christianity today identifies its *doctrinal teaching* as one with the early undivided Church of Jesus Christ of the first eight centuries. Regarding its beliefs about salvation the Orthodox Church draws on the whole of the early biblical and patristic tradition.

The Presbyterian Church, *historically* finds its origins in the reformation movements of the 16th century and in particular with John Calvin's teachings in Geneva, and more specifically with the development of the Reformed tradition in Scotland in the work and writings of John Knox (1513-1572). Its *administrative* order is based on a combination of clergy and lay governance, generally described as "presbyterian" (rule by "elders" in a representative system of Church government), which specifically does not include bishops ecclesiastically understood. Generally, its *doctrinal positions* are various forms of the Reformed (mainly Calvinist) teachings which are expressed in the *Longer and Shorter Westminster Confessions*. In its teachings about Salvation, it holds that it returns to a biblical understanding, which had been either forgotten or suppressed by the historic pre-reformation Church.

Salvation in Orthodox Teaching

A common way of indicating major distinctions between religious bodies is to identify positions, practices or teachings which distinguish them as important emphases. Thus, for example, one could say that the Roman Catholic Church in the area of Church administration is distinguished by belief in the Bishop of Rome, that is, the Pope as the supreme and single head of the earthly Church. Similarly, one could say that the Orthodox Church is governed as a family of self-governing local Churches, whose leader as "first among equals" is the Ecumenical Patriarch of Constantinople.

In a similar way, the "Orthodox Salvation Story" could be succinctly characterized as sharing progressively in Christ's restoration of humanity to the fullness of the image and likeness of God. We call it "Divinization." Here is a very brief outline of the Orthodox Salvation Story.

Humanity was created in the image and likeness of God, understood as both the gift and potential to realize in freedom God's purpose for human beings to become "God-like" in so far as it is possible for created human beings to do so. Sin is understood as the breaking of the fitting relationship between God the Creator and created human beings. In "Adam" (meaning "human being") sin darkened and weakened all of our God-given capacities and caused separation from communion with God. The result was that our human mind, will and desiring were all distorted. Humanity had fallen under the dominion of Death, Sin, Evil and the Devil. Though some of God's original gifts remained, there was no saving power in them.

Through a series of actions God began to prepare the way of salvation by choosing the Hebrew people to be a means for ultimately redeeming and restoring humanity to the potential of God-likeness. In time, the Father sent the Second Person of the Holy Trinity, the Son, to take on complete human nature (mind, soul, body-but without any sin). Thus, in the one person of Jesus Christ we see two complete natures, the divine and the human. We call this the Incarnation. It was necessary for our salvation.

The work of salvation conducted by Jesus Christ consisted of teaching, healing, guiding, and directing our lives toward God-likeness. Through His death on the Cross and His victorious Resurrection He conquered the controlling power and dominion of the demonic over our lives.

We appropriate and share in the saving work of Jesus Christ personally, sacramentally, spiritually, morally and ecclesially in an ongoing and growing process in which we begin, sustain, and realize God's purpose of growth toward communion with Him, always supported by the living presence of the Holy Spirit. We can do none of this alone. But, God does not force us, either. We "work out our salvation" in free cooperation with the essential support of Christ and the Holy Spirit.

Thus, the Orthodox say concurrently and without contradiction:

"I was saved" through Jesus Christ's saving work, especially His sacrifice and death on the Cross and His victory over the powers of Death, Sin and Evil, through His Resurrection from the dead on the third day. Without Christ, there is no salvation.

"I am saved" in the sense that I personally share in the redemptive work of Christ, beginning with my personal baptism in the Death and Resurrection of Jesus Christ. Once that has happened, I am part of the "Body of Christ, the Church," I am no longer under the determining influence of the demonic, I am member of the "household of God," and I have begun a never-ending life-long journey to grow toward rebuilding the God-like image God intends me to be.

"I am being saved" means that the Christian life is an ongoing process of breaking habits and practices and ways of thinking which contribute to my separation from God and God-like ways. It also means that with God's grace I strive to please the Lord and be "built up" more fully. I cannot do this without God, nor can I do it outside the Body of Christ, the Church. Prayer, Worship, Sacramental Life (especially communing the Body and Blood of Jesus Christ), Good Works, Discipline (such as fasting and self-control), Moral Living and above all, Love, contribute to the process of "being saved."

"I will be saved" means that the fullness of salvation comes to all those who believe and grow toward God-likeness as part of God's redemptive plan of salvation which will be fulfilled when Jesus Christ comes again to judge the living and the dead, and fulfill His Kingdom which will have no end.

Space does not permit me to expand this bare outline of the Orthodox Christian understanding of Salvation as I've presented it here. For every assertion, however, I can assure you that there is biblical and early Church support.

55. SALVATION TEACHINGS: ORTHODOX AND PROTESTANT

Q. I attend a private school run by the Presbyterian Church. I have had conversations with my history and bible teachers about differences between the Presbyterian Church and the Orthodox Church, such the place of the saints in the Christian faith. One topic that isn't clear to me is the differences between the Calvinist/Reformed view and the view of the Orthodox Church regarding salvation. In my school they teach the Calvinist view, which I find difficult to grasp and it seems to contradict itself sometimes. Could you please write a short response that I could present to my class on this subject?

– G. J. K., Tampa, FL.

A. Last week we described the backgrounds of the Orthodox Church and Presbyterianism, and we then described the Orthodox "Salvation Story." In this column, we will describe the historic and present positions of the Presbyterian Church regarding salvation and add some final perspectives about understanding the Christian Salvation story.

Presbyterian Salvation Doctrine

One of the difficult things in discussing beliefs within Protestant Churches, of which the Presbyterian Church is one of many, is that on the one hand there are often historic documents which are referred to as representative of the body's beliefs. On the other, the "private interpretation" of the Bible fostered by Protestantism means that these beliefs may be individually modified and sometimes even rejected publicly. As we saw above, the Presbyterian Church in this country is rooted in Calvinism and the teachings of the Scottish reformer John Knox.

The Westminster Assembly (1643-49), held in London, produced the The *Westminster Confession*, which has been foundational for Presbyterians. Based on it are the *Longer and Shorter Catechisms*.

Three main themes regarding salvation were originally part of Presbyterian belief. The first is the teaching that the sin of Adam and Eve was totally corrupting for humanity. Sin, understood primarily as violation of God's law, caused a complete moral, spiritual, breakdown of the original justice with which God created humanity.

The second was "double predestination." This teaching emphasized that God, from time immemorial, predestined those who would be saved and those who would be damned. The "saved" are called by God to justification, and respond with faith, by which they are justified, adopted and sanctified. Those who are not "predestined" cannot be saved, regardless of what they do.

The third historic Presbyterian teaching is the understanding of Jesus Christ's saving work based on Jesus' death on the Cross by which He received the penalty, condemnation and curse due to humanity for its total sinfulness. Referred to theologically as the theory of "penal substitutionary atonement," it is historically a core Protestant doctrine, which is understandable primarily in legal terms.

Later, Presbyterians tended to tone down or even eliminate one or more of these three emphases. Today, one can find "Orthodox Presbyterians" who maintain all three; many Presbyterians have rejected the "double-predestination" teaching or re-interpreted it. The substitutionary atonement teaching remains central to conservatives, while other "main-line" Presbyterians may emphasize other theories of the atonement, seeking to incorporate the sovereignty of God in social and legal institutions.

Thus, it might be fair to say that Presbyterian salvation teaching is characterized by focusing on the death of Christ on the Cross, understood as Jesus bearing, by substitution, the punishment due humanity for its utter sinfulness. Out of this flows the emphasis on free and undeserved justification before God.

A Comprehensive Approach to Salvation

These two approaches to salvation, are the **distinctive** approaches of the Orthodox ("Divinization") and the Presbyterians ("Justification"). There is, however, another approach which we also find in the Orthodox Christian tradition. It is a *comprehensive* approach to salvation which understands the different biblical references to salvation, not as contradictory or mutually exclusive explanations, but representations of different aspects of a full and multi-faceted work of salvation by God for humanity.

The truth is that the Bible and the early Church's teachings about salvation are a rich tapestry of images. The following is a modified version of what may be found in my book *Health and Medicine in the Eastern Orthodox Tradition.*

The focus of the Orthodox church on Christ's victory over death (as the summation of all evils), leading to salvation understood as a process of growth in God-likeness (Divinization), though a central interpretation, does not exhaust the various dimensions of salvation, all of which are biblically rooted.

These dimensions may be explored in the celebration of the Feast of the Elevation of the Holy Cross (September 14). The service of the day is filled with hundreds of allusions and references to other perceptions and understandings of salvation. Here is neither homogenizing of theories nor an undue subordinating of approaches to salvation nor an unbiblical contrasting of perceptions about salvation. Rather, one after another, each vision and understanding of salvation presents its own witness, providing us with a comprehensive mosaic of inter-illuminating understandings of salvation.

One vesper hymn sung at this feast-day service summarizes these understandings, presenting salvation successively as justification, as the deception of the devil, as release of human beings from subjugation to demonic forces, as the washing away of sin by the blood of Christ, as substitutionary redemption, as the assumption of humanity's guilt by the innocent One, as the overcoming of original sin, as the restoration of Eden, as suffering for the remission of sins, as divine condescension and mercy for the salvation of all humanity!

> Come, all you peoples, and let us venerate the blessed Wood, through which eternal justice has been brought to pass. For he who by a tree deceived our forefather Adam, is by the Cross himself deceived; and he who by tyranny gained possession of the creature endowed by God with royal dignity, is overthrown in headlong fall. By the blood of God the poison of the serpent is washed away; and the curse of a just condemnation is loosed by the unjust punishment inflicted on the Just. For it was fitting that wood should be healed by wood, and that through the Passion of One who knew not sin should be remitted all the sufferings of him who was condemned because of wood. But glory be to You, O Christ our King, for Your dread dispensation towards us, by which You have saved us all, for You are good and You love humankind.

Thus we see that the approach to salvation is of a piece with all of the Church's life: it is comprehensive and inclusive and consequently avoids reducing things to a single idea or teaching. Nevertheless, a central theme of the Orthodox understanding of salvation "Divinization," gives it a wholistic perspective and coherence.

The Mosaic of Salvation

An analogy from art may be helpful. We do not have a pile of colored stone cubes, the tesserae that artists use to create a mosaic. Rather, we have a beautiful mosaic icon with pattern and form and themes such as Christ's justifying of humanity through His death on the Cross along with the triumph of Christ over the forces of death and darkness through His Resurrection, together with many other dimensions of Jesus Christ's saving work for humanity.

Thus, we have a comprehensive and inclusive approach to salvation, which holds all the dimensions of salvation together, in a unified and meaningful image of Christian faith and life.

56. SALVATION, SUFFERING, AND SACRIFICE

Q. Is suffering necessary for salvation? That is, why couldn't Jesus die a "natural" death (old age) and then be resurrected?

–B.G., W. Roxbury, MA.

A. This question addresses a central aspect of our Christian faith–the saving work of Jesus Christ.

The Dimensions of Christ's Saving Work

It is important, before addressing this question, to point out that the saving work of Jesus Christ is multi-faceted. In truth, the Bible and Holy Tradition express many different aspects of the "how" of our salvation in Jesus Christ. The idea of sacrifice is just one of many dimensions, though it is an extremely important one. But it must be seen in the context of "the mystery of Christ" (Ephesians 3:4), which is God's "plan for the fullness of time, to unite all things in him, things in heaven and things on earth" (Ephesians 1:10).

Suffering and Sacrifice in the Old Testament

Christ's suffering and crucifixion are key elements in His work of salvation for humanity. How did this come about?

The idea that sacrifice and its related suffering are associated with redemption and salvation is at the very core of the Old Testament way of thinking. From the very beginnings of the story of the Hebrews, the forgiveness of sin and the restoration of broken relationships with God were related to sacrifice and the shedding of blood.

Critical to this understanding is the Passover story. When the tenth plague was about to be visited on the Egyptians and their Pharaoh, the smiting of the first born son of every family, the Hebrews were saved from this punishment. In the book of Exodus (chapters 11-12), we read that Moses instructed that each Hebrew household was to kill a one year old lamb on the 14th day of Nisan. They were told to take some of the blood and splash the door posts and lintel of the door of each house with it. They were to roast the lamb and the family was to eat it with unleavened bread and bitter herbs. That night, the Lord "passed over" all the houses of Egypt, and all first-born sons died, except those in the houses of the Israelites, which were marked by the blood of the Passover Lamb. Then, Moses led the Israelites from Egypt, through the Red Sea on their way to the Promised Land.

Later, when the Jewish people were established in the Promised Land, sacrifices were made by the priests at Passover in the Temple. The Lamb in this context came to be understood as the chief sacrificial victim, giving its life for the salvation of the people. Additionally, sacrifices were continuously offered in Hebrew worship. The sacrificed animal bore the sins of the people.

Because the lamb, in particular, is innocent, pure, meek and gentle (2 Samuel 12:3), it came to be that the Prophet Isaiah's vision of the coming Messiah as an innocent Suffering Servant pointed to the need for sacrifice of the one who was to be the Savior: "He was oppressed, and he was afflicted yet he opened not his mouth: like a lamb that is led to the slaughter, and like a sheep that is before its shearers is dumb, so he opened not his mouth" (Isaiah 53:7).

Jesus Christ - The Sacrifice

In the New Testament, Jesus Christ is understood as the fulfillment the Old Testament prophesies regarding the Messiah. One of the images regarding Him and His saving work is that He is referred to frequently as the "Lamb of God" (John 1:29 & 36, Acts 8:32, 1

Peter 1:19, and twenty-eight times in the book of Revelation). Thus, St. John the Baptist says about Christ, "Behold the Lamb of God, who takes away the sin of the world" (John 1:29).

Christ as the sacrificial Lamb of God is the fulfillment of the original Paschal event for the salvation of the whole world. St. Paul made the identification when he wrote "Christ, our Paschal Lamb, has been sacrificed" (1 Corinthians 5:7).

Combined with the New Testament and early Church's understanding of Christ as the "Suffering Servant" (Acts 3:13, 4:27, 30), Jesus Christ's Passion, Crucifixion and Death became the way of salvation. Fulfilled in the person of Jesus Christ for the salvation of the world, the image of the "Lamb of God" expresses the sacrificial death of the innocent Son and Servant of God on the Cross. We read: "In (Christ) we have redemption through his blood, the forgiveness of our trespasses, according to the riches of his grace which he lavished upon us."(Ephesians 1:7-8).

Jesus Christ - The High Priest

Christ's sacrificial death is especially highlighted in the New Testament book of the Epistle to the Hebrews. There the sacrifices of the Temple and the sacrifice of Christ with His death on the Cross are closely related. So it speaks of Christ "having been offered once to bear the sins of many" (Hebrews 9:28). But this points also to the fact that there is a difference. In the Temple worship the temple priests must repeatedly sacrifice the animals and sprinkle their blood on the worshipers, symbolically cleansing them of their sins.

In Hebrews, Christ is both the one who is sacrificed and the one who performs the one truly effective sacrifice. The Son of God became man, "so that he might become a merciful and faithful high priest in the service of God, to make expiation for the sins of the people" (Hebrews 2:17), Therefore our Savior is the "high priest of our confession" (Hebrews 3:1). As such, "although he was a Son, he learned obedience through what he suffered; and being made perfect he became the source of eternal salvation to all who obey him, being designated by God a high priest after the order of Melchizedek" (Hebrews 5:8-10).

This idea is also expressed by the Church Fathers and in the Liturgy of the Church. An early writing about the year 130 A.D., the Epistle of Barnabas, describes Christ's Crucifixion as taking place "so that we might be cleansed by the remission of our sins, which cleansing is through the blood of His (Jesus) sprinkling." St. Basil (330-379 A.D.) said, "He offered Himself as a sacrifice and oblation to God on account of our sins." As the Cherubic Hymn is sung in the Divine Liturgy, the Priest prays, "In truth You are the One who offers and in turn is offered . . . O Christ our God."

The answer is clear. Christ had to suffer and to die in order fulfill prophesies that God had prepared as the Lamb of God and as our High Priest for our salvation. As if to answer your question, Tertullian (160-225) affirms "It was necessary for Him to be made a sacrifice for all nations."

Suffering and Evil

57. SUFFERING AND GOD

Q. Why does God allow suffering? Is God either uncaring or incapable of helping? Is faith in God no longer justifiable? Does God know? Does God care? Is God a loving God? Is God blameless? Is God parental? Does part of the answer lie in the concept of Free Will, which allows for both good and evil outcomes? Please discuss the Orthodox concept of Free Will. *– T.N.A., Akron, OH.*

A. The answer to your question requires, first, a broad outline of Christian teaching, and then a response to the issue.

Basic Christian Teaching

God the Father (with the other persons of the Holy Trinity) created everything that exists out of nothing, giving it its order and structure and purpose. Humanity however, rebelled against God, sinned and suffered the consequences of breaking our relationship with God. Humanity and the world have been redeemed by God the Son (together with the other persons of the Holy Trinity) who took on human nature in Jesus Christ, taught, healed, guided, directed, died and was resurrected. By acceptance of Christ's saving work through baptism and the sacramental life, the life of discipline and communion with God, each of us may appropriate the saving work of Christ into our own life. God the Holy Spirit (together with the Father and the Son) is present in all life, but especially in the life of persons growing toward the fulfillment of God's purposes, supporting, strengthening and enabling the believer to struggle against evil, suffering and difficulty, in the hope of God's eternal kingdom.

Theodicy

Your questions address the issue that philosophers and theologians call *"Theodicy"* (Theh-OH-deeh-see), that is, how does one understand the existence of a Good, All-knowing and All-powerful God in the face of the existence of evil? On the one side of the equation is the understanding conveyed to us by Divine Revelation that God loves humanity, cares for our well-being, and is fatherly, loving, forgiving and compassionate toward us. On the other is the great suffering that human beings experience.

For some, suffering is an argument that the God of Divine Revelation cannot exist. For others, the God of Divine Revelation exists and our perception of suffering is mistaken or illusionary (the Christian Scientist religion). But for most Christians, the God of Divine Revelation exists and human suffering is real. Theodicy accepts that understanding and seeks to find a resolution.

Free Will or Self-Determination?

The final part of the question above focuses the answer on Free Will; that is, the choices that people make. Right choices bring them into communion with God, His spiritual and moral universe. The result is the experience of goodness and happiness. Wrong choices break communion with the source of Goodness (God) and then people face the consequences of their actions, which can bring suffering and pain. But life is complex, so that often evil people cause suffering among good people; sometimes self-righteous good people cause additional suffering for bad people. Sometimes, both good and evil people suffer in the face of natural disasters, so that in the light of our limitations, even good motives sometimes produce bad consequences. As we said, the issue is a complex one.

Behind it all, however, is the question of choice. In the Old Testament story of Adam and Eve, the message is that humanity as a whole has broken its relationship with God, in whose image it has been created. Humanity and the created universe are consequently, "out of kilter" with ultimate reality. We live in a distorted, broken and corrupt world. The Christian's task as part of the people of God, the Church, is to struggle against evil, sin and suffering. Consequently, both in an ultimate sense and in a personal and social sense, the primary responsibility for suffering is human choice.

"Free Will" is a more or less philosophical term. It assumes that there is a faculty called "the will" which is distinct from the mind and human impulses, and which controls our choices and actions. The Church Fathers, especially of the Greek East, almost never used the term "Free Will" ("*eleuthera thelesis*" or "*eleuthera boulesis*"). Rather, they chose to use the term "*autexousion*," which means "self-determination." We can choose right and wrong as whole persons, using our minds, emotions, choosing ability, spiritual orientation, relationships, etc. If we reject what is good, in a moral universe, some evil will be the consequence, on ourselves, but also on others. The result covers much of human suffering. But to do away with human "*Autexousion*," (self-determination) would in effect dehumanize us. If we couldn't make those choices, we would be like robots and not human. Self-determination makes goodness, virtue, heroism, and creativity possible. But self-determination, by definition also makes evil, sin and suffering potentially unavoidable. Because we are human, we make self-determining choices that often produce suffering. But because we are human, we can also make choices that bring joy, fulfillment, satisfaction and most of all, the realization of our God-like humanity.

Understanding Suffering in the Human Condition

So it would be correct to say that evil exists because of sin. Sin is breaking the relationship between ultimate reality (God) and His creatures who have self-determining capacities (angels and human beings). Suffering arises from this broken condition (sometimes called "The Fall").

Sometimes our suffering results from our own bad choices (example: breakdown of liver function in an excessive drinker). Sometimes suffering of others is the direct result of wrong or evil choices (example: the over 1600 "missing" in Cyprus as a result of the decision by Turks to invade Cyprus). Sometimes events of nature may cause suffering among human beings (example: floods and hurricanes). In the latter case, it is not a specific evil human action that is the cause of the suffering, but the broken condition of creation.

Christian Response to Suffering

The most important practical aspect of this understanding of suffering is that whatever its source, our faith in Jesus Christ, our self-determination and the grace of God are our major resources for dealing with suffering. We find strength in our suffering from the fact of Jesus Christ's own suffering and death on the Cross.

In the first letter of Peter in the New Testament, the issue of suffering because of persecution is dealt with. Yet much of what is said there also helps us face any kind of suffering.

For example, St. Peter calls Christians to trust in God patiently when undeserved suffering comes:

> One is approved if, mindful of God, he endures pain while suffering unjustly. For what credit is it, if when you do wrong and are beaten for it you take it patiently? But if when you do right and suffer for it, you take it patiently, you have God's approval. For to this you have been called, because Christ also suffered for you, leaving you an example that you should follow in his steps. (1 Peter 2:19).

When we suffer because of no fault of our own we are still considered by the Bible to be blessed if we are in communion with God. St. Peter says: "even if you do suffer for righteousness' sake, you will be blessed. Have no fear of them, nor be troubled, but in your hearts reverence Christ as Lord. . . . Keep your conscience clear, so that, when you are abused, those who revile your good behavior in Christ may be put to shame." (1 Peter 3:14-16).

Suffering that arises not from doing wrong, but comes as we live our lives in faithfulness to God bears in it seeds of rejoicing, because in our suffering, we will ultimately find reward in Christ's eternal Kingdom. For the Christian, St. Peter thus says, "But rejoice insofar as you share Christ's sufferings, that you may also rejoice and be glad when his glory is revealed" (1 Peter 4:13). And he adds in 1 Peter 4:19 "Therefore let those who suffer according to God's will do right and entrust their souls to a faithful Creator," showing the source of our strength in suffering is trust in God.

Counsel For Times of Suffering

St. Peter gives every believer this counsel and this promise in the face of suffering:

> Cast all your anxieties on him, for he cares about you. Be sober, be watchful. Your adversary the devil prowls around like a roaring lion, seeking some one to devour. Resist him, firm in your faith, knowing that the same experience of suffering is required of your brotherhood throughout the world. And after you have suffered a little while, the God of all grace, who has called you to his eternal glory in Christ, will himself restore, establish, and strengthen you (1 Peter 5:7-10).

58. IS GOD CRUEL?

Readers note: The Religious Question Box column recently received a long letter, which reacted strongly to some statements in previous columns about the goodness of God. It is possible only to present some sentences that give a flavor of the statement, and summarize the balance, since it was not a question, but the expression of an opinion.

Q. In World War II, I was a member of the U.S. Armed forces. I served as a medic. Over in Europe, every day, thousands upon thousands of bombers filled the skies of Europe with their horrible thunder of death...and you come up with the statement: "Just as our Lord suffered for the salvation of the world." What salvation of the world are you talking about? After 2000 years and the world with all its terrible machinery of destruction is now more barbaric, more vicious, more criminal, and it practices more savagery than ever before. Of all the religious beliefs of this earth, the religion of Christianity is the one that throughout the ages has practiced more savagery than all the other religions of this earth put together.... Not that the unfortunate Jesus wanted it this way. He was a good guy. Yet God killed 12,000 children when Jesus' parents took him to Egypt. Who really killed those children? Herod? Of course not. God was the killer. God could have told Herod not to do it.

Non-thinking religious people think that God created everything we see and don't see... Which means God within six days, just by snapping his fingers created those trillions of huge suns, plus endless species of animals, plus deadly germs...and horrible diseases. A God with all the power could very easily save the world by just snapping his fingers, and without sacrificing his so-called "beloved son" by killing him on the cross.

I wish you would visit just one home where the man of the house has been struck down by one of God's most horrible diseases, Alzheimer's. Praise the Lord, the merciful and compassionate! He is so good! Or people with strokes... Or see God's endless brutality by visiting a children's hospital, or a school of the blind...or brainless children. God is so good! Or go to Ethiopia to see how God punishes the people for their sins! God kills them by starvation, one of the most agonizing deaths known to man.

Yes, Fr. Harakas, you are a good God's lawyer. Keep praising the most vicious, most criminal creature that the ignorant mind of mankind ever imagined that exists... a vile creature that people give the name "God" to Religion? It stands for hate, blood and tears.

– A.L., Marblehead, MA.

A. It is not easy to read this letter. It is not so much the ideas expressed in it; they are standard issues in the philosophical and religious discussions in textbooks about the problem of the existence of evil and a good God. It is rather the passion and hurt and sensitivity for human suffering expressed in this letter. It is so unfortunate that this sensitivity is channeled in the wrong direction. Nevertheless, there is much that can be learned from this writer's expression of compassion for those among us who suffer.

Is God Cruel?

The first thing which needs to be done in order to respond to this statement is to correct some of the erroneous understandings about the Christian faith and the existence of evil. It would take many columns to discuss this issue adequately. Here, nothing more than a very sketchy outline of a response can be made.

The initial confusion about the Christian teaching in this letter is the idea that the Christian Church's teaching implies that God created the world with evil in it. The Bible's teaching, of course, is just the opposite. "...and it was good" is the phrase which teaches that the creation left the hands of God good and without evil.

Most commentators on the creation story, including many of the Church Fathers, understood the creation of the world as a long-term process. The "six days" are a literary device to show the developmental plan of the creation. It was not a "snapping of the fingers" sort of thing. Those words imply a misunderstanding of how God relates with His creation. This phrase seems to imply that Christianity teaches that God is some sort of oriental potentate who arbitrarily switches things around in a capricious way. It has never been a teaching of the Orthodox Church that God acts in such a way in regard to His creation.

Some of the Issues

The issue of evil and the good God is best addressed under the headings of "the laws of nature," "the freedom of humankind," "the existence of sin."

The Laws of Nature: Many of the issues which seem to describe natural phenomena as evil, such as a landslide which destroys a village, would require "the snapping of the fingers approach" to be avoided. In effect this would mean that the laws of nature could never be relied upon. If all the functions of nature, from atoms to chemical reactions, from the laws of thermodynamics to the engineer's calculations of stress, could not be relied upon in ordinary life, there would be chaos. Much of what is called "evil" is the result of mistaken decisions taken by human beings. We could not even exist in a world where the laws of nature were capricious. As a result, their stability and trustworthiness is a sign of God's goodness.

The Freedom of Humankind: The Orthodox Christian teaching is that God created intelligent creatures with the potential of fulfilling themselves by freely choosing to remain in communion and relationship with God. But to be able to freely choose to be in harmony with God's will also means that we can choose to break that relationship. We are confronted with God's expectation of us to do what is good. We must choose. It is just perverse logic to blame God for the evil consequences of human decisions. God did not build bombers and bombs to destroy cities. Sinful and compromised human beings did.

Why did God create us with the ability to choose? To have made us incapable of choosing between right and wrong would mean that we were essentially programmed to do what is good. We would not be free. We would not have self-determination. We would not be "the image and likeness of God." We would not be human beings any more. Giving us self-determination to choose is also a mark of God's goodness.

The Existence of Sin: The Church has understood, from the beginning, that our sinful condition has not only distorted our relationship with God, but in addition, it has corrupted our relationships with our own selves, with our neighbors, and with the rest of creation. This condition of fallenness describes the human situation. The evils which today's letter writer describes are not the result of God's will for us. Nor do they represent how God made His creation. Sin and evil are not of God, they come from us, His creatures.

Salvation

Christ came into the world to lead us out of this condition of sin. His coming was motivated by God's love for humankind. Christ's death on the Cross and His victory over death, sin and evil through His resurrection was not a magical act, a "snapping of the fingers." It was the restoration of the possibility for human beings to rebuild their relationship with God, find their true purpose, and grow with the help of the grace of God, toward the fulfillment of the goals for which we have been created. This means, as self-determining persons, we are to make the choice to conform to the will of God for us, and to act in conformity with His will in goodness and love for others.

In this perspective, every occasion of human suffering, or the potential for human suffering, is an opportunity and an invitation for other human beings to be "the hands of God" in providing compassionate and loving assistance to those who are in need and are suffering. Our model for this is, precisely, Jesus Christ who though innocent of any sin Himself, suffered for our salvation out of love and compassion for a suffering creation.

A Challenge to Christians

As hard as it was to read this letter, since it blasphemed our Lord with horrible accusations and characterizations, its challenge to every reader of this column must be acknowledged. God is not cruel. God loves and cares for His whole creation.

But this letter indirectly points to the Christian affirmation that God expects His followers to do His will. Today's letter writer challenges each of us to assume the role of being agents of God's love and compassion for all who hurt, suffer, and find themselves in despair or adversity and affliction.

The anxious concern for those who suffer evident in this letter is something we Christians need to cultivate in ourselves. It might be valuable for us to re-read the letter above. But we should substitute our own names where God's name is used. Were we to do that, I am afraid our letter writer's criticisms would have much greater justification.

59. GOD AND EVIL

Q. Every time I see a blind child...Every time I see a deaf child...Every time I see a deaf and blind child...Every time I see a child born in such a way that it has to be forever rolled in a chair...I think of the good Lord our God the merciful, the compassionate, who creates those unfortunate children every year by the endless thousands.

–A. L., Marblehead, MA.

Q. Why does God cripple people and give them pain or hardship?

–A. T., East Longmeadow, MA.

Q. Can theologians continue to assert that God did not create evil? It seems as if this creation allowed for evil potentially which according to Aristotelian metaphysics implies that God is responsible for the actual presence of evil in the world. Why are theologians reluctant to trace the origins of evil to God Himself?

– G. L., Brookline, MA

A. The first comment above is from a long letter to the "Question Box" from a reader who speaks here in an ironic manner to underscore his disbelief in the existence of God. He feels the evidence of evil in the world is a strong argument against belief in God. The second question came from a child, who is a believer, but puzzled with what seems to be the conflict between the message she has received that God is good, and the message that God is the creator of all things. In this, her puzzlement is similar to the first writer's.

The third question is from a first year theology student. His question is fundamentally the same as the unbeliever's and the simple believer's questions. How can the Christian faith assert that God is the source of all that is good, that God is the creator of the world and all that is in it, yet deny that God is responsible for the evils that exist in the world?

A Long-Standing Question

I chose to present this question from the three perspectives of this week's questioners to show that the problem of "Evil and a Good God" is a legitimate question which is not motivated only by unbelief. It arises in the believing heart as well as in the mind of the committed and knowledgeable Christian. To fully explore this question requires a great deal of exposition, for which there is too little space in this column. So, the most I can do is provide the most bare outline of a response.

Fundamental Truths About God

Theologians of the Church, based on Divine Revelation, affirm the truths about God that help create the dilemma expressed by today's questions. God is good. In fact, God is *the good*. He is the source of any good there is. Conversely, evil is the absence of the good. Therefore, evil occurs only where there is no communion with God.

Further, Christian theology says that God is all-powerful and can do anything He wants. So the question of God's desire to see suffering and pain eliminated is raised.

In addition, God is the Creator of all that has been created. There is nothing that exists which has not been originally created by

God. These theological truths create the problem. If God is good, and evil exists, and God has created all things, and God is all-powerful, then it would seem reasonable to say, as our first year seminarian argues, that God is also the source of evil in the world.

Many people in seeking to explain away the problem eliminate one of these theological truths, and feel that they thus resolve the question. For example, recently, a Boston area Rabbi wrote a book trying to explain "why innocent people suffer." His answer was that God was not strong enough to change things for the better, so therefore, it is not really His fault. But doing this does violence to truth, which God has made known to us through Divine Revelation. A God who is powerless before evil is not the God of the Bible.

But there is also another truth, which the Church affirms. The truth of freedom and the potential that created reality has to share or not share in God's goodness. Let us see how that influences the way the Church responds to the question of a "Good God and the existence of evil."

The Condition of Sin

The resolution to the dilemma from the Christian point of view is not to deny that God is good, nor to deny that He is the creator of all things, nor to deny that evil exists, nor to deny that God is able to do what He wants. Rather, it points to the fact that the world is not the world that God created. It is a world that has in many ways turned its back on God, which has rejected communion with Him. It is a world that is distorted, fallen and unfulfilled precisely because it is out of communion with God.

Why would God allow such a thing to happen? Because to create humanity without the ability to choose between good and evil, would mean that God would have created robots, rather than human beings made in His own free image and likeness. To be free means, ultimately, to have the ability to say either "yes" or "no" to God. To say "no" to God is to say "yes" to the absence of good, which is evil. As the highest element of all of creation, we humans have infected the whole of creation. The whole world suffers as a result of this separation of creation from the Creator. The Church calls this "the condition of primordial or ancestral sin."

Evil and Evils

There are many kinds of evils. Most of the evils we suffer are the result of human sin, which we inflict upon one another. The victims of war are not killed by God, but by other human beings using their self-determination not for the good but for evil. The victim of slander is not humiliated by God, but by a sinning human being. The condition of sin has distorted the very structures of our created world. Who knows what harm we have done to the gene pool in humanity by our abuse of technology? The deformed children of which the first questioner speaks have not been created fresh by God, but by parents who unwittingly and through no willed fault of their own, share in a genetic heritage long ago weakened and distorted. This too, is part of what is called the original condition of sin. There are voluntary evils; and there are systemic evils. They exist not because God willed them, but because creation has separated itself from the source of all that is good, that is, from God.

The Redeemer and Our Hope

The saving work of Jesus Christ is precisely God's answer to evil in the created reality. He is the victor over all of our enemies: death, sin, evil in its multitude of forms. With His resurrection He has overcome them in principle and in substance. He now makes it possible to begin sharing in the condition where sin no longer reigns -His Kingdom. The Kingdom is where God, who is fully and truly good, reigns. But as long as there is disharmony based on the rebellion of the creature against the Creator, evil and evils will continue to exist in this world. Not because God wills it, but because creatures do. In this situation, God continues to treat us with compassion, mercy and love. He even helps us transform the evils that we suffer into means of growth and spiritual maturation. To blame God is to avoid the real cause of the evils we suffer. Honesty demands more of us.

Icons

60. ICONS AND FAITH IN GOD

Q. Are icons in Church more important than our faith in God? Doesn't God and His presence—our faith in God—take precedence over icons? Don't the icons on the iconostasis impart the meaning of the Christian faith, the presence of God and all the doctrine's of the Church? And aren't the icons elsewhere around the Church supposed to play that role of complementing the Christian truth, serving God, His presence and His truth in the Church?

– A. C. D., Clinton, MA.

A. No, icons are not more important than our faith in God. Yes, in stark and absolute terms, God's presence and our faith in God do take precedence over icons. Yet, we need to understand that God's presence among us has been made visible and concrete, so divine presence and the use of icons are not contradictory. Let's see what we mean by that.

The ancient Hebrews were given the Ark of the Covenant (Exodus 25) as well as the written Word of God in what we now call the Old Testament. In Christ's Incarnation (when the second person of the Holy Trinity, the Son, took on human nature), God became a human being of flesh and blood, and dwelt among us (John 1). His presence and power were manifested in physical deeds such as healing. His Word is communicated to us through the New Testament, a physical thing. According to the Bible, the created world itself "manifests" the divine presence. For example, Jesus teaches that the lilies in the field have a message for us from God (Matthew 6:28-30). In all these, the "presence" of God is made manifest to us.

Icons do the same thing. The mistake is to see icons as something different from all those other God-manifesting material things and to separate God so sharply from them. Icons neither substitute for the presence of God, nor are they antagonistic to the Christian's faith, nor do they stand in opposition to faith and the awareness of the presence of the living God. They are important aids which make us sensitive to the divine presence of God in our lives. They point to the truths of the Christian faith and serve to bring us into the presence of the Lord.

Understood and used properly, icons are part and parcel of our experience of God.

61. ICONS AND THE TEN COMMANDMENTS

Q. If the Ten Commandments say, "Thou shalt not make images and worship them," why do we worship the icons which we make?

– *S.K., Chicago, IL.*

A. This question is legitimate and fair. Of course, when the Church makes and uses icons, it is fully aware of the commandment that you refer to. So that means that both in understanding and in practice, the Church sees the making and the using of icons as something different than the worshiping of images. Let us see how.

The Old Testament Background

The commandment against images is related to the pagan practice of erecting statues of pagan gods. Offerings of various kinds were made to the gods in front of the statues. This practice is called "idolatry," i.e., "the worship of idols."

We need to first note what immediately comes before the commandment about images that you describe. The text reads in Exodus 20: 3 "You shall have no other gods before me." The context about images, thus, is about the worship of false gods, about idolatry, about

Hebrews who were tempted to follow the religious ways of their pagan neighbors. It is a demand of loyalty to "Yahweh," the God who revealed Himself to His chosen people, the Hebrews.

Immediately following the instruction that the Hebrews are to believe in no other god, we have the commandment that you refer to. Here is the whole text:

> You shall not make for yourself a graven image, or any like-ness of anything that is in heaven above, or that is in the earth beneath, or that is in the water under the earth; you shall not bow down to them or serve them; for I the LORD your God am a jealous God, visiting the iniquity of the fathers upon the children to the third and the fourth gener-ation of those who hate me, but showing steadfast love to thousands of those who love me and keep my command-ments (Exodus 20:4-6).

You will note that a strict reading of this commandment would literally prohibit any artistic activity, other than making designs that did not represent anything. The way the commandment reads, it is clear that its purpose, on the one hand, is to keep people from idola-try, that is, the worshiping of false gods. On the other hand, its pur-pose is to move people to love the true God and to keep His com-mandments.

The commandment clearly prohibits the making of images of false gods and worshiping them. But in the Old Testament, it is also clear that it did not mean that artistic objects were prohibited, even when it was connected with the worship of God. For example, we read in the same book of Exodus where we find the commandment about graven images, instructions to the Hebrews on how to make the tabernacle, the center of worship for the Hebrews. "According to all that I show you concerning the pattern of the tabernacle, and of all its furniture, so you shall make it" (Exodus 25: 9). One part of the tabernacle was the "mercy seat." Here are the biblical instructions for the making of the mercy seat.

> Then you shall make a mercy seat of pure gold; two cubits and a half shall be its length, and a cubit and a half its breadth. And you shall make two cherubim of gold; of hammered work shall you make them, on the two ends of the mercy seat.
>
> . . .The cherubim shall spread out their wings above, overshadowing the mercy seat with their wings, their faces one to another . . . And you shall put the mercy seat on the top of the ark; and in the ark you shall put the testimony that I shall give you.
>
> There I will meet with you, and from above the mercy seat, from between the two cherubim that are upon the ark of the testimony, I will speak with you of all that I will give you in commandment for the people of Israel (Exodus 25:17-25).

This is a very important passage for understanding the question of the use of icons in the Orthodox Church. It points to God's commandment that certain "graven images" of angels be used to adorn the mercy seat of the tabernacle. So, the important thing about the commandment is not strictly speaking, the image itself, but the use to which it is put. The focus of the commandment is the use of images for the worship of false gods, that is, idolatry. Further, this passage is important because it makes the mercy seat, with its two cherubic angel figures the precise location where the Hebrew people would "meet" with God: and hear Him speak to them, and receive His commandments. "There I will meet with you, and from above the mercy seat, from between the two cherubim that are upon the ark of the testimony; I will speak with you of all that I will give you in commandment for the people of Israel." A person could assume that the mercy seat was a sort of prototype of the icons used in the Orthodox Christian Church today!

The Christian Tradition

The Christian Tradition from the beginning rejected the worship of images as idolatry. It has never changed this position. However, also from the very beginning, as early as the catacomb period, Christians drew representations of holy persons and events. The Christians also showed respect for the persons and events thus represented. In this they had a common and ordinary practice as a model. It was the custom when a high dignitary visited a city, his portrait would be set up in front of him. The people would salute the dignitary by reverencing his picture. This was a generally accepted way of showing respect.

So, it was natural to bring this practice into the Church. The greeting or expression of respect was a formal kiss. The important point is that it was not "worship" then, just as it is not now worship. It is honor and respect. The Seventh Ecumenical Council in 787 made the point clearly. The honor given to the icon is transferred to the person or event depicted in the icon. But it is not worship, which only belongs to God. Like the mercy seat of the tabernacle, the icon is a place where we meet God and holy persons and events. We celebrate the icons on the first Sunday of Lent. On that Sunday, one of the hymns puts it all in perspective, showing the connection between the tabernacle practice and the icon. In part, it says:

> The grace of truth has shown forth, and the things which were foreshadowed of old have now been fulfilled openly; for behold, the Church has put on the incarnate likeness of Christ...in accordance with the foresign of the tabernacle of the (Old) Covenant, that, keeping the Icon of him whom we worship, we may not go astray.

So we see that worship belongs only to God. The icon points us to Christ and His saints. We honor them through the use of icons. This is not idolatry. Icons do not violate the commandment.

62. THE STATUS OF PAPER ICONS

Q. The quote below was printed in a monthly church bulletin. I was always under the impression that printed paper icons which had not been blessed or which were not being used for devotion could be discarded. This is the quote: "Please be advised that any and all icons are holy by virtue of what they are: images of the divine world. There have been incidents in the past several years where not only printed but also paper ones have wept with miraculous myrrh. Therefore these icons are not to be thrown away in the garbage. Please use them in your home during prayer-time or bring them back to church, or burn them in your fireplace. *—M.E., Boston, MA.*

A. I am sure that this concern may have passed through the minds of many of the readers of the "Religious Question Box." Most of the icons that we see in Churches are painted and not printed. They are usually painted on wood panels or canvas. Most often, they are in some kind of frame.

Some "Paper Icon" Background
In ancient times, icons, often very beautifully done, were painted in hand copied manuscripts -on paper, that is. Such books, of course, were preserved and cherished. They were never deliberately destroyed. With the advent of printing, things changed. The advent of relatively inexpensive color printing brought into being a whole range of icons printed on paper. Some are high quality multi-colored icons that are mounted on wood panels and used in Churches in the same way as hand painted icons.

On the other end of the spectrum, they have been printed in thousands and thousands of copies in books, magazines, the covers of church bulletins, as small "handouts," and are often used as decorations in printed material of different sorts. These mass produced "icons" have instruction and inspiration as their main purposes. Normally, they are not reverenced. Yet, this is not always the case. Some of us have cut out a bulletin icon and framed it, not simply because it was pretty, but precisely because it was a holy reminder. Most of us, also, have paper icons at our home iconostasis.

Making Sense of Paper Icons

With such a wide range of uses of paper icons, it was inevitable that the disposal of perhaps hundreds of such representations would become a concern.

There is no formal guidance about this question to my knowledge in the tradition of the Church. We need to think about it and come to a conclusion. The concern expressed in the church bulletin quoted in today's question is certainly understandable, even if the logic is a bit flawed. The only paper icons that have been reported as flowing tears have been in churches where they were part of the worship of the Church. To my knowledge there have been no reports of tears from icons printed in books or periodicals or from icons tucked in people's wallets.

Nevertheless, respect for icons is an important part of the Church's tradition. The Church struggled for over two hundred years in the eighth and ninth centuries during the "Iconoclastic Controversy" precisely over the issue of respect or *timee* for icons.

Yet, there seems to be something excessive in a stance that would require us to go through every religious magazine, tear out every representation of an icon and burn those pages before we could discard the magazine. There is also something legalistic, fearful and pharisaic about doing something like that. It doesn't seem to fit the Orthodox Christian commitment to freedom and spiritual understanding. We need somehow to be discerning about this issue.

Reverence In Disposing of Icons

We can narrow the question down by stating clearly that any icon of any sort that has been blessed, either by anointing, by means of a specific prayer of blessing, or by being left on the altar table or in the Church for a period of time, should never be discarded thoughtlessly. This would surely be irreverent. The time honored way of disposing of such icons when they can no longer be used is to burn them and scatter their ashes upon the earth.

Next, I think that it would also be the appropriate thing to burn a worn out icon, which though not blessed, has been used in the home, auto or elsewhere in a sacred way. If an icon has served as an aid to worship or for overtly religious purposes, it must be respected as such.

That leaves the "illustrative" type of icon. For example, some parish bulletins include sketches of the icon of their patron saint. Line drawings and photos of icons illustrate articles in periodicals. Are these the same as the icon in a church that is reverenced and censed as part of the worship? It is clear that they are not.

The key is the intent. We should think of such "icons" not as icons, but as illustrations of icons, since they were not created with the intention of being used in a sacred way or as part of worship, but only for the purpose of illustration or education. They are not icons in the full sense of the word.

What To Do With Paper Icons

If, however, you have any doubts about such an illustration, then I would say, save it or display it. If you must dispose of it, then do as the church bulletin says and burn it or return it to your Church. But in the main, I don't believe that we do anything disrespectful if in the normal course of disposing of magazines we also dispose of "illustrations of icons."

You may be interested in "The Paper Icon Project." It invites people to send good quality color paper icons (no Christmas cards, bulletin pictures, calendar tops, etc.) for distribution in mission fields. Collect them and send them to the Orthodox Christian Mission Center, P.O. Box 4319, St. Augustine, FL 32085.

63. DISPOSING OF CHURCH ICONS

Q. When Icons are taken down from the Iconostasis, what is the procedure and canon a church must follow before and during that happening. What is a congregation to do with the Holy Icons which are taken down? Should they be taken away, say to the town dump, or is there a better place for them? *—A.C.D., Clinton, MA.*

A. There does not seem to be any official direction on this matter, either directly in the Canons of the Church or in the policy of the Archdiocese, as my inquiry of the Chancellor's office of the Archdiocese informed me.

The Rudder

But there is mention of the subject in the book commonly used for reference to the Holy Canons, the *Rudder*, or the *"Pedalion"* as it is known in Greek. The passage in question refers to the discussions of the Holy Fathers at the Seventh Ecumenical Council in Nicea in 787. The passage from the Rudder says:

> The holy icons are not adored on account of the material, but on account of the likeness which they possess to the ones pictured by them. Hence the Fathers of the present Council in some addresses said that when the wood forming the shape of the Cross in crucifixes becomes decomposed, it is to be burned; and when the paint and outlines of the pictures in the icons become utterly effaced-i.e. so as to be no

longer recognizable -the wooden board left is burned as use-less wood. Some persons however bury such icons out of reverence. (*The Rudder,* tr. by D. Cummings, Chicago: The Orthodox Christian Educational Society, 1957, p. 419.)

A Difficult Situation

I suppose that a similar approach could be used when replacing icons. Often this is done when we replace the 'westernized' types of icons with more traditional 'byzantine' style icons. I know many Priests who find it difficult to deal with this situation, so they often end up in a storeroom or closet where they are neither disposed of nor are they any more venerated.

A Practical Experience

In my experience at Annunciation Church in Newburyport, Mass., which burned down a number years ago, we were able to save a great many of the icons, but they are in various stages of damage due to the fire. Some of the icons were so badly damaged, we had them burned at a crematorium and the ashes were then placed among other items in the cornerstone of the new Church.

The old Iconostasis Icons were of superior byzantine style, done at the Holy Mountain, but they were too many and too big for us to use in our smaller Iconostasis. We saved all we could, and they were respectfully stored. Some of the icons were very badly blistered. Some were in good enough shape to be restored. The parish has looked into the possibility of doing that. When and if they are restored, we will try to make the smaller ones available to parish-ioners, should they want them. The larger ones from the Iconostasis will be made available to any Orthodox Church which might be able to use them. Those which cannot be restored will be burned. No con-sideration was given to burying the icons.

Handling the Situation

All of this has gone on through a cooperative process involving the Priest, the Church Council and some interested lay-persons. The congregation has been informed of the process through the parish bulletin. In any case, we have not treated the icons which are no longer being used with disrespect. We seek to honor them and to do what we can to continue their use. Those which cannot be kept, we are seeking to dispose of in a respectful manner.

I hope this answer assists you in finding answers to your questions, since, beyond what I quoted above, there do not seem to be any further guidelines of an official character.

64. ICON OF HOLY TRINITY

Q. Why does the icon of the Holy Trinity have the Father pictured on it when man doesn't know what the Father looks like?

– J. K., Montreal, Quebec, Canada.

A. Strictly speaking you are absolutely right. In the Gospel of John we read "No one has ever seen God; the only Son, who is in the bosom of the Father, he has made him known" (John 1:18). In another place in the New Testament we read: "No man has ever seen God..." (1 John 4:12). Elsewhere, Jesus taught His disciples that "...the Father who sent me has himself borne witness to me. His voice you have never heard, his form you have never seen..." (John 5:37).

This teaching is also the teaching of the Fathers of the Church. So, for example, St. Gregory the Theologian taught that God "...is like some great Sea of Being, limitless and unbounded, transcending all conception of time and nature, only indistinctly perceived by the mind, and that very dimly and scantily...God then is boundless and hard to understand, and all that we can comprehend of Him is His boundlessness" (*Orations*, 45). The general truth of theology about the essential nature of God is that He is beyond all efforts at human description.

Describing the Indescribable

Nevertheless, the Bible, the Fathers, preachers, teachers and ordinary people do speak of God. Only we recognize that every word we say in some way is suitable to our understanding, but no way fully adequate to describe God's being. Since we must use the symbols of our language when we would speak of God, in the same way we use depictions in icons as a kind of symbolic language to present beliefs and doctrines.

The best "icon of God," the Bible teaches us, is Christ, the second person of the Holy Trinity who took on human nature and dwelt among us. St. Paul thus refers to "Christ, who is the likeness of God" (2 Corinthians 4:4) and that "He is the image of the invisible God" (Colossians 1:15). In both of these cases, the word "likeness" and the word "image" translate the Greek word, *"eikon,"* or, "icon."

The Icon of God

It is for this reason that the earliest and most popular of all icons throughout the whole history of the Church is the icon of Christ. Jesus Christ is the most striking, direct and clear image for us human beings of what God is like. Conversely, in the early history of the Church, we have almost no efforts to make icons of the Holy Trinity.

We do not have a long tradition of iconography of the Holy Trinity. It was only in late Byzantium, that the theme of the "Hospitality of Abraham" was used in icons of the Holy Trinity. But it was a rather rare icon and its history is not very clear (more will be said about the "Hospitality of Abraham" icon below).

However, in the 17th and 18th centuries Orthodox Church art succumbed to the influence of Italian Renaissance painting with its realistic style. It was only then that an icon of the Holy Trinity began to be painted more widely. But it was in the form of the Father as an "old man," with Jesus and with the Holy Spirit as a dove. It is this icon which you are referring to and which was widely introduced into our Churches. You are therefore correct in raising the question about the appropriateness of such icons. Present theological opinion holds that this kind of icon is wrong theologically as well as artistically, and should not be painted.

"The Hospitality of Abraham" Icon

What then should be painted? The most widely accepted answer to that question is the icon of the "Hospitality of Abraham" which is based on a description of God visiting Abraham and Sarah, in the form of three angels in the appearance of men. The story of how God visited Abraham and Sarah at their home by the Oaks of Mamre is told in the Old Testament book of Genesis, chapter 18. Abraham and Sarah are depicted as offering them hospitality and therefore, without realizing it, offering hospitality to God (Hebrews 13:2).

In a somewhat different form this icon has become a modern classic of an icon specifically of the Holy Trinity through the famous 18th Century work of the Russian iconographer Andrei Rublev, which depicts the Holy Trinity in the persons of the three angels only, eliminating from the icon of the "Hospitality of Abraham" the figures of Abraham and Sarah and any depiction of their home.

The reason this icon is acceptable is that it is clearly symbolic to the point that it makes no claim to any kind of "representation of God" but only points to the presence of the Holy Trinity in this world through the symbolic representation of the angels. This icon has been commented upon widely, both theologically and artistically. At the World Council of Churches Assembly in Vancouver, British Columbia, Canada, in 1983, a slide presentation with commentary was presented on the Rublev "Trinity Icon" at one of the Plenary Meetings.

Present Practice

In consulting with Iconographer Elias Katsaros of Huntsville, Alabama about his present practice in painting the icon of the Holy Trinity, he told me that most of the time he paints the icon in the form of the three angels, alone. But occasionally the Holy Trinity icon includes the figures of Abraham and Sarah together with aspects of their home, "by the Oaks of Mamre."

65. PAINTING ICONS

Q. I am a 28 year old man who finds extreme beauty in icon painting. Please inform me about how I could learn to paint icons, locally if possible.   *–G. G., Clifton, NJ.*

A. I would like to answer your question by first just saying a few words about the beauty and truth of the icons, and then, to give you some counsel and advice as to how to proceed.

What is the Beauty of the Icon?

The best way to approach the icon so as to understand its beauty is by way of theology. There are, of course, many kinds of beauty, including harmonious design, balance and color. A stroll through a major art museum will show us many forms of created beauty. A stroll through a garden, in the mountains, along the ocean or a lake or a stream, will show us another kind of beauty. Viewing animals provides us with another sense of the beautiful. When we approach people, there are some who are physically beautiful. These people are often highly appreciated in our society. But we know that there is another kind of human beauty which is much more important: it is the beauty of the soul which radiates from a life, whether the bodily appearance is beautiful or not. There is a soul beauty, a spiritual beauty which can captivate us.

Such is the icon. In its appearance it deliberately does not seek to copy the external and material beauty of worldly things in themselves. Rather, through its reverse perspective, its elongated lines, its formal drapings, and its coloring, it points to the spiritual reality of its subject. For example, an icon of Christ is not seeking to present a "photographic" representation of Christ at all. It leads us to look beyond, to the divine nature of Christ, as well. It presents to us a transfigured reality, an image of the reality of Christ who was both fully God and fully a human being in one person.

The beauty of icons comes from their spirituality, from the inner light which they seek to capture. But an icon is more than this. It is not just a "picture." In Orthodox liturgical life, the icon is "reverenced" by the faithful. That is, it is kissed, or "saluted" by the faithful as they enter the Church building, or in their own private devotions. This is not "worship" since we worship only God. It is honor and a means of communication. The Seventh Ecumenical Council, held in Nicea of Asia Minor in 787 A.D., declared the faith of the Church in regard to icons. When believers honor an icon by reverencing it, the honor is not accorded to the paint and wood which physically make it up, but is conveyed to the person or event depicted in the icon.

Thus, an icon is really not an icon unless it is also used faithfully in a devotional way. It is not just an art piece. Not just a beautiful object. In its fullness it must be part of the experience of devotion. Only when the icon enters the personal and corporate experience of prayer and sacramental life does its beauty fully express itself. The icon becomes real in the atmosphere of prayer and worship.

It is for this reason that traditionally, the first preparation for painting an icon is prayer. The act of creating an icon is itself properly an experience of worship and devotional service.

Learning More About Icons

I would strongly suggest that you begin learning how to paint icons by learning as much as you can about them in the context of faith and the tradition of the Orthodox Church. Begin learning about the faith of Eastern Orthodox Christianity, for it is in this context that iconography has developed. A book which discusses the Orthodox Faith in the frame of reference of the icon is Ernst Benz's *The Eastern*

Orthodox Church: Its Thought and Life. (Garden City, NY: Doubleday & Co., Anchor Books, 1963).

Next, I would suggest that you read some books about iconography. There are many of these in English. I would recommend that you start with a book about the history of iconography. Though there are many other good books on the subject, read a good, illustrated history of Iconography, such as *Early Christian and Byzantine Art* which is part of the Pelican History of Art series, (Middlesex, England: Pelican Books, 1980). It was written by John Beckwith.

I would then suggest you read one of the three following books on the artistic theory and theology of Iconography, so that you can have a thorough background on the subject. The most simple and clear is by Constantine Cavarnos, *Orthodox Iconography*, (Belmont, MA: Institute on Byzantine and Modern Greek Studies, 1977). A fuller treatment on the development and historical as well as theological background is Constantine D. Kalokyris', *The Essence of Orthodox Iconography*, (Brookline, MA: Holy Cross Orthodox Press, 1971); The standard theological interpretation of icons is by Leonid Ouspensky, *Theology of the Icon*, (Crestwood, NY: St. Vladimir's Seminary Press, 1978).

If you want, you could also profit by reading two short writings by Church Fathers on icons: St. John of Damascus, *On the Divine Images* and St. Theodore the Studite, On the Holy Icons, (Crestwood, NY: St. Vladimir's Seminary Press, 1980, 1981).

Then, learn something about technique by reading a handbook about icon painting: *The Painters Manual* of Dionysios of Fourna, rev. edition, translated by Paul Hetherington, (London, The Sagittarius Press, 1981). This manual teaches you how to prepare materials, describes how Old Testament themes and New Testament topics should be painted, including the parables and miracles. Sections describe how martyrdoms, church buildings and the epigrams on the icons are to be painted.

All the books mentioned above can be obtain by writing or calling Light and Life Publishing Co. or any Orthodox Bookstore. If your parish has a bookstore, check there first where they might have the book or order it for you.

You may wish to subscribe to a magazine which is published by an organization of iconographers, *Sacred Art Journal.* You can learn about it by writing to 2907 Oakwood Lane, Torrance, CA 90505.

Getting Training

The best way to learn iconography is to work with an Iconographer of good reputation. Ideally, you should study under one of the master iconographers on the Holy Mountain Athos in Greece, or with an iconographer in Greece or this country who has many years of experience and whose iconography "speaks" to you in a special way. This means that you should study the works of many different iconographers. Unfortunately, there are no schools for iconographers in this country, to my knowledge.

Since you ask that you would like to study locally, I would suggest that you visit some Orthodox Churches in the New Jersey and New York area, so as to get the "feel" of the iconography of several iconographers in the area. Speak to the parish priests of the parishes which you visit for information about the iconographers. Then, approach one of these local iconographers whose work you find inspiring and especially beautiful. It is possible that they will provide you with lessons. I am sending to you a list of Greek Orthodox Churches in your area for you to visit.

66. ICONS OR STATUES?

Q. What objection does the Orthodox Church have to three-dimensional artwork when depicting the Lord Jesus in human flesh, and the saints? In Exodus 25:18-22, Almighty God is instructing Moses to erect a Tabernacle. He said, "...make two cherubim out of hammered gold...", and in 1 Kings 6:23-32, Solomon is building the first Temple in Jerusalem, and it is stated that "In the inner sanctuary he made a pair of cherubim of olive wood, each 10 cubits high." But if we go to Exodus 20:4,5, it is stated in the Decalogue: "You shall not make for yourself an idol in the form of anything...", presumably to worship. But this is not the case in the above two references. The point of the question is that if God wanted the spiritual world depicted for His mercy seat in the Holy of Holies, could we not also depict sanctified humans—not to worship, but to venerate?   *–E.V.S., Purchase, NY.*

A. Your question reminds me of another question that was discussed earlier this year in the Religious Question Box column, in the *Hellenic Chronicle*. There the question had to do with crucifixes and whether or not the corpus of Christ on the Cross was a statue. The answer distinguished between bas-relief representations and statues. The key passage, explaining the difference, said that bas-relief representations were acceptable, and statues were not.

> Statues are defined as fully rounded figures capable of "being felt on all sides with the hand and fingers." Bas-relief representations, carvings and castings are "low relief" art forms where the figure is carved so that it projects somewhat from the background on which it is placed but is not a fully formed figure that can be felt on all sides "with the hand and the fingers." In general, this means that if a figure is not free standing, without a defined back and has a "medallion like" appearance it is not a statue, according to this definition. Consequently, though the figure is carved in part, that does not make it a statue. It must be modeled in a life-like way from every aspect and essentially free standing.

The Issue

The earlier question was based on a concern that a crucifix might be a statue and that was seen as a serious fault. Today's question takes the opposite perspective, and in essence, asks "What is so wrong with statues?" In defense of this view, the questioner presents Old Testament passages that refer to God's instructions to the ancient Hebrews to provide for some carvings in the Ark of the Covenant, which was like a traveling chapel for the Hebrews as they wandered in the desert. Subsequently, these things were placed in the Holy Temple in Jerusalem and other carvings were also made.

This is contrasted with the Commandment that rejects out of hand any idols, but in language that also seems to reject any kind of representation. The text reads as follows: "You shall have no other gods before me. You shall not make for yourself a graven image, or any likeness of anything that is in heaven above, or that is in the earth beneath, or that is in the water under the earth; you shall not bow down to them or serve them" (Exodus 20: 3-5).

Reconciling the Views

The apparent contradictions are not so clear upon investigation. On the one hand it is not clear from the Old Testament description whether the angelic representations were statues or bas-relief, as defined above. What is clear is that they are representations or like-nesses "of (some)thing that is in heaven above," not to speak of things "in the earth beneath." The implication is that when the commandment was given, the only things that were carved as images were religious statues for use in worship. Hence, "you shall not bow down to them or serve them." Otherwise, it would be a prohibition against any kind of art that required any kind of carving or modeling, which, as you point out, would seem to be violated by God Himself!

Idolatry Condemned

Clearly, there must be some other interpretation. This commandment, in fact, is a commandment against idolatry. Here both the biblical and ecclesial traditions are clear: there is absolutely no compromise with idolatry. One example from the Old Testament is found in Deuteronomy 29:16-17, where it speaks of the example of the Hebrews in Egypt and other lands, in "the midst of the nations through which you passed; and you have seen their detestable things, their idols of wood and stone, of silver and gold, which were among them." The Old Testament condemnation of idolatry is frequent and fierce, especially in the great prophets such as Isaiah and Jeremiah. Idolatry means betrayal of God! One of the things the Apostles required of new converts was that they should "abstain from the pollutions of idols" (Acts 15:20). In Church life, the Seventh Ecumenical Council was careful to show that the honoring of icons was not idolatry.

What is wrong with idolatry? Idolatry (literally, the "worship of idols") substitutes some created thing for God and makes that thing the central and key aspect of life, rather than God. Often, it is religious: "another god." But even more often, it is some other thing or experience or habit that becomes central in a person's life, displacing God. People can make their jobs into idols. Love for money or love for fame, or devotion to some cause can supplant God in their lives. Vices can become idols, such as the abuse of drugs.

Consequently, every kind of idolatry, especially immoral idolatry, should be fought against vigorously. This is what St. Paul says about this kind of idolatry: "Put to death therefore what is earthly in you: fornication, impurity, passion, evil desire, and covetousness, which is idolatry. On account of these the wrath of God is coming. In these you once walked, when you lived in them. But now put them all away: anger, wrath, malice, slander, and foul talk from your mouth. Do not lie to one another, seeing that you have put off the old nature with its practices" (Colossians 3:5-9).

Why Bas-Relief and Not Statues?

Clearly, the Orthodox Church wants to draw a sharp line between acceptable and harmless representations and the danger of promoting idolatry in areas that could be misused religiously. So, on the one hand, it does not oppose the use of statues for non-religious purposes, such as the statue of a civic leader in a public square.

Because of its Incarnational theology, based on the belief that the Son of God, the second person of the Holy Trinity, took on human material nature and dwelt among us, it has a sacramental approach to religious life. That is, material things can express spiritual realities. So long as these material things, such as the Bible or icons or church architecture, do not substitute for God, they are not idolatrous. The danger with fully rounded statues in worship is that they are too much like the idols that were worshipped and condemned throughout the Old Testament and the New Testament periods.

Some say that we are too sophisticated for idolatry, but St. Paul's admonition about moral idolatries argues against that perspective. The Orthodox Church clearly wants to draw an absolutely clear line between acceptable representation and idolatry; it draws it at the use of statues in worship.

Heaven and Hell

67. LIFE AFTER DEATH

Q. The Roman Catholic Church teaches that our spirit undergoes purification in purgatory. My Protestant friends claim that this is heresy, found nowhere in the Bible. I was wondering what the Orthodox Church teaches on this, and on what grounds do they teach it?   *– P.K.J., Orange City, IA.*

A. The writer of this letter to the "Question Box" is a Roman Catholic student studying at a Protestant college.

Life After Death

The teaching of the Christian Church about life after death is based on our expectation of Jesus Christ's Second Coming. As we say in the Creed, ". . . and He will come again in glory to judge the living and the dead. His Kingdom will have no end," and "I expect the resurrection of the dead." Throughout history, the Orthodox, the Roman Catholic and most Protestants, have taught that we live after our physical lives end, and that we will experience life everlasting after Christ's Second Coming. But there are also many differences among the various church bodies regarding life after death.

A case in point is the Roman Catholic teaching regarding Purgatory. This teaching is unique to Roman Catholicism: it is not found either in Protestant or Orthodox teachings.

The Roman Catholic Teaching On Purgatory

The teaching about Purgatory is that it is a place or condition of temporal punishment where people who have died while in a state of grace suffer so as to pay for the ordinary ("venial") sins they have committed. In Purgatory, the punishment that is due even for forgiven sins, but which the person did not live on earth long enough to fulfill, is cleansed. Purgatory comes from the word "purge" and the image used is a fire that removes impurities from gold when it is refined.

The Roman Catholic Catechism puts it this way:

> The Church gives the name Purgatory to this final purification of the elect, which is entirely different from the punishment of the damned. . . . The tradition of the (Roman Catholic) Church, by reference to certain texts of Scripture, speaks of a cleansing fire (1 Cor 3:15; 1 Pet 1:7). As for certain lesser faults, we must believe that, before the Final Judgment, there is a purifying fire (paragraph 1031).

The Basic Rationale

Roman Catholics, Protestants and Orthodox refer to nearly all the same passages in the Bible regarding prayer for the dead, but interpret them differently. The Protestants reject praying for the dead; the Roman Catholics not only pray for the dead, but have also developed the idea of Purgatory; the Orthodox pray for the dead, but reject the belief in Purgatory. How can such a thing be? We can begin, by looking at another passage from the official Roman Catholic Catechism.

> To understand this doctrine and practice of the (Roman Catholic) Church, it is necessary to understand that sin has a double consequence. Grave sin deprives us of communion with God and therefore makes us incapable of eternal life, the privation of which is called the 'eternal punishment' of sin. On the other hand every sin, even venial . . . must be purified either here on earth, or after death in the state

called Purgatory. This purification frees one from what is called the 'temporal punishment' of sin. These two punishments must not be conceived of as a kind of vengeance inflicted by God from without, but as following from the very nature of sin (paragraph 1472).

If you look at this passage carefully, you will see a distinction between two kinds of punishment, "eternal punishment" and "temporal punishment." The presupposition is that every sin has to be punished, even when forgiven. Though the spiritual dimension of a sin can be forgiven there remains a portion of the sin that must be paid for, worked off, or redeemed by good actions or deeds. This "temporal punishment" is at the heart of the teaching regarding Purgatory.

Roman Catholics hold that there is no purpose to praying for the dead if that prayer doesn't help them remove the "temporal punishment" due their sins, if they didn't do it for themselves in this life. This eventually led to the practice of Indulgences, according to which, living persons could do good works to erase the "temporal punishment" of deceased persons.

Orthodox Approaches

Contrary to this view, the Orthodox Church thinks differently on this subject. The most important question is the nature of sin and its forgiveness. Sin consists of both deeds and the dispositions of our soul. Whenever these are contrary to God-like living, they separate us from communion with God. Rather than understanding sin primarily as a violation of a divine law that requires punishment, the Orthodox Church emphasizes the broken relationship with God in sin. For this to be overcome, we must repent wholeheartedly and call upon God's mercy for forgiveness of our sins.

If that repentance is genuine and sincere, then God forgives our sin. All of it. There is nothing left for us to do, other than make restitution to someone we may have harmed, not as "punishment," but as an expression of our true repentance. When we repent of our sins, we are fully cleansed. We see this with clarity in the Holy Sacrament of Confession, about which Jesus said to His Apostles "Receive the Holy Spirit. If you forgive the sins of any, they are forgiven" (John 20:22-23). So no punishments are required or demanded. God is merciful and forgiving for all those who truly repent and commit themselves to living according to His will in an ongoing spiritual effort to be God-like in our lives.

So where does that leave us regarding praying for the dead? In a paradox. Repentance is possible only in this life, as far as we know. If a person died in a state of unrepentance, it would logically mean that he/she died with sins unforgiven. Our Orthodox faith, however, would have us pray for the souls of the dead, imploring God to be merciful to them. It is not a question of guarantees, or being punished or relieving punishment. It is an appeal to the love and compassion of God.

An analogy is when a loved one is sick and in danger of death. The physicians give us no hope. Yet, we still pray, asking that God mercifully extend the earthly life of our relative or friend. We know that there is no guarantee that our prayer will be answered as we want it answered. Yet, we pray anyway. So it is with the Orthodox way of praying for the departed dead. God is Lord. We appeal to His kindness, compassion and tender mercies for the departed. The rest is up to God. So we pray, "May the Lord God place his/her soul where the righteous repose. Let us ask for the mercies of God, the kingdom of Heaven, and the forgiveness of his/her sins from Christ our immortal kind and God."

68. GOING TO HELL

Q. If God is such a loving and forgiving God, how can he send anyone to Hell!

–J.K., Moline, IL

A. On the surface, your question has a kind of logic to it, and you are not the only person to raise the question. In many ways, it is a very modern question because of the way twentieth century people understand love and forgiveness. In other ways your question also repeats a very old understanding of how persons eventually end up in hell. So there are some things which need to be clarified in your question. Once these are made clear, the answer to your question will become self-evident. Let's look at these various aspects of your question.

A Loving and Forgiving God

For modern people, a serious misconception about the meaning of love has become widespread. People often confuse love with indulgence, that is, with never saying no to anyone, with giving people what they want and ask for, with short-term giving of pleasures. This is not the biblical understanding of love. Love is to be concerned about the genuine well-being of a person for their own sake, and not for any benefit of the person who loves. Love is selfless concern and action for the genuine good of another. The greatest act of love was the sending of God's Son, Jesus Christ, into the world to teach, heal, die for our sins and to conquer sin through His Resurrection, for the sake of the salvation of the human race. God loves us for our present and eternal benefit: our salvation. *If we don't receive that act of love and make it our own, God cannot change the inevitable consequences of our sinfulness.* He cannot and will not force us into heaven!

So, the same thing has to do with forgiveness. Forgiveness is meaningless unless there is repentance. God is forgiving and always waiting -in fact, anxious- to forgive us. The condition that makes that forgiveness possible is our repentance. To repent means that we are genuinely sorry for a wrong act or thought, that we resolve to not repeat it, that we are willing, if necessary, to make recompense for it. In practice, the Orthodox Church calls us to repent continuously, as, for example the "Jesus Prayer" when repeated throughout the day has us say, "Lord, Jesus Christ, Son of God, have mercy on me, a sinner." Any forgiveness that could come without heartfelt repentance would be "cheap grace," and could not really change our lives.

When there is true repentance on our part, God forgives. Without it, there can't be any forgiveness. So our eternal destiny as well as the quality of our present lives is lived either in heaven or hell, depending on God's response to our genuine needs and our repentance. The wonderful thing is that God is always ready to respond to our need for salvation and to our repentance. The whole Christian Tradition assures us of that. But it does not mean that God is a sentimental pushover for all our self-indulgent desires. Salvation is serious business!

Who Sends Whom To Hell?

There is a 19th century icon that presents Jesus as a Judge seated on a throne at the end of the world, making decisions about who goes to heaven and who goes to hell. The unfortunate implication of this icon of the Last Judgment is that somehow, God arbitrarily makes an off-the-cuff decision at that moment, "sending" us in either direction. However, that is not a correct interpretation.

The Bible and the Church's Faith are clear in teaching that the Kingdom of Heaven is already begun in and among us in this life. Eternal life, understood as communion and relationship with God doesn't begin at death, but right now, in this life. Hell also begins in this life. When we are separated from God, when we break our communion with Him, when we live our lives in ways that are contrary to the God-like way human beings ought to live, then hell has begun for us, already! Is not a drug-addict in hell? Is not a criminal already in hell? Are not liars, or persons who have hope only in material things, or selfish egotists, for example, already living in hell?

The final judgment at Christ's Second Coming will confirm what already exists in us. There is nothing arbitrary about God's judgment at all. If in this life we seek to live close to God, seek to obey His will, respond to His love and forgiveness with love for Him and with love for our neighbor, if we witness to our faith with regular church attendance, participation in the sacramental life, share our resources to help those in need and to do the work of God, we are already sharing in the life of heaven. If we do none of these, if we do the opposite of these things, then we have already consigned ourselves to hell.

Of course, the loving and forgiving and merciful God is waiting-anxiously waiting-for those of us on the way to hell to genuinely repent and change our ways.   If we do that in this life, *He is always ready to forgive us.*

The Bible and Hell

In the light of the above, the seriousness of the doctrine of hell is evident. The New Testament is uncompromising about it. Here are just a few passages which you might wish to contemplate.

Jesus taught in His Sermon on the Mount, "I say to you that every one who is angry with his brother shall be liable to judgment; whoever insults his brother shall be liable to the council, and whoever says, 'You fool!' shall be liable to the fire of hell" (Matthew 5:22).

In the same place, Jesus taught us in a dramatic and exaggerated way, to make His point that we should do everything possible to avoid sinning, with these memorable words: "If your right hand causes you to sin, cut it off and throw it away; it is better that you lose one of your members than that your whole body should go into hell" (Matthew 5:30).

To the hypocritical scribes and Pharisees, He threw out the challenge: "You serpents, you brood of vipers, how are you to escape being sentenced to hell? (Matthew 23:33). The whole Parable of the Rich Man and Poor Lazarus (Luke 16:19-31) shows Jesus' teaching of heaven and hell dramatically and clearly. The teaching of the Bible is clear, those who live lives of sin without repenting, without accepting the forgiveness of God, without communing with God, and without faith, will undergo "a punishment of eternal fire" (Jude 7).

Now Is the Time!

In his *1st Treatise on the Priesthood* St. John Chrysostom said the following about heaven and hell.

> The majority it is true of those who are not very sensibly minded propose to be content with escaping hell; but I say that a far more severe punishment than hell is exclusion from the glory of the other world, and I think that one who has failed to reach it ought not to sorrow so much over the miseries of hell, as over his rejection from heaven, for this alone is more dreadful than all other things in respect of punishment. (Sec. 12).

This is serious business! There is no compromise or softening or "explaining away" of the doctrine of hell in the New Testament or in the Church Fathers. It is real. It begins now. It lasts forever. So don't be fooled. Now is the time to do something about it. The "something" we all need to do is to repent, and to repent continuously, accepting daily what we say in the Creed, that Jesus came into the world to save us, and what we say in the Divine Liturgy repeatedly, "let us commit ourselves and one another and our whole life to Christ our God."

69. HELL AND GOD'S GOODNESS

Q. Your book *The Orthodox Church: 455 Questions and Answers* mentions some quotes about Hell. Frankly, one of the things I find very incompatible with my image of God as a loving being is a hell where one suffers. Is the devil in charge of hell? Would a loving God allow anyone to suffer this way?   *–G. E., Sacramento, CA.*

A. It is interesting to note that in the book there are questions and answers on heaven, but none on hell! Strangely, in the book hell is not even mentioned in the "Index of Topics." So the question is a timely one and useful.

The New Testament Teaching About A Merciful God

The Church's teaching is based on what has been revealed to us in the Scriptures and in the ongoing Holy Tradition, both forming a single source of teaching regarding truths about God, human existence, redemption and salvation.

It is, of course, true that the Church knows God to be merciful and forgiving. The life of the Holy Trinity is love, and in Himself and in His relationship to us, "God is love" (1 John 4:8). God's love for us is expressed in many ways. He created the world, gives life to us, provides for us. Especially we know the love of God in that He sent His Son, Jesus Christ, into the world for our salvation. "For God so loved the world that he gave his only Son, that whoever believes in him should not perish but have eternal life" (John 3:16).

Though we constantly rebel against God's will, He is consistently patient with us. He is *"makrothymos"* -long-suffering; *"polyeleos"* -full of mercy; *"philephsplachnos"* -lovingly compassionate; *"eleimon"* -forbearingly merciful. He awaits our repentance and our turning back to Him in whose image we have been created. God does not force us into relationship with Him. One of the inviolate things He has given to us is self-determination. We can choose to belong to His household, or we can choose to stay out of it. That is why Jesus "said to all, 'If any man would come after me, let him deny himself and take up his cross daily and follow me'"(Luke 9:23).

But what of those who continue to live apart from God? What shall we say about the person who rejects God throughout this life on earth? This willful rejection of God is what we take with us into eternity. What we are in this life in regard to our relationship with God, we take into the next. God's "judgment" is really nothing other than what we have prepared for ourselves. The unrepentant person, by his or her own decision is both unwilling to know God and takes that unwillingness into eternity.

The New Testament Teaching About Hell

There are several words in the Bible and the Patristic Tradition that are usually translated as "hell" in English. In the Old Testament, often the word is *"sheol"* meaning sometimes the place of all the dead, though in some passages, it is expected that the dead will not remain there forever (Psalm 16). In the New Testament, a frequently used word for the state of the unrepentant who reject God and His ways is *"Gehenna,"* that is, the final place of the wicked after the Last Judgment. Another term used is "Hades" meaning primarily the state of waiting for souls of the deceased before the Last Judgment. The word "hell" itself is an Anglo-Saxon word without direct connection with the biblical words.

We can see that the New Testament presents Hell as a lost opportunity for those who deny God. Given human self-determination, it must exist. Note how the two following passages express this.

The passage from John 3:16 quoted above, teaching that God's love for the world was so great that He sent his Son into it for our salvation, continues with these words that show that separation from God in eternity is our own doing.

> For God sent the Son into the world, not to condemn the world, but that the world might be saved through him. He who believes in him is not condemned; he who does not believe is condemned already, because he has not believed in the name of the only Son of God. And this is the judgment, that the light has come into the world, and men loved darkness rather than light, because their deeds were evil. For every one who does evil hates the light, and does not come to the light, lest his deeds should be exposed" (John 3:17-20).

Similarly, the passage quoted above from the Gospel of Luke, quoting Jesus saying that whoever so chooses may follow Him, continues with these words:

For whoever would save his life will lose it; and whoever loses his life for my sake, he will save it. For what does it profit a man if he gains the whole world and loses or forfeits himself? For whoever is ashamed of me and of my words, of him will the Son of man be ashamed when he comes in his glory and the glory of the Father and of the holy angels" (Luke 9:24-26).

Hell Is A Clear Biblical Teaching

In many different ways, the New Testament teaches the existence of Hell. It uses many different images and characterizations, but all clearly indicate that after death there is a situation in which people who simply had no place for God in their lives in this life, will continue that way in the next. Except that since the afterlife consists of either communion with God or no communion with God, the latter is not a pleasant experience, since there is nothing else.

So, for example, those who refuse communion with God are "cast into outer darkness" with "weeping and gnashing of teeth" (Matthew 25:30, 13:42). Another biblical image of hell is "everlasting fire prepared for the devil, and his angels" (Matthew 25:41). Elsewhere, it is said that these go "into hell (*'Gehenna'*) into unquenchable fire." St. Paul teaches that this becomes a time of God's just wrath, that brings "tribulation and anguish" (Romans 2:5, 8 and following) or "destruction" (2 Thessalonians 1:9). In the Book of Revelation, the "second death" (the first is the spiritual death in this life) leads to the symbolic description of being cast into a "lake which burns with fire and brimstone." These characterizations should not be understood literally. We don't know exactly what either heaven or hell will be like. But these images of hell graphically show us how separation from God is not to be desired.

The Source of Our Understanding

While everyone is entitled to make the choice about what they will believe, there is a certain inconsistency in picking and choosing what we want from God's revelation of Himself and His ways to us. If we accept the message of God's love for humankind, of our creation with the freedom to choose for or against Him, but reject the consequences of that choice, then we must acknowledge that we are not being consistent.

70. FREEDOM TO CHOOSE IN HEAVEN?

Q. Are those souls who are in Heaven capable of sinful thoughts or deeds? Or does one relinquish the ability to choose between right and wrong when one joins the Church Triumphant? If one still does have that choice, could one get booted out of Heaven, as Lucifer was, after being admitted?   *–J. K., Phoenix, AZ.*

A. Let's begin by pointing out that Divine Revelation gives us very little detailed information about the here-after. Most of the descriptions of heaven and hell are graphic picture-images intended to convey simple truths: hell is bad to be in; heaven is good to be in. What makes hell bad is that it is a state or condition of not being in communion with God. What makes heaven good is precisely that those in heaven are in communion and relationship with God.

Here is an outline of what the Orthodox Church teaches about life after death.

WE Prepare Our Place In Eternity: God the Father, through the saving work of His Son Jesus Christ, and by means of the sanctifying work of the Holy Spirit, offers salvation to everyone. Our response to God's gracious offer of salvation and redemption determines our place in or out of His Kingdom in eternity. In short, once we become followers of Christ, God lets us make the daily choices that lead eventually to heaven or to hell.

The Partial Judgment: When we die, we begin immediately to experience a foretaste of heaven or hell. This means that until the End-Times, when Christ "will return to judge the living and the dead," those who know God through lives of faith, prayer, worship, sacramental life, obedience and service, will be in some measure of communion with God. Those who rejected God, who lived lives of faithlessness, who ignored God in this life, who did not follow His way, will have a foretaste of separateness from all there is in the next life: God.

The General Judgment: In the Creed we profess to believe that "He shall come again to judge the living and the dead." This will be the end of history as we know it. In chapter 25 of the Gospel of Matthew we have a dramatic description by Christ as He, the Great Judge of the End Times, separates the "sheep" from the "goats." We do not know when that will occur, so the teaching of both Bible and Church is that we should always be ready in a spirit of repentance, faith, commitment to the Lord, obedience, love and prayerful worship. Anything else regarding the End Times (the date, the Anti-Christ, the "millennium", the details of the presently deceased, etc.) are simply not discussed in our sources of Revelation or are so unclear, that the Church avoids speculation.

Mutual Prayer Between Heaven and Earth: Because the Church is one, and loves (selfless concern for the welfare of the other), the Church believes that there is a bond of prayer between those who have gone on and those of us in the Church Militant on earth. Thus, we believe we can ask for the intercessionary prayers of holy persons who have died (the saints). We, on the other hand, can offer prayers on behalf of relatives and friends who have died, believing that in some way our prayers help them.

Are Those In Heaven Free To Leave?

You can now see that your question refers to a condition which has not yet occurred, since the General Judgment has not taken place. The dead, saints and sinners alike, are in a condition of fore-tasting their eternal reward or punishment. However, the Church is so confident about its saints that even now they are thought of as in Heaven, precisely because their lives on earth were characterized by deep and abiding communion with God.

Let us suppose, anyway, that the Last Judgment has taken place, and those who loved God and served the Lord on earth are now in communion with God in Heaven. Would they want to leave from the presence of God? Could they?

Resources From Our Faith

Let's look at some of the resources available to us in Orthodox Christianity to see if we can answer this question. First, let us assume that when we die we still have the ability to choose to leave heaven.

"The Company of the Saints": If is true that "bad company ruins good morals" (1 Corinthians 15:33). Then the opposite must also take place: being in good company fulfills and satisfies all that is good in us. In heaven we are "in the assembly of the holy ones" (Psalm 89:5) and in the company of "saints and apostles and prophets" (Revelation 18:20). Heaven is an experience of being in the company of all those who love and serve God. Why would we want to leave their company for the failed and disgraced?

In the Light and In the Darkness: One of the favorite images of the godly way of life is that it is light, and that separation from God is darkness. In this life, to be a Christian is to "turn from darkness to light and from the power of Satan to God" (Acts 26:18). According to the Bible, "the Father . . . has qualified us to share in the inheritance of the saints in light. He has delivered us from the dominion of darkness and transferred us to the kingdom of his beloved Son, in whom we have redemption, the forgiveness of sins" (Colossians 1:12-14). Why would we want to leave the light for eternal darkness?

Beauty, Pleasure and Delight: Communion with God is a pleasing and satisfying experience, beginning now, but lasting forever in heaven. A hymn from the *Triodion*, the Orthodox Lenten Service book, puts it this way:

> O precious Paradise, unsurpassed in beauty, tabernacle built by God, unending gladness and delight, glory of the righteous, joy of the prophets and dwelling of the saints, with the sound of thy leaves, pray to the Maker of all, May he open unto me the gates which I closed by my transgressions, and may he count me worthy to partake of the Tree of life and of the joy which was mine when I dwelt in thee before.

Why would we want to leave the fullness of happiness of Heaven for the pain and suffering of separation from God?

Freedom and True Freedom

There is an understanding of Freedom as "Self-Determination," that your question relates to "the right to choose." Apart from the secular understandings of the idea of "rights," it has to be pointed out that the right to choose freely is a gift from God. In some potential sense, that right to choose would remain in us in Heaven. "Now the Lord is the Spirit, and where the Spirit of the Lord is, there is freedom" (2 Corinthians 3:17).

More important is the freedom we have in our inner person to be true to our creation in the image and likeness of God. To be free this way is to be fully integrated, without contradicting impulses, with our God-given created condition. A person who is free in this sense has no temptation to deny his or her own divinely created nature as a person who is God's image and likeness. By Christ, believers have been ultimately freed from every contrary impulse. In Christ "every one that believes is freed from everything from which you could not be freed by the law of Moses" (Acts 13:39).

That is why in Heaven, just as the angels are firmly rooted in their loving obedience to God, human beings will have reached a stage of permanent and undeviating communion with God, so that they simply would not choose to leave their fulfilling relationship with God, as members of His eternal Kingdom, because they would never have any desire to leave His presence.

71. DO PETS GO TO HEAVEN?

Q. Do pets go to heaven when they die?　　　*–R. H., Townsend, MA.*

A. This is a sympathetic question and it is understandable, at least by pet owners who come to love their dogs and cats and other household pets. Those of us who have pets in our homes often come to be attached to them and sense a certain response they have for us, which we interpret to be love. Their behavior often is comforting and provides us with a feeling that they are "almost human." From this kind of affection come questions such as this one, "Do pets go to heaven?"

A Short History of Animals and Pets

For the greater part of human history and in many places in the world to this day, animals were and are not thought of as pets. They were, rather, perceived as aids to human life. Animals are sources of food and clothing, and are used as means to assist human beings in their varied endeavors. For example, chickens and cattle are raised and cared for by farmers for meat and milk production. Similarly, sheep provide wool for humans to turn into clothing and cloth. Dogs serve as hunting animals and warn of strangers. Horses provided transportation for the movement of individuals, for commerce and trade, and for military purposes.

St. Hilary of Poitiers (315-367) expressed the Church's attitude toward animals, when he wrote:

that there is not a single animal or plant in which the Creator has not implanted some form of energy capable of being used to satisfy man's needs. For He Who knew all things before they were, saw that in the future man would go forward in the strength of his own will, and would be subject to corruption, and, therefore, He created all things for his seasonable use, alike those in the firmament, and those on the earth, and those in the waters.

A Change in the Appreciation of Animals

With just a few exceptions of the extremely rich and pampered classes in antiquity, this was the general situation until the rise of capitalism provided enough wealth, so that some people could afford to breed, maintain, and care for animals in their homes as companions and pets.

Thus in earlier times, animals that we think of as pets were not particularly highly regarded. For example, in ancient times dogs were thought of as scavengers; wild and dangerous threats to human life. So, they came to exemplify bad and evil things. The image that was dominant was a pack of wild dogs threatening human life and society. By extension, to call a person a "dog" was an insult.

Even the Bible uses this kind of language. Here are just a few examples. "Do not give dogs what is holy; and do not throw your pearls before swine, lest they trample them under foot and turn to attack you" (Matthew 7:6); "It has happened to them according to the true proverb, The dog turns back to his own vomit, and the sow is washed only to wallow in the mire" (2 Peter 2:22); "Look out for the dogs, look out for the evil-workers" (Philippians 3:2); "Outside are the dogs and sorcerers and fornicators and murderers and idolaters, and every one who loves and practices falsehood" (Revelation 22:15). The Psalm that is interpreted as referring to Christ's Crucifixion is another example: "Yea, dogs are round about me; a company of evildoers encircle me; they have pierced my hands and feet" (Psalm 22:16-18).

However, the new situation is that animals of all kinds have not only been domesticated, but have become our household companions and are considered to be family members. (At this very moment, as I am writing these lines, our beloved and gentle pet dog Rusty, is curled up at my feet -and our rambunctious cat "Taffy" is putting her paws on the keyboard, as I sit in front of the computer!).

Thus, there has been a sort of revolution in thought about pets. As we have noted, sometimes we still use the term "dog" as an insult. But more often than not, we attribute virtues of loyalty, and faithfulness in our pets; and then compare them with the treachery, meanness, and ignoble character of some human beings. Famous is the poet Byron's *Logicians Refuted* where he writes:

> The dog to gain some private ends,
> Went mad and bit the man,
> They swore the dog had lost his wits,
> To bite so good a man,
> The man recovered of the bite,
> The dog it was that died.

So, no wonder that the question arises, "Do pets go to heaven?"

Why Pets Do Not Go To Heaven

In the Creation story in Genesis, a very important distinction is made between animals and human beings. Human beings were created not only out of the same material that the animal world was created, but also with the "breath of God," "in the image and likeness of God" (Genesis 1-2). What precisely is this difference?

We could say that animals do have a soul, in the sense of a life force and the basics of perception, response, the ability to learn, instinct, and so forth. What they don't have is the "image of God" in them. St. John of Damascus (675-749), summarizing the faith of the Church, refers to the distinctive aspect of human nature as "reason," saying "the human being is a rational and intelligent animal." Another word he uses to indicate this difference is "mind." This creates a meeting place between human beings and God; a meeting place that animals do not have. So, when St. John of Damascus speaks about Jesus' Incarnation (the Second Person of the Holy Trinity, taking on human nature), he contrasts the human mind as the image of God, with "the soul of an irrational animal." He says in his *Exposition of the Orthodox Faith*:

> Therefore, God the Word, wishing to restore that which was in His own image, became man. But what is that which was in His own image, unless mind? So He gave up the better and assumed the worse. For mind is in the border-land between God and flesh, for it dwells indeed in fellowship with the flesh, and is, moreover, the image of God. Mind, then, mingles with mind, and mind holds a place midway between the pureness of God and the denseness of flesh. For if the Lord assumed a soul without mind, He assumed the soul of an irrational animal.

The Kingdom of God Is For Human Beings

The Kingdom of heaven, then, is for human beings. We have no evidence anywhere in the Scriptures or in the Tradition of the Church to support the idea that animals, which do not have a "rational soul," are destined for heaven-or for that matter, for hell. Only human beings face that double potential destiny.

In the meantime let us enjoy our pets, but not at the expense of our responsibility for our fellow human beings. Pets and animals are part of God's creation, for which we have a moral and spiritual responsibility. The Old Testament speaks of the proper care of domesticated animals (1 Kings 4:31-34, 1 Kings 18:5, 2 Kings 3:17, are just three examples). Jesus accepts as necessary and right the care of animals (Luke 13:15). The humane treatment of animals, including our domesticated pets, is part of our Christian responsibility to our environment. Let that be fulfilled, and I trust that God will be pleased.

End Times: Christ's Second Coming

72. IS CHRIST COMING SOON?

Q. Is the Second Coming of Christ near?   *–E.L., Athens, Greece*

A. The answer to your question is not simple and straight-forward. In fact, we do not know the answer; but we can give some kind of answer in three ways: "maybe," "not your concern" and "yes". Yet, these answers are not contradictory. Paradoxically, they are part of a single response to your question.

The Expectation of the Second Coming

Because Jesus has promised His coming again to judge the world, Christians expect that He will return one day. Jesus said, "...when I go and prepare a place for you, I will come again and will take you to myself, that where I am you may be also." (John 14:3). The parable of the Second Coming, describing the judgment of Christ, separating the good from the evil (the sheep from the goats) in the 25th chapter of Matthew also teaches the Second Coming of Christ. "When the Son of man comes in his glory, and all the angels with him, then he will sit on his glorious throne..." (Matthew 25:31). There are many other biblical passages that speak of it. Thus, the Church has always expected Christ to return in a Second Coming. In the Creed, we say, "And He shall come again in glory to judge the living and the dead; Whose Kingdom shall have no end...I await the resurrection of the dead." The question that you ask however is when the Second Coming will take place, that is, whether it will happen soon. Do we have answers for that?

The Second Coming Might be Soon

It is interesting that in different places in the Bible there are passages which indicate a kind of "order of events" which will take place before Christ's Second Coming. Yet these are very difficult, if not impossible, to put together into a coherent pattern.

For example, in 1 Thessalonians, St. Paul says, "The day of the Lord will come like a thief in the night" during a time of peace and security. But in 2 Thessalonians we read, "the day will not come, unless the rebellion comes first, and the man of lawlessness is revealed...." If we add the difficult-to-understand passages of the Book of Revelation to this mix, we can do one of two things.

On the one hand it is possible to spend a lifetime trying to make sense out of the passages so as to harmonize them and make predictions about the Second Coming, according to our subjective understanding. Thus, many Protestants fight among themselves under the banners of Pre-Millenarianism, Millenarianism, various sorts of Dispensationalism, Theologies of the Anti-Christ, etc. Some have predicted the Second Coming, sold their homes, put on white robes, climbed some mountain, and awaited the Second Coming. All have been disappointed.

The other way of dealing with those passages which describe the end times and the return of Christ is to understand them as pointing to the return of Christ itself and the fact that we should be ready for it. This has been the way of the Orthodox Church. Often the parable of the "Ten Wise And Ten Foolish Virgins" is interpreted by the Church to mean that the Second Coming could take place any time; but, in any case, unexpectedly. The main message is that we are to be alert and ready, for the Lord can return at any time. For example, in Holy Week we sing the hymn of the Parable of the Bridegroom:

Behold the Bridegroom comes in the middle of the night, and blessed is the servant whom He shall find watching; and again unworthy is he whom He shall find heedless...

In short, the Church's use of those passages is to tell us that we should be ready spiritually and morally every day, in repentance, obedience, loyalty, and devotion to Christ.

The Date of Christ's Return?

The whole concern about the date when Christ will return is not the business of Christians. That is what we learn from the New Testament. Jesus Himself says: "But of that day and hour no one knows, not even the angels of heaven, nor the Son, but the Father only....Watch therefore, for you do not know on what day your Lord is coming....Therefore you also must be ready; for the Son of man is coming at an hour you do not expect." (Matthew 24:36, 42, 44). So also St. Paul: "As to the times and seasons, brethren, you have no need to have anything written to you. For you yourselves know well that the day of the Lord will come like a thief in the night." (1 Thessalonians 5: 1).

On the basis of this, St. Paul counsels:

> Now concerning the coming of our Lord Jesus Christ and our assembling to meet him, we beg you brethren, not to be quickly shaken in mind or excited, either by spirit or by word, or by letter purporting to be from us, to the effect that the day of the Lord has come. Let no one deceive you..." (2 Thessalonians 2: l-3a).

Our job is not to be concerned whether His coming is to be sooner or later. We are not to anticipate the date, whether it be imminent or delayed. We are not to get excited and worked up about the date. Rather, ours is another responsibility: to be always ready.

Jesus is coming soon: FOR YOU!

The Bible is clear that what we do in this life is what will determine our eternal destiny. If we are close to God in this life we will be close to him in the next. If we are far from God in this life, we will be far from Him in the next. Heaven and Hell are a continuation of our lives on earth. That is why we are to be ready at all times. But if He doesn't come in our lifetime, then, you and I will go into eternity at our deaths, already prepared for the judgment. Our eternal destiny will be set. St. Paul teaches that to those who are faithful and who suffer for the Gospel, God will "grant rest," and that in them Christ "will be glorified." But they "who do not know God," and "who do not obey the Gospel of our Lord Jesus...shall suffer the punishment of eternal destruction and exclusion from the presence of the Lord and from the glory of his might." This will take place "when the Lord Jesus is revealed from heaven with his mighty angels in flaming fire" (1 Thessalonians 1:5-12).

Since we are taught in the parable of the Rich Man and Poor Lazarus, that those who die already begin to experience their eternal reward or punishment (Luke 16:19-31), the Orthodox Church teaches that when we die, we begin immediately experiencing a foretaste of our eternal destiny. This is known in theological terms as the "Partial Judgment," in contrast to the "General Judgment," which will take place at Christ's Second Coming.

This means that for each of us, personally, the consequences of the Second Coming will begin taking place at our death! In effect, relatively soon (for who knows when he or she will die?) we will each face our own personal equivalent foretaste of the Lord's Second Coming.

Is Christ Coming Soon?

He may come soon. He may not. Our task is not to calculate the date of His Second Coming, but to be always ready. Whether He comes in our lifetime or not, when we die we will face our personal equivalent of Christ's Second Coming. Is Christ coming soon? Maybe; Not our concern; Yes, for sure!

73. THE END TIMES AND THE PRESENT TIME

Q. When Christ returns and His Church is raptured, which Christians or which bodies do we believe will be raptured? (This is round-about way of asking, "In Christ's eyes, who or what makes his Church on earth today?") —*B. N., Waltham, MA.*

A. Let us begin by defining what we are talking about; then we'll briefly describe these teachings in their various forms; then we will assess them from an Orthodox perspective.

What Is Meant By These Words?

Eschatology refers to the events which will take place at the end of the world as we know it. (In Greek and in theological language "Eschatology" comes from the Greek word "*Eschaton*," meaning "the end" or the "last thing"). The most clear definition of this teaching is in the Creed: the "Lord Jesus Christ...will come again in glory to judge the living and the dead. His kingdom will have no end....I expect the resurrection of the dead. And the life of the age to come."

We should note that this statement speaks of the Second Coming of Christ (the First Coming was His birth through the Theotokos, His earthly ministry, ending with His Ascension) as a single event. Thus, when the end time comes, Jesus will return, a general resurrection of the dead will occur, a general judgment of all will take place, and the Kingdom of God will be fully realized.

Rapture teachings exist only among Evangelical Protestants. "Rapture" teachings hold that the Second Coming of Christ will be in two stages. Some of these people teach that the two phases of Christ's return will be separated by a period of seven years of a "Great Tribulation Period." Accordingly, it is held that the Antichrist will rule the world during this period. They teach that the first period, before the Tribulation is called the "Rapture," when dead Christians will be raised, and living Christians will be lifted up to meet with

Christ in the air and will therefore avoid the Antichrist's Tribulation because they are with Christ in Heaven. After the Tribulation, Christ will descend from heaven a second time, with those Christians who were taken up in the Rapture. He will destroy the Antichrist, judge the nations and set up an earthly Kingdom which will last for one thousand years. This one thousand year reign is what is being talked about with the word Millennianism. But those persons who accept such teachings differ significantly among themselves. Here are some of their differing views.

Different Views

Pretribulational Premillennialism: The teaching described above is "the dominant eschatological position among evangelicals today," according to the evangelical Protestant periodical *Christianity Today*. It is known as "Pretribulational Premillennialism." Contemporary Evangelical Protestants also understand this scenario in political terms in reference to Israel, Russia and Armageddon, i.e., a final battle between forces of good and evil ending with the second eschatological coming of Christ. The millennium will then begin and Christ will reign on earth for a thousand years with Jerusalem as its capital city. This view is the interpretation found in the commentaries in the widely used "Scofield Bible."

However, though this is the dominant view among Evangelical Protestants, it is not the only one. There are three others. I describe them through quotations from the periodical mentioned above, an authoritative source for Evangelical Protestantism.

Posttribulational Premillennialism: "Also known as *historic* premillennialism, this view predicts that Christ will return in a single event after the period of intense persecution of the church known as the Tribulation. Immediately after Christ returns, the Antichrist and his followers will be destroyed and Israel will repent and be saved. The promised messianic kingdom (millennium) will be established for 1,000 years, after which the rest of the dead will be raised, the final judgment effected, and the new heaven and the new Earth will begin."

Postmillennialism: "This eschatological outlook anticipates a period of unprecedented revival in the church prior to the return of Christ...As a result, the entire world will experience conditions of peace and economic improvement that will gradually improve until Christ returns. During this millennium, Christian values and principles will dominate, though not every person will become a Christian."

Amillennialism: The preceding are the main views of Evangelical Protestants regarding the end times. There is, however, one other view among the Evangelicals which is called by them "Amillennialism." It means that there will not be a one thousand year reign of Christ on earth. As described by *Christianity Today* it comes closest to the Orthodox position, which we now turn to for a closer look.

Orthodox Eschatology

Central to all of these views is "Millennialism" which is also known as "Chiliasm," from the Greek word *"chiliasmos"* meaning "teaching about the thousand years." The early church did have some people who taught some forms of "Millennialism." They were influenced by Chapter 20 of the Book of Revelation together with Jewish Apocalyptic writings. These, however, are understood correctly as not dealing with the end of the world, but in reference to the Messianic ministry of Christ, that is, by Christ's First Coming.

In his commentary on the Book of Revelation, St. Andrew, Bishop of Caesaria (6th Century) expressed the Orthodox view. The "one thousand year reign of Christ" when the controlling power of the Devil is contained (when "Satan is bound") refers not to the end times connected with the Second Coming of Christ, but with the First Coming. It is precisely the victory of Christ over death, sin, evil and the Devil, through His resurrection, which we celebrate at Eastertime.

As one Orthodox author puts it, "The 'first resurrection' of Revelation 20:5-6 thus refers to the spiritual state of the believer after Baptism. The 'second death' is the condition of those who live in the 'Christian centuries' but who consciously reject the Baptism of Christ." The biblical language of "meeting Christ in the air" needs to be understood as a dramatic image of Christ's return at the end of the world. Without the "chiliasm" doctrine, there are no stages or phases, but only the "Second Coming" as described in Isaiah 65:17-18, Matthew 12:28, Luke 17:20-21, Matthew 7:21-23, and Romans 14:17. Therefore, there is no so-called "Rapture"

The proper interpretation of those passages is that they are ways the Bible speaks of Christians being in the household, domain and Kingdom of the glorified Christ.

74. "TOLL HOUSES" AND THE END TIMES

Q. I've read that some Orthodox teach about "demonic toll houses" that a departing soul after death has to go through. Supposedly, the soul has to be escorted by Angels who will defend the soul if that person had a good life. If the soul is found above reproach it continues to climb to the Lord. Otherwise the demons take control over it and take it down to the black pits. Some say that there are twenty such "Toll Houses" on the way to Heaven or Hell. Can you tell me if the Church has taken a clear position the teaching of "Toll Houses"?

– P. C. L., Worcester, MA.

A. A question similar to this one was answered fourteen years ago. I share it with the readers of the "Religious Question Box" again, but significantly revised and updated.

"Toll Houses"?

The idea that when we die we have to go past a number of "Toll Houses," detaining the soul for testing of the sins which it has committed and requiring payment for them, is a dramatic way of showing our moral and spiritual responsibility for our lives in this world. The main proponent, in our times, of the "Toll House" teaching was Fr. Seraphim Rose in his book *The Soul After Death*. He was a convert to Orthodoxy from a California based religious sect. The group he led and which still exits, is not associated with any of the canonical Patriarchates or Autocephalous Orthodox Churches.

"Toll houses" at most, might be called a *"theologoumenon"* (that is, an optional theological opinion), but for the vast majority of Orthodox teachers of the faith of the Church, such views are either unknown (not mentioned at all); acknowledged as having some minor elements of tradition supporting them, but not official doctrine; or, finally, simply erroneous misinterpretations, to be condemned. It is this last opinion that many critics have adopted regarding the "Toll Houses" teaching of Fr. Rose. The most thorough critic of this teaching is Fr. Michael Azkoul, in his book, *Toll-House Myth: The Neo-Gnosticism of Fr. Seraphim Rose.*

I tend to agree that the "Toll House" teaching is not to be found in the authentic teaching of the Orthodox Church and that speculation on it is not spiritually or theologically good. I would suggest, instead, that you read some of the preceding accounts of Orthodox teachings regarding Eschatology [the doctrine of the last things], for authoritative understandings of the Church's doctrine on the last things.

Older, but still useful is Frank Gavin's, *Some Aspects of Contemporary Greek Orthodox Thought*, if you can find it in a library or used book store. A bit polemical, but more theologically correct, it appears to me, is Lev Puhalo's *The Soul, The Body, and Death.* Another older book that addresses the eschatological teachings of the Orthodox Church is the book by the first Dean of Holy Cross School of Theology, Bishop Athenagoras Cavadas, titled *World Beyond the Grave or the Afterlife.*

For a middle of the road, and generally accepted perspective, read Constantine Callinicos' *Beyond the Grave: An Orthodox Theology on Eschatology*. Newer works are by Hierotheos Vlachos, *Life After Death*, as well as the acclaimed book by N. P. Vassiliadis, *The Mystery of Death*.

To my knowledge, the most recent book about Orthodox Eschatology, written from the perspective of a convert from Protestantism to Orthodoxy, is Dennis Engleman's *Ultimate Things*.

For two short summaries of Orthodox teaching on eschatology, read Bishop (Now Metropolitan) Maximos Aghiorgoussis' "The Dogmatic Tradition of the Orthodox Church," in *A Companion to the Greek Orthodox Church* and John Karmiris', *A Synopsis of the Dogmatic Theology of the Orthodox Catholic Church*, chapter XI.

The "Last Things"

So that this question is not left "hanging," I think it would be good to conclude this column with a brief discussion about the "Last Things" from the perspective of the Orthodox Church. The Orthodox Church has just a few things to say about what will happen at the end of time and when each of us dies.

"Eschatology" is the teaching that refers to the events which will take place at the end of the world. All history is under God's Judgment. The most clear expression of this teaching is in the Creed. The relevant passage says that the "Lord Jesus Christ...will come again in glory to judge the living and the dead. His kingdom will have no end....I expect the resurrection of the dead. And the life of the age to come."

The Creed speaks of the Second Coming of Christ (the First Coming was His earthly ministry) as a single event. Thus, when the end time comes (the time of which only the Father knows), Jesus will return, a General Resurrection of the dead will occur, a General Judgment will take place, all will receive their place in Heaven or Hell, and the Eternal Kingdom of God will be fully realized.

In the meantime, upon death, people experience a "Partial Judgment." This means that they immediately have a "foretaste," of their eternal destiny. The Orthodox Church teaches that those who share most fully in communion with God, the Saints, are part of the Church Triumphant. They can pray for us before the throne of God. Conversely, we Orthodox believe that those who are part of the Church Militant (still in this life, fighting against the temptation of sin for our salvation) can pray for our relatives and friends who are experiencing the Partial Judgment. So we conduct services of intercession for them. This is similar to any prayer we say for anyone in any situation. We pray with confidence that the Lord hears us, but there is no fore-ordained response to our prayers. We do our part by praying for the deceased. God responds as He sees fit.

Finally, our task is always to be ready to prepare for our death. Remembrance of our death grants us the blessing of a right perspective about life. Our spiritual condition becomes uppermost. Our worldly material condition loses importance. The issue is "What am I doing to prepare myself to meet my Maker?"

Speculating about the end-times, worrying about the new millennium, trying to figure out the details of what happen after we die, are irrelevant activities for the Orthodox Christian, or for any Christian. Sooner or later our time will come. How will we stand before God? That is the real question that each of us must answer.

Theology and Life

75. THEOLOGY AND ORDINARY CHRISTIANS

Q. In light of the sophisticated theological issues which lie at the core of the many church body divisions, what posture is incumbent on we relatively unsophisticated lay people as we grope to be good Christians in his Church on earth today?   *–B.N. Waltham, MA.*

A. One way of answering this question is to understand theology as "studying the things pertaining to God." I limit myself here to Christian theology. The "things pertaining to God" can be understood as dealing with things "about" God; with "interpreting" the things of God; and with "communing" with God. Let's look at these as a way of finding an answer to your question.

"theology" - The Things About God

We start with what could be called "theology" (lower case "t"), which deals with "the things **about** God." We could say that "The Religious Question Box" and many of the currently published books about the Orthodox Church are forms of theology, meaning that there is an effort to explain and describe the teaching and perspective of the Church **about** the Orthodox Christian faith, life, practice, history, etc.

Much of the education seminarians and students of theology receive in schools of higher education is "about" the Orthodox faith. So, theology presents and seeks to clarify God's truth, what the Church is and to convey its message to the membership of the Church and to the world outside it. When someone asks "What is the view of the Orthodox Church on so and so topic" it is theology that seeks to answer that question.

When the response to such a question involves expressing the established teaching and practice of the Church -which covers a great deal of material, to be sure- it is a fairly straight-forward process. Both clergy and laity have a constant need for this kind of instruction and education. Much of what the Church Fathers wrote was this kind of theology.

"Theology" - Interpreting the Things of God

However, often questions regarding the actual teaching of the Orthodox Christian Faith have arisen. Often someone would try to explain an as yet unclear part of Church teaching and make serious errors in the process. When these false teachings have a direct impact on salvation, they are in need of correction.

Thus, in the New Testament, St. Paul in the book of the Acts of the Apostles "corrects" false teachings about the relationship of the Jewish Law and with new converts. In this case, he correctly "interpreted" the existing teaching to address a new issue presented by the "Judaizers" of the Christian faith. We could say that he did "Theology" (with an upper-case "T").

The great Church Fathers did the same. For example, when St. Athanasius fought the teaching of the Priest Arius in the third century, who held that the second person of the Holy Trinity was a creature, and therefore, not God, he did **Theology**. The same issue was addressed by Ecumenical Councils, seeking to clarify and put into clear formulations to protect our salvation.

In our day, this kind of "capitalized" **Theology** is being conducted in reference to serious ethical questions such as the newly raised issues of ecology and bioethics and the nature of the Church.

But this kind **Theology** is not for everyone. In fact, it is very dangerous. The classic expression of this perspective is found in what is known as the *First Theological Oration* of St. Gregory the Theologian. He says:

Discussion of theology is not for everyone, I tell you, not for everyone—it is no such inexpensive or effortless pursuit. Nor, I would add, is it for every occasion, or every audience; neither are all its aspects open to inquiry. It must be reserved for certain occasions, for certain audiences, and certain limits must be observed. It is not for all men, but only for those who have been tested and have found a sound footing in study, and, more importantly, have undergone, or at the very least are undergoing, purification of body and soul. For one who is not pure to lay hold of pure things is dangerous, just as it is for weak eyes to look at the sun's brightness" (Oration 27.3).

St. Gregory the Theologian, one of the Three Great Hierarchs of the Church, also cautions not only about who should Theologize, but also, about who should listen to, read and study, this kind of Theology:

This kind of Theology is a serious undertaking, not just another subject like any other for entertaining small-talk, after the races, the theater, songs, food, and sex: for there are people who count chatter on theology and clever deployment of arguments as one of their amusements.

But there is another kind of theology that is appropriate for everyone. We could describe this kind of theology appropriately as being written completely in upper-case letters.

"THEOLOGY" - Communing With God

In the teaching of several Church Fathers, there is, nevertheless, a third and highest level, which we could call **THEOLOGY** (all upper-case). Here we are not talking about instruction and interpretation, but true and genuine communion with God. It is in this spirit that the Church Fathers say that "True Theology is prayer," and that "The true theologian is one who prays," and that "One who truly prays is a true theologian."

Again, St. Gregory the Theologian in the same place puts it well for us:

> I am not maintaining that we ought not to be mindful of God at all times . . . . It is more important that we should remember God than that we should breathe: indeed, if one may say so, we should do nothing else besides. I am one of those who approve the precept that commands us to "meditate day and night" (Psalm 1:2; Joshua 1:8), to tell of the Lord "evening, and morning, and at noon,"(Psalm 55[54]:17), and to "bless the Lord at all times,"(Psalm 34 [33]:1); or, in the words of Moses, "when we lie down, when we rise up, when we walk by the way"(Deuteronomy 6:7) or when we do anything else whatever, and by this mindfulness be molded to purity" (Oration 27:4).

What's A Layman To Do?

Thus, I think that St. Gregory the Theologian gives us the response to your question. We (clergy and laity) are not to be ignorant of the teachings of the Orthodox Faith. Because the clergy are the teachers of the faith in a primary sense, they need to be well educated in what we have called here theology," (information) and Theology (interpretation). Most clergy, however, and most lay people do not need to have much knowledge of the ongoing "sophisticated" interpretations and discussions. Only in this sense, would it be right to agree with your calling them theologically unsophisticated. There are, however, always exceptions. Keep in mind that many professors of theology are laymen. So, theology (instruction) is necessary for everyone in the Church; Theology (interpretation) is only for those adequately prepared.

St. Gregory the Theologian, thus tells us:

> So it is not continual remembrance of God I seek to discourage, but continual discussion of theology. I am not opposed either to theology, as if it were a breach of piety, but only to its untimely practice, or to instruction in it, except when this goes to excess. Fullness and surfeit even of honey, for all its goodness, produces vomiting (Proverbs 25.16[27]); and "to everything there is a season" (Ecclesiastes 3.1).

But **THEOLOGY** understood as personal communion with God in the life of the Church through prayer, worship, sacramental participation, moral living, spiritual discipline, struggle for growth in Christ and the image and likeness of God toward God-likeness is the ongoing and most important task of every Orthodox Christian, clergy and lay. This is the most important kind of theology. It is the highest **THEOLOGY**.

- A -

- B -

- C -

- R -

- S -

St. Cyril of Alexandria - 74
St. Cyril of Jerusalem - 109, 112, 150
St. Gregory of Nyssa - 106, 107, 108, 122, 149, 181
St. Gregory the Theologian - 245, 291
St. Ignatios - 86, 135
St. Irenaeus - 87, 142, 149, 204
St. John Chrysostom - 150
St. John of Damascus - 132, 135, 142, 156, 195, 250, 275
St. John of Damaskos - 87
St. John the Baptist - 107
St. Justin Martyr - 87, 205
St. Proclos of Constantinople - 74
St. Stylianos - 190
St. Theodore the Studite - 250
Static Tradition - 23
Statues - 253
Statues in Worship - 255
Statues of Pagan Gods - 236
Steadfastness - 203
Strength in Suffering - 225
Suffering - 181, 217
Suffering and Evil - 221
Suffering and God - 221
Suffering and Pain - 222
Synaxis of Archangels - 126
Synod - 175
Synod of Jerusalem - 42
Systemic Evils - 233

- T -

Talmud - 128
Teaching About Hell - 266
Teaching and Perspective of the Church - 289
Temple - 219
Temptations - 159
Ten Commandments - 38, 236
Theanthropos - 79, 149
Theology - 248, 289

THEOLOGY - Communing With God - 291
Theology - Interpreting the Things of God - 290
theology - The Things About God - 289
Theology of Iconography - 250
Theosis - 159
Theotokos - 75, 186, 281
Theotokos in the Orthodox Tradition - 193
Thousand Year Reign - 103
Tobit - 127
Toll Houses - 284
Toll Houses and the End Times - 284
Tradition: Different Kinds - 22
Traditional Teachings of the Church - 30
Traditions of Men - 23
Transfiguration of Jesus Christ - 71
Trinitarian - 65
Truly Christ is Risen! - 88
Trust in God - 225
Truth, The - 53
Truth and the Life of God - 21
Truth of God - 163
Truths about God - 265

- U -

Unblemished Lamb of God - 79
Understanding Who Jesus Christ Is - 81
Unity of the Church - 175
Unity of the Faith - 166
Unity of the Spirit - 108
Unleavened Bread - 218

- V -

Victorious over Death - 93
View of the Church - 41
Violation of a Divine Law - 259

Virgin Mary - 192
Virtue - 203
Virtues - 160, 189
Voluntary Evils - 233

- W -

Walk by the Spirit - 108
Was Jesus Christ Really
   Being Human? - 59
Ways of Knowing God - 8
We are Sinners - 77
WE Prepare Our Place In
   Eternity - 268
What is the Church? - 163
Who Died on the Cross? - 78
Why Innocent People Suffer - 232
Why Were Human Beings
   Created? - 139
Wickedness - 137
Will of God - 146
Work of Christ - 198
Work of Salvation - 198
World Council of Churches
   Assembly - 247
Worship - 122, 149
Worship of Idols - 236
Worshiping of Images - 236
Wrath of God - 202

- Z -

Zoroastrianism - 127

SCRIPTURE VERSES

Acts 1:8 - 107
Acts 1:16 - 111
Acts 2 - 21
Acts 2:1-4 - 117
Acts 2:2 - 107
Acts 2:27 - 85
Acts 2:31-32 - 85
Acts 2:4 - 108
Acts 2:42 - 114
Acts 3:19 - 90
Acts 4:26 - 90
Acts 5:32 - 115
Acts 5:42 - 90
Acts 9:22 - 90
Acts 10:36-37 - 90
Acts 10:39-43 - 91
Acts 13:39 - 271
Acts 13:52 - 113
Acts 15:20 - 254
Acts 18:18 - 24
Acts 20:27-30 - 176
Acts 26:18 - 270
Colossians 1:12-14 - 270
Colossians 1:15 - 246
Colossians 1:18-23 - 177
Colossians 1:21 - 91
Colossians 1:21-23 - 95
Colossians 2:8 - 21
Colossians 3:5-9 - 254
1 Corinthians 1:22-25 - 69
1 Corinthians 2:9, 11 - 139
1 Corinthians 5:7 - 219
1 Corinthians 6:19-20 - 115
1 Corinthians 11:2 - 21, 63
1 Corinthians 11:20 - 29
1 Corinthians 11:23 - 63
1 Corinthians 12:3 - 115
1 Corinthians 12:11 - 107
1 Corinthians 12:27 - 160, 174
1 Corinthians 13:10,12 - 169
1 Corinthians 14:1 - 119
1 Corinthians 14:12 - 115, 119

John 6 - 200
John 6:53 - 204
John 10:24-25 - 17
John 10:29 - 17
John 10:30 - 17
John 12:38 - 14
John 13:18 - 14
John 14:3 - 97, 277
John 14:6 - 17-18
John 14:16-17 - 20
John 14:25-26 - 20
John 15:26 - 105
John 16:13 - 108
John 17:12 - 14
John 20:22-23 - 260
1 John 3:5 - 77
1 John 3:10 - 135
1 John 3:14 - 91
1 John 4:7-12 - 182
1 John 4:8 - 181, 265
1 John 4:12 - 245
1 John 5:20 - 54
2 John 2-3, 9 - 53
Isaiah 53:7 - 218
James 5:16 - 187, 188
James 12:4 - 71
Jude 7 - 263
1 Kings 4:31-34 - 275
1 Kings 18:5 - 275
2 Kings 3:17 - 275
Luke 4:18 - 107
Luke 4:18-21 - 14
Luke 9:23 - 155, 265
Luke 9:24-26 - 267
Luke 10:21 - 113
Luke 12:11-12 - 114
Luke 12:12 - 108
Luke 13:15 - 275
Luke 16:19-31 - 100, 263, 280
Luke 23:43 - 84
Luke 24:34 - 91
Luke 24:5 - 200
Luke 35:36 - 134
Mark 1:8 - 107

Mark 1:9-11 - 67
Mark 3:28-29 - 134
Mark 4:11 - 176
Mark 9:7 - 68
Mark 12:6-8 - 68
Romans 1:7 - 185
Romans 3:20-26 - 202
Romans 5:9-11 - 203
Romans 5:10 - 199
Romans 5:12 - 91
Romans 5:12,14,17,19,21 - 152
Romans 6:3-5 - 94
Romans 6:3-11 - 207
Romans 6:3-14 - 200
Romans 6:23 - 91
Romans 8:6-8 - 91
Romans 8:22 - 180
Romans 8:29 - 200
Romans 9:1 - 114
Romans 12:2 - 203
Romans 12:11-18 - 116
Romans 14:17 - 113
Matthew 3:16 - 107
Matthew 5:22 - 263
Matthew 5:30 - 263
Matthew 5:48 - 158
Matthew 6:28-30 - 235
Matthew 7:6 - 273
Matthew 12:32 - 109
Matthew 16:15 - 81
Matthew 16:15-18 - 171
Matthew 16:16 - 81
Matthew 17:3-9 - 68
Matthew 18:15-17 - 172
Matthew 23:33 - 263
Matthew 24:36, 42, 44 - 99, 100, 279
Matthew 25:30, 13:42 - 267
Matthew 25:31 - 97, 277
Matthew 25:41 - 267
Matthew 27:51-53 - 84
Matthew 27:52 - 86
Matthew 28:6 - 200
1 Peter 2:2 - 119
1 Peter 2:22 - 77

1 Peter 3:10-12 - 115
1 Peter 3:14-16 - 225
1 Peter 4:13 - 225
1 Peter 5:7-10 - 225
2 Peter 1:4-7 - 203
2 Peter 1:17-18 - 68
2 Peter 2:22 - 273
2 Peter 3:18 - 119
Philippians 2:8 - 92
Philippians 2:10 - 88
Proverbs 3:13-14 - 146
Proverbs 6:23 - 146
Proverbs 12:26 - 146
Proverbs 15:3 - 154
Proverbs 25:16[27] - 293
Psalm 8:4-5 - 146
Psalm 16 - 266
Psalm 19:1 - 122
Psalm 22:16-18 - 273
Psalm 33:6 - 111
Psalm 44:21 - 154
Psalm 51:11 - 106
Psalm 66:19-20 - 113
Psalm 85:10 - 30
Psalm 88:2 - 30
Psalm 103 - 110
Psalm 104:21 - 122
Psalm 104:31-35 - 123
Psalm 118:142 - 31
Psalm 119:30-34 - 31
Psalm 139:2 - 106
Psalm 139:7 - 111
Revelation 14:19, 19:15 - 93
Revelation 22:15 - 273
Revelation 22:16-17 - 112
2 Samuel 12:3 - 218
1 Thessalonians 1:5-12 - 100,280
1 Thessalonians 1:6 - 113
1 Thessalonians 5:1 - 99, 279
1 Thessalonians 5:2 - 97
1 Thessalonians 5:16-19 - 113
1 Thessalonians 5:19 - 108
2 Thessalonians 1:9 - 267
2 Thessalonians 2:l-3a - 99, 279

2 Thessalonians 2:3 - 97
2 Thessalonians 2:15 - 63
1 Timothy 2:8 - 115
1 Timothy 3:14-16 - 173
1 Timothy 3:15 - 139
1 Timothy 3:15 - 4, 19
1 Timothy 4:1-2,6 - 176
2 Timothy 1:13-14 - 114
2 Timothy 3:5 - 25
Titus 3:5 - 119
Wisdom 1:7 - 111
Zechariah 1:6 - 112
Zechariah 7:12 - 112